UPSTATE UNCOVERED

UPSTATE UNCOVERED

100 Unique, Unusual, and Overlooked Destinations in Upstate New York

CHUCK D'IMPERIO

excelsior editions

AN IMPRINT OF STATE UNIVERSITY OF NEW YORK PRESS

Photograph on the cover of Nipper taken by Michael P. Farrell courtesy of the *Times Union*.

Published by State University of New York Press, Albany

Excelsior Editions is an imprint of State University of New York Press

For information, contact State University of New York Press, Albany, NY
www.sunypress.edu

Production, Ryan Morris
Marketing, Kate R. Seburyamo

Library of Congress Cataloging-in-Publication Data

Names: D'Imperio, Chuck, author.
Title: Upstate uncovered : 100 unique, unusual, and overlooked destinations
    in upstate New York / Chuck D'Imperio.
Description: Albany : State University of New York Press, 2017. | Series:
    Excelsior editions | Includes index.
Identifiers: LCCN 2016021653 (print) | LCCN 2016024276 (ebook) | ISBN
    9781438463704 (pbk. : alk. paper) | ISBN 9781438463711 (e-book)
Subjects: LCSH: Upstate New York (N.Y.)—Guidebooks. | Upstate New York
    (N.Y.)—Description and travel.
Classification: LCC F126.8.D56 2017 (print) | LCC F126.8 (ebook) | DDC
    917.47/104—dc23
LC record available at https://lccn.loc.gov/2016021653

10 9 8 7 6 5 4 3 2 1

To Trish—

My beloved life and traveling companion,

from whom all good things flow.

♦ ♦ ♦

Author's Note

As with any of my books let me make two upfront observations.

First, *where is Upstate?*

As I have mentioned in all my other writings, for the sake of simplicity I consider anything in New York State that is *not* in New York City or Long Island to be Upstate. I know this flies in the face of those diehards who insist that there are rigid demarcation lines between the "Capital District" and "Central New York," "Western New York," and other regions. I understand that. Trust me; I know where Upstate New York is. I was born here (Delaware County), live here (Otsego County), and will probably end up here forever. And besides, the title of this book is easier to digest than if I more correctly titled it *Upstate Uncovered: 100 Unforgettable, Overlooked Destinations, Landmarks, and Historical Sites That Are Located throughout the State of New York but Not Found in the Five Boroughs of New York City or Long Island.* That would be a mouthful for sure!

As with all travel guides, I issue this gentle warning. If you set out on a journey to explore any of these hundred destinations, which I hope you do, be sure and use the contact information I have included to check the entries out before hitting the road. You never know when hours will change, places will close or move, or other important tourist or visitor information will be altered between the time this book is printed and the time of your visit.

Contents

Upstate Uncovered is divided into five loosely defined geographical regions to help readers create their own itineraries when seeking out sites covered in the book.

REGION TWO

Finger Lakes

♦ ♦ ♦

*Including parts of Cayuga, Chemung, Onondaga, Ontario,
Seneca, Wayne, and Yates Counties*

REGION THREE

Central New York

◆ ◆ ◆

*Including parts of Chemung, Chenango, Cortland, Delaware,
Fulton, Herkimer, Madison, Montgomery, Oneida,
Onondaga, Otsego, and Schoharie Counties*

REGION FOUR

Catskills, Hudson Valley, Capital District

*Including parts of Albany, Delaware, Dutchess, Orange, Rensselaer,
Saratoga, Schenectady, Sullivan, Ulster, Washington,
Westchester, and Rockland Counties*

REGION FIVE

North Country and Adirondacks

*Including parts of Essex, Franklin, Jefferson, Oswego,
St. Lawrence, Warren, and Washington Counties*

Introduction

Over the last decade I have written more than a half-dozen books about Upstate New York, each with a different topic (famous grave sites, little-known museums, historic monuments, and popular foods from Upstate, among others). After ten years and more than forty thousand miles traveling, researching, interviewing, and writing, this is my ultimate tribute—an ode, if you will, to wonderful Upstate New York.

Upstate New York is packed with fascinating places to see, explore, and revel in. We are often thought of as the "weak-sister" region, overlooked by our big-shouldered neighbor to the south. And you will find no bigger fan of the Big Apple than me. But Upstate is special, in so many ways.

Our beauty is unmatched, and our small cities and towns hold many interesting historical tidbits. Our people, past and present, have been instrumental in forming our great nation and continue to lead the way into its future. Our universities are among the best in the country, our museums are the ark that holds the story of America, and our great outdoors, from the Gunks to the Finger Lakes to the Tug Hill Plateau and the roar of Niagara, offers some of the best natural wonders you can wish for.

Upstate is the birthplace of the potato chip, IBM, sponge candy, chicken riggies, the American Navy, Endicott-Johnson Shoes, four U.S. presidents and eleven U.S. vice-presidents, salt potatoes, General Electric, and those little evergreen-tree air fresheners that hang from a million rearview mirrors. The greatest names in sports are enshrined in our Halls of Fame for baseball, boxing, horse racing, and more. Singer Kate Smith saw the moon come over her mountains (the Adirondacks) from her home in Lake Placid. Glenn Curtiss licked his rivals the Wright brothers time after time and earned U.S. Pilot License #1 while living in Upstate. When Laura Ingalls Wilder wrote her classic *Farmer Boy*, she was talking about a little house in Upstate New York, *not* a house on the prairie. Our wines are award-winning, our canal was an engineering marvel, and Sam Patch leaped his way into the history books out in Rochester. The Busch family may have made their beer in St. Louis, but they grew their hops in Otsego County. The largest wheel of cheese was made here, and the largest pancake griddle flipped the biggest pancake in the world in Upstate. It's true—there's a photo of it is in this book. L. Frank Baum first dreamed up *The Wizard of Oz* in Chittenango, and the Cardiff Giant enjoys his stony, eternal nap at the Farmer's Museum in Cooperstown.

Frederick Douglass, John Brown, Gerritt Smith, and Harriet Tubman all carved their names in the holy book of emancipation in Upstate. Lucille Ball grew up here, and in death came back home to rest forever. Schoharie County was General Washington's "Breadbasket of the Revolution," and President U. S. Grant died on a lonely Upstate mountaintop overlooking the Saratoga battlefield. We are RCA's giant rooftop Nipper in Albany and we are the Kazoo Museum in Eden. We *were* once the Onion Capital of the World and we still *are* the Chicken Wing Capital of the World. We are the Roscoe Diner, the Moosewood Restaurant, Dinosaur Barbecue, and a motel made out of railroad cabooses in Avoca. And we are the home of the only two-story brick outhouse in the East.

We are Uncle Sam's bustling Troy riverfront and Grandma Moses's quaint and quiet Hoosick Falls. We are maple syrup buckets and endless snowmobile trails. We are salmon runs and Howe Caverns. We are Ithaca's gorgeous gorges and Hurley's historic houses.

This book is not a definitive book on Upstate New York by any means. No such book can ever be written. *Upstate Uncovered* is rather my own personal journal of places I have visited over the last decade that I encourage you to also visit. I assume nothing. Maybe everybody is already aware that the last operating U.S. Army ship deployed in the D-Day invasion is docked in Upstate New York. Maybe everyone knows that Sherrill is New York's smallest city and that Wyoming's street lamps are lit entirely by natural gas. Maybe you all know already that Rod Serling included memories of his Upstate upbringing in his *Twilight Zone* stories. Maybe not.

It is almost impossible to take a leisurely drive with me. Ask my wife. I have to stop at every historical marker ("Look, honey, the second known death from a bee sting," in Royalton), every historic building ("Hey, it's the largest cement building in the world," in Cuba), and every natural phenomenon along the way (Chimney Bluffs State Park will leave you scratching your head, for sure). I love to explore and I always ask questions. Always. How else would I have found out that the Schuyler Mansion in Albany has played host to more important and famous people over the years than any other home in the United States except the White House?

There are libraries filled with books about New York City, its history and people. I wanted this book to be the same kind of work about my Upstate New York. In fact, surprisingly, one of the largest audiences for this book (as well as my previous works) is in the five boroughs of New York City. No longer are we strangers to them, located somewhere north of the Tappan Zee Bridge and miles from civilization. Over the years the symbiotic relationship between "Upstate" and "Downstate" has manifested itself in a myriad of ways. Take a look at the residency numbers from several rural counties in Upstate for example. In a handful of them, the majority of homeowners are from the metropolitan area. These "second-home" owners swell our ranks in the summer and during hunting seasons. For generations, downstaters have vacationed in our region, from Lake George to the Catskill Game Farm to Niagara Falls. They have sent tens of thousands of their children to Upstate colleges, from the Rochester Institute of Technology to Cornell to RPI to Colgate to the Culinary Institute of America and to the many seats of learning found in "SUNYland," an area north of the New York State Thruway that hosts nearly a dozen State University of New York schools, including Canton, Brockport, Plattsburgh, Utica, Oswego, and more.

Some may wonder who picked these 100 entries? Well, that would be me. There was no criterion that had to be met for inclusion in the book. Having worn out several sets of tires traveling the byways of Upstate as I wrote seven books about the region, I simply used my intuition as to what I thought my readers might like to learn about. (Surely, the book could have had three hundred entries; we shall see if a second volume lies in the future.) I like these choices. Some are fun, many more are important. All are interesting. For example, some will question whether Albany's Hook and Ladder Company 4 fire station is in fact "Upstate's Most Beautiful Fire House." Well, it is to me, and my purpose for dubbing it so is to have you drive by it some day and see if it measures up to your expectations.

I have also included a section in each chapter titled "Other Nearby Attractions or Sites." Here I have pinpointed other interesting places to visit near the chapter's subject. This is intended to make your visit to these places as far-reaching as possible. There is just so much to see in Upstate!

There are a number of famous birthplaces in this book. Again, New York being one of America's original thirteen colonies, I could write a whole book on birthplaces, and perhaps title it *Upstate New York: Birthplace of a Nation*. I kept my birthplaces down to a dozen or so for this volume. I think the ones I chose reflect the diversity of the region, from Whitehall, the "Birthplace of the American Navy," to Monticello, the "Birthplace of the Bagel-making Machine."

The facts included in all of these entries are what make Upstate so unique. Yes, we are for the most part rural and sparsely populated. It is no joke that in most places we *do* have more cows than people. Yes, our economy suffers more deeply and for longer than in other regions in the state. Young people leave and for the most part do not come back. And don't get me started about the winters. But we have fought valiantly in America's wars, we have been beaten down and gotten back up, we have invented and created our way into the history books, and we have been the scene of many momentous achievements over the last two hundred–plus years. Achievements by such giants as Cornell, Edison, Morse, Woolworth, Eastman, Carrier, Trudeau, Corning, Westinghouse, Singer, Remington, and the Messrs. Wells and Fargo. All great stories, American stories.

Most of the above-mentioned names and events, and dozens more, are covered in this book. My desire is that you read *Upstate Uncovered* and then shove it under your car seat or stuff it in your glove box. And then, on a glorious day filled with Upstate's legendary autumnal bliss, while you are out for a drive on a back road, you might pull this book out from its hiding spot and thumb through it. And stop—right there, just up around the corner—and take a look.

You never know what you will find in our beautiful, historic and wondrous Upstate New York.

Chuck D'Imperio
upstatebooks@yahoo.com

REGION ONE

Western New York

◆ ◆ ◆

*Including parts of Allegany, Chautauqua, Erie, Livingston,
Monroe, Niagara, and Steuben Counties*

Roque on the Village Green

Angelica
Allegany County

Roque is the name of the game.

The sign on the outskirts of the village of Angelica refers to it as "A Town Where History Lives." It is a beautiful little community of about a thousand residents, but as far as history goes, not much of it is visible.

However, if you do a little digging, Angelica has some great stories to tell. Some of the former residents here have tales that leap off the pages of early Western New York history.

Angelica Schuyler was the eldest of the fifteen children of General Philip Schuyler. She married a wealthy British businessman and politician, John Philip Church. They lived in London and Paris for a time and returned to America in 1797. For their efforts to finance the American Revolution, she and her husband were granted ownership of a hundred thousand acres in western New York. Their son, Philip, came to Allegany and Genesee Counties and mapped out the design of the village named in honor of his mother. Having spent several years in Paris, they designed this little community with Parisian nuances, such as wide boulevards and a circular village green in the center. Angelica's younger sister, Elizabeth, was the wife of Alexander Hamilton. The pistols used in his duel with Aaron Burr on July 11, 1804, were kept for many years in Angelica.

Oliver Norton Smith was born in Angelica on December 17, 1839. Smith was Brig. Gen. Daniel Butterfield's company bugler. The general wrote "Taps" at Harrison's Landing, Virginia, in July, 1862, and Smith became the first bugler ever to play it in public.

Angelica resident Calvin Fairbank is a legend in the story of the Underground Railroad. He helped nearly fifty slaves escape to the North. He was captured several times and tried and convicted twice in Kentucky. He suffered unimaginable degradations while serving nineteen years in prison after his convictions. It is reported that he withstood his jailer's lash like no other, having been on the receiving end of more than thirty-five thousand lashes.

These stories rank up with the greatest tales of Upstate New York.

Now, let's talk about croquet. Well, actually let's drop the "c" and the "t" and talk about "roque" (pronounced "roke").

"Nobody knows where the idea of the game really came from well over a century ago," David Haggstrom told me. He is a native Angelican and is also the library director at nearby Alfred University. "Yes, it has many similarities to the game of croquet, but the two most glaring differences are the mallets and the balls. Our mallets are short-handled and have large faces. Croquet uses long handles, and mallets with smaller striking faces. They also use wooden balls. Ours are made out of rubber, very similar to a bowling ball."

So what is the mystique of this little-known game?

"A couple of generations ago, when people lived in an unhurried time, some local men got together and established a roque court right here in the middle of our famous park. Roque was established already, although nobody knows from whence it began. In fact, it was an Olympic sport at the 1904 Summer Olympics in St. Louis. Only one nation submitted a team. The United States.

"When the sun went down in the old days, a lot of the senior men in Angelica would gather at the court in the park. Spirited games of roque would begin, and many times they lasted well past midnight. It is a beloved tradition in our town, and we believe we are the only place left in America that still plays it regularly. During the hype of the 1904 Olympics, roque was declared the 'Game of the Century,'" he chuckled.

I asked him if there are set rules for the game.

"I'm sure somebody around here wrote them down a long time ago. You know, court size, dimensions, and such. It is pretty similar to croquet, really. But nobody ever seems to know where those rules ended up."

"So, do you still play?" I asked.

"Yes. I use my father's mallets. Some of my friends use their grandfathers' equipment," he told me.

Every year, in August, Angelica has a big community-wide festival called Heritage Days. One of the centerpieces of the event is the big roque tournament.

"That really draws a big crowd," Haggstrom said. "Even *CBS Evening News* sent a crew here in 2013 to see this unknown game that was being played in a little Western New York village. That was pretty exciting. We try and get the younger boys interested, but times are a lot different now."

I had to ask. "Do women play?"

"No. They never have. Historically and currently we can never find a woman who has played roque in Angelica."

"Are they allowed to play?"

"Well, I asked a man that years ago, and he said women would certainly be welcome to play but they had to bring their own roque balls and mallets to the court. And they don't make them anymore," he chuckled. "Also, a 1936 article from our newspaper, the *Angelica Advocate*, suggested

5

that women shouldn't play because their big dresses and hoop skirts would inadvertently (or on purpose) move the ball around the court to a more favorable position for the player."

Other Nearby Attractions or Sites

A leisurely stroll around Angelica will reveal many architectural surprises. Most of the buildings are original to the early and middle 19th-century. To evoke Paris, the planners laid out a village where a large circular park is the centerpiece. Around the park you will find many old homes, five churches (some with original Tiffany stain glass windows), a courthouse with a lighted cupola, and the village post office which has been in operation for over a century. In the center of the park is the village green where croquet (um, I mean roque) tournaments are still held.

Just on the edge of town is Angelica's historic Until the Day Dawn Cemetery at the end of East Main Street. Calvin Fairbank is buried here (lot 182.2) and a plaque on his gravestone tells of his heroics along the Underground Railroad.

More than a dozen New York State forests are located within 30 miles of Angelica. One of the best is Bald Mountain State Forest just two miles east of the village. Hiking, camping, hunting and snowmobiling are all very popular here.

Essentials

What: America's oldest roque court
Where: The Park, Angelica; Allegany County

Contact

Angelica history, tourism, and events: www.angelica-ny.net

2

The Caboose Motel

Avoca
Steuben County

A night on the rails.

"We have seventeen modern rooms at our motel, but most of our customers want to sleep out there in one of those cabooses," Patricia Thomas said. She is the owner of one of the most unusual overnight stays in Upstate New York.

As we walked out to the five 1917 railroad cabooses for a closer look, I asked Patricia where they originated from.

"They are all 1917 original cabooses that actually rode the American rails for decades," she began. "They come from five different major railway companies, and we have placed a sign on the front of each one telling where it came from. We have 'train enders' from the New York Central, the Pennsylvania Railroad, the Erie, the Great Western, and the Nickel Plate Railroad. People are always curious about that last one. It is a rare one. The Nickel Plate Road was the nickname for the New York, Chicago, and St. Louis Railroad."

All of the cabooses were standing in line on a set of original railroad tracks. "The cars were brought up by train to Wayland, just a few miles from here. We then had them brought over on flatbed trucks. They were a mess. But they sure cleaned up nice," she laughed.

I told Patricia I would like to see the inside of the Nickel Plate Road caboose. "Sure," she said. "Everybody does."

We entered the small space, stepping over a steel grate deck that I imagine old trainmen had stood on for many years waving to little kids by the crossing gates as the train roared through the midwestern towns and cities. Once inside, I was amazed at how much room there was. I would never call it spacious, but it was about the equivalent of an average camper. There were all the modern amenities you would want for a basic overnight visit: shower, toilet, lights, heat, and a small sitting room. This caboose could sleep four comfortably, six in a pinch. It was light and airy and had plenty of storage space. To reach one top bunk bed you had to climb up the original metal toe holes inserted for the shorter conductors of the day.

As I stood there I could easily imagine spending the night in a caboose. Not for the sheer comfort of it, but for the sheer history of it. I could almost imagine myself being gently rocked to sleep as the train chugged along the rails to points unknown. I could also almost hear the sounds of the train below me, the click-clack sound of the rails, the distant whistle, the . . . hey wait a minute! I really could hear them!

"We love to do that," Patricia laughed. Each caboose comes with an audio system that you can turn on which plays actual train sounds much like I described. Patricia had secretly turned the speakers on as I was standing in the middle of the caboose daydreaming. It was pretty neat, I must admit.

"So, who are your typical customers?" I asked.

"We are right in the thick of the Finger Lakes, so we do get a lot of tourists. And we get a large segment from the model-train hobby groups. Train fanatics come from all over the world to spend the night in one of our cabooses." She showed me the guest books, which had names from Germany, South Africa, Australia, and France.

"In fact, we just had a guy spend the night who actually was an old trainman who had spent time riding the rails and sleeping in an old caboose like this one. He was ninety-two years old and he said it was a dream come true to stay here."

I noticed a little sign telling about geocaching.

"Yes, we are listed as a geocaching site. We get people from all over coming here trying to find our little treasure. It is under one of our cabooses. Our handle is 'Night Train in Avoca.' It is a lot of fun and we get a lot of 'hunters' here. The only rule we have with the geocachers is that they cannot come here at night. That's all we need—one of our guests stepping out at midnight to find people crawling around under the caboose with flashlights," she laughed.

"What is it like owning a caboose motel?" I asked Patricia.

"It is magic. We love those old train cars and to see the look on people's faces when they walk inside is well worth the work here. Especially the little kids. They just squeal. It is a business, so there is a lot of maintenance and paper work and stuff. We are always fixing a roof here or a wheel there or some wiring someplace. But we accept that. They are each a century old after all. But it is also a piece of real history. And that is what makes it all so special. In 2012, *USA Today* came out for a look and wrote about us. They called us one of 'The Top Ten Places to Stay Overnight in a Vintage Motel.' We were the only place listed from New York State. We think that was pretty special, too."

Other Nearby Attractions or Sites

Avoca is located in the Finger Lakes region of Upstate New York. There are several well-known wineries within a short drive of the motel.

The Caboose Motel offers picnic areas, gas grills, and camp fires. While relaxing outside your caboose some night, take a look behind it. There in the neighbor's back yard is a large stone farm silo. Walk over—the neighbors allow you to come and take a look. The structure is obviously quite old. This silo, and the accompanying stone-foundation farmhouse, were Underground Railroad way stations. The silo and the house were once connected by secret tunnels.

Essentials

What: The Caboose Motel

Where: 60483 NY Rt. 415, Avoca; Steuben County

Contact

The Caboose Motel: www.caboosemotel.net. The caboose rooms are open seasonally, usually from June until October. The rest of the motel is open year-round.

3

The Bare Knuckle Boxing
Hall of Fame

Belfast
Allegany County

The champion's barns.

Riding through the rolling hills and dales of Allegany County in western New York the average passerby would not think twice when passing a small cluster of white buildings, barns and such, situated behind a white picket fence. What a missed opportunity.

"I like to say I have the most famous barns in sports history," Scott Burt told me. He is the owner and operator of the Bare Knuckle Boxing Hall of Fame in Belfast, N.Y. "Yessir, if these old barn walls could talk."

Scott Burt was born and raised in tiny Belfast, and as he grew up he always heard the story about the famous "boxing barns" in town. "Little did I know that many years later I would be in a position to buy these old buildings. And I am glad I did."

The barns are the actual training facilities of the legendary John L. Sullivan, the "King of Bare Knuckle Boxing." Sullivan, under the tutelage of the famous boxing coach William Muldoon, came here to train for his big boxing comebacks in the 1880s.

"Muldoon owned these barns," Burt said. "He was quite a legendary figure in his own right. He is considered to be America's first physical fitness trainer. He even trained Harry Houdini and Theodore Roosevelt. Muldoon coined the word 'sweater' to describe the knit training outfit Sullivan wore as well as coming up with the word "long johns" because his boxer preferred to use training shorts that were longer than others.

"In 1887, John L. Sullivan was one of the most famous men in the world. But he was definitely on the decline. His boxing days were over when Muldoon finally met him, drunk in a bar in New York City. Sullivan was bragging that he could still fight, while Muldoon knew that the champ was at the end of his days. He was deathly ill, walking on a crutch and certainly in no shape to fight anybody, especially in a defense of his championship. Sullivan was probably an alcoholic and was challenged to defend his title by Jake Kilrain, one of the greatest fighters of his time."

To get the fatigued and sickly Sullivan to fight at all took a little bit of chicanery on several fronts. Richard Fox, the editor of the *National Police Gazette*, awarded a bejeweled championship belt to Kilrain in 1887, naming him the world champion. This galled Sullivan, who then had his own belt made.

"I have the only replica of that belt here at my barn," Burt said. "The original cost a hundred thousand dollars and was paid for by his fans in Boston. Sullivan finally got irked enough by this pugnacious challenge from Kilrain that a fight was scheduled. Trainer Muldoon took control over Sullivan's boxing future and brought him to remote western New York to train him right here in little Belfast."

Why out here? I asked.

"Well, Muldoon owned this farm and it was far from the booze and loose women that were contributing to the champ's decline in New York City. Once here, Muldoon worked Sullivan to unimaginable levels. One day he took Sullivan fifteen miles out from Belfast and told him to get out of the wagon and walk home. Another time, trying to get the champ to start running again, Muldoon actually chained Sullivan to the back of a wagon and raced him through town with the locals all cheering and jeering at the fighter racing to keep up. Muldoon put him on a diet of meat and stale bread. When Sullivan relapsed into his old ways and showed up stinking drunk at the barns, Muldoon would chain him in a small cell to sleep it off."

I asked if this perhaps had a negative effect on the strengthening of the champ. "No, Sullivan responded well to this training. Although there were little slip-ups. In fact, when I bought the training barns in 2009, we had to move the building three blocks to its present location. In doing so, we uncovered a little trap door under the floor of the 'dry-out cell' that Sullivan was placed in when he got drunk. Under that trap door we found a jug of whiskey wrapped in a newspaper. It was more than a century old. The champ was still able to get his way after all," Burt laughed.

By the time of the world championship fight against Kilrain, John L. Sullivan was running twenty miles a day while holding six-pound dumbbells. His weight had dropped from 260 to 210 and he went into the fight a five-to-one underdog.

On July 8, 1889, Jake Kilrain from Baltimore, stepped into the ring with John L. Sullivan in front of three thousand fight fans in tiny Richburg, Mississippi. This fight would be the very last championship contest of the bare knuckles era. The fight employed the standard London Prize Rules, which were much harsher and more brutal than the Marquis of Queensbury Rules employed thereafter. The rules stated that a round was to be defined as a period of boxing that lasted until one of the combatants was knocked to the ground.

On that day, the fight lasted more than seventy rounds and was finally declared over when Sullivan, who was himself beaten so badly that he vomited in the ring during the forty-fourth round, knocked Kilrain down in the final round. Kilrain's corner called for the end of the fight because they feared their boxer would die in the ring.

John L. Sullivan went on to fight several more times and was the first American athlete to earn more than a million dollars. He retired to a life of booze, gourmet food, and numerous romantic liaisons, and when he died in 1918 at age fifty-nine, he was broke.

"The history at these barns is like no other. Sure, you have fancy halls of fame with large committees, and wealthy donors and gala celebrations. But here, in Belfast, we have the real thing," Scott Burt said. "Burt Sugar, the legendary owner of *Boxing Illustrated* and arguably the greatest boxing expert in America, once told me, 'Scott you have it all. There is nothing like it in sports history in America. It is the only museum in the world dedicated to bare knuckles boxing, and it is right here in a building that was a key part of that history. Your building, these barns, are the greatest item in your collection. This is real history.'"

The barns of Belfast contain many unique and precious artifacts of the dawning of boxing in America. "We know that Muldoon built these barns in 1884, because we found that in his own handwriting in a grease pencil on the floor joists. We still have some of the items that John L. used in his training, like the heavy iron rings which he used for weight training. They are still hanging from the ceiling, untouched since the 1880s. Muldoon built Sullivan something he called the Repose Room, which is a highlight of the tour I give of the barns. The room is resplendent in solid wood wainscoting on the walls and ceilings, appointed with elegant bookcases and lamps, as well as every comfort feature you can imagine. This is where the trainer would bring the champ to relax when things got a little tense around here. You can still see the couch that Sullivan rested on and the plush chair that Muldoon sat in."

The front of the museum area features two life-sized statues of Sullivan and Muldoon. "These are quite the works of art," Scott said. "They are solid marble. The only problem was I couldn't find any local carvers who would make them for me."

So where did they come from? I asked.

"I hired ten Buddhist monks from Vietnam to carve them for the museum. And they did a magnificent job."

Other Nearby Attractions or Sites

Belmont is located nine miles south of Belfast on NY Rt. 19 S. It is the county seat of Allegany County. The Belmont Literary and Historical Society Free Library is one of the most photographed buildings in the village. It is a tri-corner structure erected in the 19th century vernacular public architecture style. The 1893 red brick building features a balcony over the front door and a three story clock tower.

Essentials

What: John L. Sullivan training barns (Bare Knuckle Boxing Hall of Fame)

Where: Hughes Street, Belfast; Allegany County

Contact

Bare Knuckle Boxing Hall of Fame (tours are given): www.bareknuckleboxinghalloffame.com

4

Anchor Bar

Buffalo
Erie County

The birthplace of the Buffalo chicken wing.

I worked in my parent's grocery store when I was a kid in the 1950s and 1960s. My dad was a butcher, and I saw him cut up maybe a half-million chickens over the years. The chickens themselves would end up whirling around on a glorious, brightly lit rotisserie, five on a skewer, all the while browning and crisping and sizzling like a food arcade pinball machine. But what about the rest of the chicken?

Well, in those days the lowly innards were basically an afterthought. I can't tell you how many times I reached my hand deep inside the cold, clammy chicken and hauled out that little mysterious bag of unwanted parts. My father tried frying the livers and breading them, but no one really bought them. The necks were saved for a couple of old ladies who liked to throw them into their chicken stocks. The gizzards were saved for a couple of old men who liked to give them to their even older dogs. And the chicken wings?

Nothing.

They would stay on the chicken as they spun around on the rotisserie, all trussed up with string to keep them from hitting the heating elements. Most of the time they burned anyways. And most of the time they ended up in the garbage. Until a fateful day in the 1960s, the unwieldy, boney, cumbersome, and tasteless chicken wing was relegated to the dustbin of food history. Kind of like the lonely Maytag repairman of poultry parts.

Then along came Teressa Bellissimo. And she turned it into a grazing icon.

Ms. Bellissimo was the owner of the Anchor Bar in downtown Buffalo in the 1960s. The bar had been there since 1935. The legend goes that one cold winter night, March 6, 1964, the owner's son, Dominic, was tending bar when his buddies stopped by for a beer and something to eat. It was late in the evening. Having closed down most of the kitchen already, Mama Teressa deep-fried some chicken wings and served them up to her son and his friends. She drenched the tasteless wings in Frank's Hot Sauce, poured out a glob of bleu cheese dressing onto the plate, and garnished it with some leftover celery stalks. Problem solved. The doomed wings were cooked and served. The young men were delighted with the new tasty treat. And a legend was born.

The Anchor Bar continued to serve up chicken wings in hot sauce. Originally they just gave them away to thirsty bar patrons, but eventually as demand grew, they started charging for them. Still their popularity grew and with it so did the restaurant. A half-century later, the Anchor Bar sells them by the hundreds of thousands a year.

Today the deep-fried chicken wing that first appeared in the Anchor Bar backroom a half-century ago is the top food snack item in America. Whole restaurant chains dedicated solely to the hot wing have popped up all over the country. The frozen food aisles in our grocery stores offer dozens of different types and tastes, and they have become the top item at tailgating parties. Nearly thirty billion wings are sold each year. And speaking of tailgating, a record 1.3 billion wings were sold for parties surrounding a single day, the 2013 Super Bowl. That's a lot of wings, hot sauce, and celery!

I have eaten at the Anchor Bar in Buffalo several times. When I visit I often wonder what the place was like back a few decades when it was still a little bit of a secret. A corner watering hole at heart, the Anchor Bar has a large, muscular, circular oak bar in the main room. A series of television sets rings the barroom, all of them on a sports channel. Motorcycle memorabilia, an old jukebox, eight-by-ten black-and-white autographed photos of bygone movie and TV stars, a jumble of old license plates on the wall, kitschy statues and bric-a-brac make the large room seem small and close and very comfortable.

Today, forget it.

Like Yogi Berra once said, "Nobody goes there anymore. It's too crowded."

Waits of thirty minutes or more to get a seat at the "Home of the Original Buffalo Chicken Wings" are routine. Charter buses pull in to the expanded parking lot. International tourists are an ever-growing clientele. A seat at the bar is as rare as a snowless Buffalo December day. But still they come. And for good reason.

The wings here are memorable. They come out in piles, in mountains, on large trays, a steaming heap of bright orange, crispy hot wings accompanied by an empty "bones bowl." Wet naps are required. Thousands will be served during your brief visit here. The wings are cooked to perfection, and the sauce, although a shocker at first, ends up striking just the right balance of hot and tangy. The atmosphere is one of controlled mayhem, which is part of the fun of the Anchor Bar experience. Most everybody orders wings here; after all, that is why they came. I don't even know if they offer salads on the menu, and if they did who would dare order one.

No visit to Buffalo, or even western New York, would be complete without visiting the Anchor Bar. Be prepared to wait in line for a seat, and be ready for a harried, yet fun, experience inside (they are busy, selling more than seventy thousand pounds of wings a month). But whatever you do, come. And enjoy. The Anchor Bar is about as close to a national food shrine as it gets in America.

Other Nearby Attractions or Sites

The city of Buffalo pays tribute to their signature food with a gigantic festival every Labor Day weekend. The National Buffalo Wing Festival is the largest food festivals in New York with over 100,000 in attendance annually. The festival is held at Coca Cola Field, the home of the minor league Buffalo Bisons baseball team. The stadium holds more than 18,000 fans. The event spills over throughout the city with many featured attractions, live music, chicken wing eating contests and more. Since the festival began in 2002, it is estimated that more than three million chicken wings have been sold. The event is a major city fundraiser which helps fill the coffers of many Buffalo non-profit agencies.

Essentials

What: The birthplace of the Buffalo chicken wing

Where: Anchor Bar, Buffalo; Erie County

Contact

The Anchor Bar: www.anchorbar.com

The National Buffalo Wing Festival (also known as WingFest): www.buffalo wing.com

Buffalo tourism, history, and events: http://www.visitbuffaloniagara.com

5

The Edward M. Cotter

Buffalo
Erie County

The oldest active fireboat in the world.

People sometimes forget that Buffalo is a major port city. At one time in its history it had the third most active waterfront in the East. Today, a ride through the area reveals shadows and ghosts from its halcyon era. Intricate series of boat slips and harbor sites appear around every turn. Ships come and go as they ply Lake Erie laden with cargo bound for Canada or the American Midwest. Dozens of monster silos create their own kind of odd landscape along the waterfront. Most are empty and forgotten, but many still carry giant signs on them and are clearly still in use.

As a major industrial port, Buffalo was a key player in much of America's history, from the early Erie Canal days (it was the western terminus) through World War II. In fact, one of the finest naval floating museums is found here along the waterfront. The Buffalo and Erie County Naval and Military Park features three of the Navy's best-known ships still afloat; all are open for public tours. Here is the mighty USS *Little Rock* (1943), the first ship named after that Arkansas city. The sixteen-hundred-ton submarine USS *Croaker*, which saw heavy action in the last year of World War II, is also docked in Buffalo. Perhaps the ship with the most famous name here is the USS *The Sullivans*. This destroyer saw action in both World War II and the Korean War. It is named after the five Sullivan brothers who died in a submarine attack on their ship in 1942. It was the greatest loss of life in a single family during World War II.

In another section of the Buffalo waterfront, across town from the newly developed Military Park, is a different famous ship, which carries a name few remember. This boat really does have a unique story to tell!

The *Edward M. Cotter* is a fireboat. It was built in 1900 and is still in use. On the day of my visit, I followed twisting Ohio Street along the industrial area of the lakefront. Construction cranes crowded next to empty warehouses, which were all overshadowed by looming cement silos. Local blue-collar pubs showed their dimly lit insides through open doors on this warm afternoon. This area is known as Silo City. At one time five thousand people worked in Silo City unloading as much as two-and-a-half million tons of grain an hour!

The grain elevators and silos, built between 1860 and 1920, are a formidable and yet somehow graceful exclamation point to the city's thriving past. Company names adorn the tops of the silos, some from current users and others from companies that departed long ago. The biggest tourist draws here are the six hundred-foot grain silos painted like Labatt Blue beer cans. They are referred to as "The World's Largest Six-Pack."

I finally spotted the silo that said General Mills on top. I was told this would be my directional marker to find the *Edward M. Cotter*. At the dead end of the road I came on a very small, one-room firehouse. Tied up next to it, positively gleaming in the August sunshine, was the boat.

The *Cotter* is a fully functional, operating fireboat. It is painted a dazzling red, and all the accoutrements of what we know to be a fireboat are on display. Hoses, fire axes, life preservers, round portholes, nautical ropes, searchlights, a powerful water cannon on top, the glass-walled captain's wheelhouse, the anchor. They are all there. Just like in the books we read as a youngster. The *Cotter* appeared as if it were ready to steam out onto Lake Erie at a second's notice.

The *Cotter* began life as the *William S. Grattan*. Her main duties were patrolling the busy harbor area and performing all-important ice-breaking chores during the hard Buffalo winters. On several occasions, the *Grattan* played a key part in dramatic events at the port. Perhaps the worst incident in the boat's long history happened on July 28, 1928. A barge laden with five thousand barrels of crude oil caught fire and the *Grattan* responded. Eventually, she too was engulfed in fire, and the ship's crew had to swim through flaming oil-soaked water to safety. One death, several injuries, and a heavily charred fireboat were the results of this tragedy.

Later, the *Grattan* was repaired and emerged with a new name, the *Edward M. Cotter*. He was a well-known firefighter and a popular leader of the Buffalo fire union.

In 1960, the *Cotter* sailed to Canada to help extinguish a grain elevator fire. In doing so, she became the first U.S. fireboat ever to cross international borders to assist in a fire.

The *Cotter*, a proud bridge connecting Buffalo's past and present, is a beloved icon in the city and is open for tours. The boat was designated a National Historic Landmark in 1996.

Other Nearby Attractions or Sites

The aforementioned Silo City is really a sight to see, unlike anything else in New York State outside of New York City. Efforts are underway to make these monuments to the past accessible to the general public. One company has purchased some silos and is turning them into "faux rock climbing walls." Another company now gives guided tours of Silo City that are popular with both locals and tourists. A few intrepid companies are taking over a few of the silos for new business endeavors. For instance, Labatt, of "World's Largest Six-Pack" fame, intends to use their newly purchased silo as a catalyst for a brewery and entertainment venue.

Essentials

What: The *Edward M. Cotter* Fireboat

Where: 155 Ohio Street (berth), Buffalo; Erie County

Contact

Edward M. Cotter (fireboat): www.emcotter.com

Buffalo: tourism, events and information www.visitbuffaloniagara.com

Silo City guided tours: http://explorebuffalo.org/regularly-scheduled/silo-city-grounded

Silo Rock Climbing: www.facebook.com/SiloCityRocks

6

A Forest of Tree Letters

Canisteo
Steuben County

The world's largest living sign. Photograph courtesy of Dylan McCaffrey.

Writer, researcher, entrepreneur, artist, and all-around publicity-hound Robert Ripley (1890–1949) must have loved seeking out the odd and unusual items in Upstate New York to wow his readers with. Many of them have roots right in this book. Ripley's "Believe It or Not" was a publishing sensation, corralling millions of followers in print and on radio and television.

Ripley once wrote about singer Kate Smith's island home in Lake Placid, calling it "the smallest recording studio in the world." He once featured Upstate's Annie Edson Taylor, the first person to survive going over Niagara Falls in a barrel, in a famous cartoon panel along with an alligator with a rubber tail. He wrote about Greene County's Pratt Rock in a nationwide cartoon, calling it "New York's Mt. Rushmore." He made Albion, in Orleans County, famous by writing about it twice, first for the curious "Church in the Middle of the Street" and second for Culvert Road, the only place where a road goes underneath the Erie Canal.

But surely Mr. Ripley was stymied for words when he arrived in Canisteo in Steuben County to seek out and research "The World's Largest Living Sign." I've seen it several times and yes, it is hard to describe.

In 1933 students in the local school planted more than 250 Scotch Pine trees on a hill overlooking their school. The trees spell out "CANISTEO" in letters so perfectly aligned that it must have made their handwriting teacher beam. The natural lettering stretches over ninety feet long, over a field more than three hundred feet wide. The living sign is perfectly positioned in on a north-south axis, and even today pilots flying overhead use this oddity to get their bearings.

A sign at the village limits of Canisteo tells of its famous forest feature. The day I was there, in the summer when school was out, I was really impressed by the sign and how beautiful it looked. So how do locals feel about this oddity? It wasn't long before a car pulled up in the empty school parking lot, and I got to find out.

"Yup, it has been here on that hill forever," Toby Johnson, seventy-six, told me. He is a lifelong resident of nearby Hornell. "People think it's crazy but we love that sign. It is funny to see, but people come up to the school (Canisteo-Greenwood Elementary School), get out, and take pictures of it all the time. Just like you are," he laughed.

"It is amazing how clear the letters are spelling out 'Canisteo.' They say that when airplanes go overhead the pilot will tell the passengers to look out their windows so they can see it. I used to have a cousin back in the 1970s who had to mow around each and every one of those trees. He said it was a pain in the neck. I guess every town has to be known for something, and for Canisteo it is that darn tree sign. But stay away from it around St. Patrick's Day," he chuckled.

For many years huge flocks of turkey vultures would fly back to Canisteo on March 17 to nest after the winter. They would make the living sign their home. The community has held many "Turkey Vulture Festivals" to celebrate the returning of these birds to their famous sign.

On July 15, 2004, the National Park Service certified the Canisteo Living Sign as a National Historic Site.

Mr. Ripley would have been flummoxed had he been aware of another, larger living sign located in South Bend, Indiana. That sign spells out "STUDEBAKER" at Bendix Woods County Park. The location is a former aviation proving ground for the Studebaker Company. This sign was planted five years after the Canisteo one. But with a word like Studebaker, well, it is obviously much larger. The Indiana sign is a half-mile long and consists of an amazing eight thousand pine trees. There is no record of Mr. Ripley honoring this sign, but the folks at the *Guinness Book of World Records* have certified it as the "World's Largest Living Advertising Sign." It too is registered as a National Historic Site.

The Canisteo sign is easily viewed from the parking lot of either the Greenwood High School or Elementary School. If you want a closer look you can walk up to the field behind the school, or find access to the sign from an adjoining cemetery.

Other Nearby Attractions or Sites

Five miles north of Canisteo is the small city of Hornell. If you are going to watch the turkey vulture spectacle at the Canisteo Living Sign some St. Patrick's Day, spend the rest of the day in Hornell. This city of under ten thousand throws the biggest Irish party in the region. Mayor Shawn Hogan, first elected in 1986, is (at the printing of this book) still mayor. He is the longest-tenured city mayor in New York State. Every year, for more than a quarter-century, Mayor Hogan has been the "star" of the event, figuring out a new and unique way to ride in the parade. His mode of transportation has varied from an 1898 locally made automobile to a cardboard airplane to a farmer's manure spreader to a horse!

Hornell is the birthplace of two famous celebrities. Actor Bill Pullman, who played the president of the United States in the 1996 hit movie *Independence Day*, was born here in 1953. Artist Frank Kelly Freas was born here in 1922. He was the chief cover artist for *MAD Magazine* and the creator of its mascot, Alfred E. Neuman. Actor Bob Crane, who starred in the classic television comedy *Hogan's Heroes*, got his first radio DJ job at Hornell's WLEA radio station in 1950.

Essentials

What: The world's largest living sign

Where: 120 Greenwood Street, Canisteo; Steuben County

Contact

Canisteo history and events: www.canisteo.org

Hornell St. Patrick's Day Parade: http://www.corningfingerlakes.com/events/hornell-st-patricks-day-celebration

Ripley's Believe It or Not: www.ripleys.com

7

Athenaeum Hotel

Chautauqua
Chautauqua County

The queen of the lake.

To call the Athenaeum Hotel grand would be a monumental understatement.

The hotel, the largest wooden building east of the Mississippi, is the regal centerpiece of the famous Chautauqua Institution. Built in 1881, just seven years after the institution was founded, it has over 150 rooms, a cavernous dining room, a welcoming awning-covered veranda, lush landscaping, and a breathtaking lakeside location. In the old days steamboats and pleasure craft would bring well-heeled guests to the hotel by the hundreds.

The cost to build the hotel was $125,000, making it at the time one of the most expensive such structures of its kind. Construction was financed by a small group of investors who wanted to provide lavish accommodations to the rich and famous who visited here. Automobile maker Clement Studebaker was one of the original investors. Another was wealthy Ohio industrialist Lewis Miller. Miller's daughter, Mina, married inventor Thomas A. Edison. Perhaps trying to keep familial feathers unruffled, Edison saw to it that the Atheneum Hotel was the first fully electrified hotel in America.

The Chautauqua Institution was founded to become training grounds for Methodist ministers. Today, many of the original religious connotations can still be seen throughout the 750-acre community. There is a Christian Science House, a Lutheran Home, a Disciples of Christ House, and a Hall of Christ. The entire community, including all the nearby clustered eighteenth- and nineteenth-century cottages, the Athenaeum, the amphitheater, the bell tower, and the grounds, were registered as a National Historic Landmark in 1989 for their history and architectural significance.

"I started coming here as a kid and at age seventy-two, and I am still here," Rich Fischer told me. He is a longtime volunteer at the Institution. "It is a magical place. In the winter months the gates are open and people can come and go as they please. A couple hundred residents stay here all winter. But in the summer season, the gate is closed and entry is restricted and admission is charged. We can get ten thousand visitors over a busy weekend," he told me.

Chautauqua is famous for bringing in an A-list of speakers, celebrities, and entertainers for residents and visitors to enjoy. A half-dozen U.S. presidents have stayed here, from U. S. Grant to Bill Clinton. Kings and queens have vacationed here, and the list of entertainers who have performed at Chautauqua is exhaustive. "We recently had writer Ken Burns here for a whole week," Rich told me. "Our amphitheater, which was built in 1892, holds five thousand people, but somehow we managed to get over six thousand in every night to hear Mr. Burns."

I asked Rich what makes Chautauqua unique and special to both him and those who own the little Victorian cottages that dot the grounds. "I think it is because you can really live 'the good old days' here," he said. "People know each other here, they watch out for their neighbors. The houses are beautifully cared for, and everyone takes pride in their home. Automobiles are frowned upon in the close quarters of the Institution, so at night you will see people out walking or riding their bikes around. There are ice cream socials and concerts and a beautiful lakeside to stroll along. In the evening, I dare say that almost nobody locks their door. It is just a wonderful slice of Americana here."

Rich showed me the list of current entertainers, and it was impressive. "Country music singer Vince Gill stayed for two hours after his concert and shook every hand in the audience," he said. I asked him if they always got the biggest stars.

"Let me show you something, Chuck," he said to me as he opened up a file drawer. "In here is a brochure from every year over the last four decades. Each brochure lists the entertainment for the year. Pick a year." Okay, I thought. I'm ready to play. "How about 1983?" I said.

After a brief search Rich brought out a triple-folded 1983 brochure for the summer events at the Institution. And he started to read. "Well, the season began with Bob Hope and then next came Kris Kristofferson, Dinah Shore, a Roger Williams piano concert, Ginger Rogers, Arlo Guthrie and Pete Seeger, Harry Belafonte, Bobby Vinton, the Tommy Dorsey Orchestra, Ray Charles, and then Tennessee Ernie Ford. Oh, and the lectures that summer were by three famous politicians of the time: Eugene McCarthy, John Anderson, and Robert Taft."

I have had the Sunday brunch at the Athenaeum, and it is spectacular in a muted, elegant "Gilded Age" sense. The dining room is high-ceilinged, light, and breezy with wide windows showcasing the rich blue waters of Chautauqua Lake. The food was sumptuous and the wait staff service impeccable. After a royal repast it seemed only right to shuffle out to the massive two-story front porch, park myself in a rocking chair, and watch the strollers wander by, the boats ply their way up the lake, and the birds flit around the giant flowering bushes along the staircase. It was sublime.

Other Nearby Attractions or Sites

There is no need to add extra stops to your visit to Chautauqua. There is plenty to see and do right here on the grounds. They have an ice cream parlor, a well-stocked bookstore, walking paths, barber shops, a fitness and wellness center, an art gallery, a general store, a medical center, and almost universal Wi-Fi service. The community also has its own police and fire departments. An active list of concerts, lectures, and exhibits should keep everybody busy. But to me the most unusual site to see at Chautauqua is one that is often overlooked.

Palestine Park is a scale model of the Holy Land. The park is spread out over small dunes and mounds and gullies to recreate the towns, villages, rivers, and stream of Palestine. Chautauqua Lake doubles as the Mediterranean Sea. Since the park is built low to the ground, many visitors don't see it at first. As you walk among the tiny white buildings representing Jericho, Jerusalem, Bethany, and the Mount of Olives you will feel like a giant striding across the landscape. It is quite an incredible historical oddity and in fact, it was the first landmark built at the Institution (1874). It is said that it was laid out near the lake's edge so that visitors disembarking from the passenger steamers of the day would have to "walk through the Holy Land" to get to the Institution.

Scheduled tours are given to explain Palestine Park, usually on Sundays.

Essentials

What: The Athenaeum Hotel

Where: Chautauqua Institution, 1 Ames Avenue, Chautauqua; Chautauqua County

Contact

Athenaeum Hotel: www.atheneaum-hotel.com

Chautauqua Institution: www.ciweb.rog

8

The First Chapter of the American Red Cross

Dansville
Livingston County

Upstate's angel of mercy.

Long before Clara Barton (1821–1912) settled in Dansville, the community was known as a center for healing and wholesomeness through "Our Home on the Hillside" a spa and health institute opened here in 1870 by Caleb Jackson, a popular health guru of the day. Jackson believed in water cures, hydrotherapy, strict diets, fresh air, exercise, and creative pharmacology. The sanitarium was an elaborate series of brick buildings constructed on a hill overlooking the village of Dansville. Hundreds were employed here, and at its peak the spa was one of the largest in the world and catered to more than twenty thousand customers annually.

Oh, and he invented the very first breakfast cereal, which he served at Our Home on the Hillside. It was called "Granula."

Barton was already internationally famous for her relief work when she came to rural Dansville for rest and recuperation from exhaustion in 1881. A pioneer nurse, Barton was well known throughout the land for her activities during the Civil War. She was in charge of battlefield hospitals, organized a corps of nurses, and tended to wounded soldiers often while they were still on the battlefield. One story that grabbed the headlines concerned the time she was tending a wounded soldier at the height of a pitched battle. An enemy bullet came crashing through her medical tent, pierced a hole in her nurse's blouse, and struck and killed the man she was tending.

She had just returned from a speaking tour and investigative journey exploring the already established Red Cross organization in Europe. When back home she set her mind to found an American Red Cross, and she formulated her organizational plans while at the health spa. Her first chapter in the United States was opened in Dansville, and it is still there.

Today the Clara Barton American Red Cross Chapter #1 serves a dozen local communities. When it first opened its doors on August 22, 1881, there were just fifty-seven members. Annual dues were twenty-five cents. Just two weeks after the chapter opened, the group responded to its first disaster.

The great "Thumb Fire" on the upper peninsula of Michigan was one of the most disastrous fires of the nineteenth century. The fire, fed by drought and high winds, scorched more than a million acres in a single day. The toll was horrific. Over three hundred people died and more than five thousand lost their homes, jobs, and crops. The monetary damage was over three million dollars.

Clara Barton, then sixty years old, raced to New York City to begin pleading for resources and funds. She spoke tirelessly about the tragedy and handed out flyers and pamphlets all over the city asking for donations. The Dansville Chapter, being the only Red Cross office in the United States, acted as the lead relief agency for the fire in northern Michigan. Eight large crates of supplies left Dansville for the disaster site. Mark Bunnell, the son of the Dansville newspaper editor, and Mrs. Julian Hubbell, a young Dansville chemistry teacher, accompanied the relief supplies. They had also collected three hundred dollars from the Dansville community as a donation for the stricken communities devastated by the fire.

On September 4, 1881, the now iconic Red Cross flag flew for the first time over an emergency relief camp in the United States.

This was the first of thousands of emergency relief actions that the American Red Cross has engaged in for well over a century. The success of the relief agency in the fire in Michigan galvanized support for its growth and expansion, and in a short time American Red Cross chapters sprang up all over the country.

And it all started in little Dansville, N.Y.

The first Red Cross office was located in St. Paul's Lutheran Church, located appropriately on Clara Barton Street. A historical marker out front gives pertinent information about the first meeting of the Red Cross held there in 1881. The church was listed in the National Register of Historic Places in 2014. The offices later moved nearby to a home donated by Frederick and Emma Noyes, who were among the original charter members of the Red Cross.

American Red Cross Chapter #1 today acts as a working relief office as well as a small museum dedicated to the Red Cross and Clara Barton's decade of residence in Dansville. Many of the items are from the Civil War era, a time when Clara Barton first became known as "The Angel of the Battlefield."

Other Nearby Attractions or Sites

The massive, sprawling Our Home on the Hill Sanitarium was purchased in 1929 by one of the earliest superstars in the health field, Dr. Bernarr MacFadden. He is called by some "The Father of American Physical Fitness." He was a wealthy and well-known man whose clients and admirers included everyone from sports stars to entertainment celebrities to President Franklin D. Roosevelt. MacFadden ran the Dansville resort until he died in 1955. It continued in various forms until it closed forever in 1971.

I have been to Dansville several times, and while the American Red Cross Chapter #1 office is very interesting, who could not help but be intrigued by the hulking castle-like campus of deteriorating brick buildings lurking beyond the thick undergrowth near the entrance to town?

The building is incredible, elegant, stunning, and unforgettable. It is also decrepit, unsafe, dangerous, and not a little spooky. I wandered in as far as I dared to get a look at it but was chased back by "DO NOT ENTER" signs, a rusty chain-link fence, and the howling of a dog, which I assumed, given the aura of the place, was a werewolf.

Dansville has recently begun celebrating their most famous resident with an annual Clara Barton Day, which involves community events, parades, and of course celebrations of Clara Barton. The museum will be heavily involved with the celebration.

Essentials

What: The first American Red Cross office

Where: 57 Elizabeth Street, Dansville; Livingston County

Contact

Clara Barton–Livingston Red Cross #1: www.redcross.org/ny/dansville/about-us

Dansville history, tourism, and events: www.dansvillechamber.com

9

Dunkirk Lighthouse

Dunkirk
Chautauqua County

The first shots of the War of 1812.

There are so many wonderful lighthouses around Upstate New York that I had a hard time figuring out which one to include. I knew I wanted to feature at least one, but which?

The Tibbett's Point Lighthouse (1854) is a marvelous structure standing proudly where "the river meets the lake" off Cape Vincent. The Selkirk Lighthouse (1838) at Port Ontario and the Salmon River is one of the oldest in America and welcomes guests to spend the evening overnight in an original keeper's home. The Hudson-Athens Lighthouse must be one of the most photographed of them all, sitting proud and stoic smack dab in the middle of the Hudson River. The Cayuga Inlet (West) Lighthouse is striking because it is the only one painted bright red. And for sure beauty it is hard to match the graceful columns that sheath the Crown Point Lighthouse on Lake Champlain. Not used as a working lighthouse since 1926, it now serves as a monument to explorer Samuel de Champlain. And it is beautiful. I mean, how many lighthouses can brag of having an actual sculpture by Auguste Rodin adorning its facade?

I chose the Dunkirk Lighthouse to represent the dozens of others in the state to be included in this book, for several reasons. It is highly accessible to tourists, and it has a full range of amenities to make a visit here satisfying, including restrooms, a museum shop, and guided tours. The view along the coast of Lake Erie is spectacular. And it has a lot of great history to it.

The first shot of the War of 1812 happened right here, just a few hundred feet out from the Dunkirk Lighthouse.

"Yes, this is quite the historical place," Dave Briska told me. He is a volunteer guide at the lighthouse and a member of the board of directors that oversees its operations. "A salt barge was heading to Buffalo and was coming past the lighthouse when a British warship appeared and started to chase it. The salt barge quickly headed into shore near the lighthouse to hide out. The warship, the *Lady Provost*, was hunting up and down the coast looking for the barge and her valuable cargo. A woman who lived near the lighthouse, known to all as the Widow Cole, saw the British ship coming and got on her horse and raced all the way to an American camp at Fredonia. There she told Captain Martin Tubbs what was happening, and he started marching to the lighthouse. His small band of militia grew along the way, adding trappers, farmers, and hunters to join the cause. By the time they got to the lighthouse, the British saw what had become a rather formidable force standing shoulder to shoulder along the bluff firing on them, and they decided to high-tail it out of there. But the war was on. And the first shots were fired on our property."

The Dunkirk Lighthouse is quite striking. It is attached to a lovely red-brick keeper's home, which is two stories tall and has many wide windows. The interior is a very comfortable living space. The house was considered quite lavish at the time, designed in the era's Victorian style.

Unlike many others, this lighthouse was originally square rather than round. A rounded shell was placed around it to make it look more compatible to the house.

"The light has a rare Fresnel lens on it, which reflects the light out over the water," Dave told me. "It cost ten thousand dollars to buy back in 1857. It still works today and is now worth a million-and-a-half dollars."

The grounds of the lighthouse are littered with all kinds of sea-going artifacts, including a number of very substantial anchors.

"Those anchors are from many of the ships that sank right off our coast. The storms come up fast and furious at Dunkirk, and hundreds of ships have gone to the bottom taking their crews with them."

I asked Dave for one of his favorite stories. He looked over a large map that pinpointed all the verified sunken ships near the lighthouse and pointed to one. "Well, they are all interesting but here is one I enjoy telling. In July of 1913, a Canadian coal barge named the *Anna Belle Wilson* sank in fifty feet of water just off our coast. A storm had swamped it. The ship had six crew members along with the captain and his wife. As they took on water and began to abandon ship, the wife put up quite a fuss about leaving behind her money on the ship. As the storm swirled around them, and the *Anna Belle Wilson* began to sink, the man and wife argued over what to do. Finally, the woman won out and they both went back into the boat to get her money. Well, the crew had had enough of that by then and they rowed off to safety to our lighthouse. Captain Barney McIntyre and his wife were never seen again."

It was clear to me that Dave Briska has had a long love affair with this lighthouse. "Yes, that is true," he readily admitted. "And my favorite place in the whole world is right up there," he said as he pointed to the top of the tower holding the light. "It is more than eighty feet up in the air, and I like nothing better than to climb up there on a nice clear day, sit in my chair, and view the world around me. On the best days, you can even see Canada, more than twenty-five miles across Lake Erie. It just doesn't get any better than that," he beamed.

The gift shop and museum features a wide array of nautical-themed items.

Other Nearby Attractions or Sites

Brocton lies ten miles to the south of Dunkirk. The town is noted for its famous highway double arch. You can't miss it. Its graceful iron beams curve over a downtown intersection like a giant spider. It is lit at night. Painted green, it is the only highway double arch east of the Mississippi. The people of Brocton are mighty proud of this oddity. They raised funds to save it from being torn down and worked for years to finally get it listed on the National Register of Historic Places (1996). Down the block is one of Brocton's most popular restaurants. It is called (of course) the Green Arch Diner.

Brocton is also the home of the late cartoonist Brad Anderson. His character, the beloved Great Dane Marmaduke, will be remembered in Brocton with a whimsical statue of the comic-strip dog on US 20. Construction of this statue was being planned as this book was about to be printed. At its peak "Marmaduke" was one of the most popular comic strips in the country, appearing in more than five hundred newspapers.

Essentials

What: The Dunkirk Lighthouse

Where: 1 Point Drive North, Dunkirk; Chautauqua County

Contact

Dunkirk Lighthouse: www.dunkirklighthouse.com

10

Vidler's Store

East Aurora
Erie County

America's five-and-dime store.

Upstate New York has no shortage of historic five-and-dime department stores in its past. Baby boomers delighted in shopping at these stores, which became the cornerstones to our small town main streets and early urban centers. Store such as Woolworth's, S. H. Kress, W. T. Grants, J. J. Newberry's, and others became the shopping malls of our youth. From small towns such as Cooperstown and Cortland to major cities like Binghamton and Albany, these stores were the places our moms could take us for a day spent entirely shopping for almost everything.

And when I say everything, these stores had it all! From clothes to safety pins and from forty-five-rpm records to the machines to play them on, these were the shopping meccas of the mid-twentieth century.

And most of them kept you in the store for the duration of your shopping marathon by giving you a place for lunch or dinner. The Woolworth's, Grants, and Newberry's chrome-and-red-leather lunch counters were stocked with homemade pies and soups; a griddle was fired up and ever ready to cook up some fancy-named breakfast special ("Early Shoppers' Start-'Em-Up Breakfast," a famous one was called), and the ubiquitous gleaming ice cream soda fountains were busy pouring us our favorite sodas and floats nonstop while mom shopped. All great memories of the days of old.

But for the most part, they are just memories. These keystones to the downtowns of the 1940s and 1950s are long gone. The last Newberry's closed in 2001. Woolworth's, which gave us the first "five-cent store" in Utica in 1878, succumbed in 1997, and W. T. Grants's lunch counter closed forever in 1976, the victim of the second-largest bankruptcy filing at the time in U.S. history.

These great stores had everything you needed under one roof. Everybody has a "junk drawer" in their kitchen today. Well, these stores were "America's junk drawers," and New York had the best ones. Vermont is known for its quaint country stores and Pennsylvania is famous for its open-air markets, Amish or otherwise. But New York was the five-and-dime capital of America.

Today, one can still experience the thrill of entering a store teeming with customers, one that still exudes family-friendliness, a store that displays everything you can imagine in a wonderful jumble of afterthought marketing. That place is Vidler's 5 and 10 in East Aurora. The store is a magical throwback to the day when family shopping was fun, when prices were low, and when the person at the cash register was usually a family member of the owner. Today you can buy everything here from a winter coat to iPod accessories to sewing thimbles to penny candy.

Vidler's began in 1930 and succeeded by supplying its customers with everything they needed at a fair price all during the Depression era. Robert Vidler was the founder, and the store is still run by the third generation of family members. Vidler's was never afraid of expanding, and as their customer base grew, so did the store, and the inventory. Today Vidler's is a hurly-burly of crowded aisles, animated displays, piped-in music, and product placement that seems to have been made up as they went along. The store now covers almost an entire city block in the heart of downtown East Aurora. That is twenty times the size of the original store started by Bob Vidler in 1930. Ask how many items they stock in the store today and the answer is "nobody really knows." At last count they carry more than seventy-five thousand different items.

It is an event to stop in at Vidler's. As you enter the front door you are greeted with one of the most familiar and reliable nostalgia triggers to get you in a friendly frame of mind: a hot, working, ever-popping popcorn machine! Go ahead and grab a bag for a dime. Everybody does.

The store is old-timey with oiled wooden floors, old cash registers, and old lighting fixtures. The help is friendly, and the mood is definitely happy. On weekends, the crowds are thick with families. On autumn weekends, parking spaces out front along Main Street can be few and far between. Between Thanksgiving and Christmas, lines snake out the front door and down the sidewalk as shoppers clamor for toys, decorations, gifts, stockings, and fruitcakes. Even though Buffalo is fifteen miles away, *Buffalo Spree Magazine* routinely names Vidler's as "the most fun place to shop in the Buffalo area."

You cannot miss the store. The exterior is a whimsical mixture of architectural styles. The canopies and awnings are old-fashioned red-and-white striped, and there is a man on the roof. And, no, it is not Santa Claus.

It is Ed Vidler, son of founder Bob Vidler. In 2009, eighty-three-year-old Ed himself pulled the curtain off a giant statue of himself dressed in his Vidler's red apron and waving to all below, and then watched as it was hoisted up by a crane and positioned over the front of his namesake store. The smiling East Aurora icon weighs in at four hundred pounds and stands (or sits) ten feet high. It is the perfect, giggle-inducing topping to a store that is beloved by its community and recognized nationally for its importance and success in carrying on the five-and-dime tradition in America.

Oh, by the way. The locals refer to the statue as "Vidler on the Roof." Perfect.

Other Nearby Attractions or Sites

This community exudes big-city amenities and small-town values. The Main Street is a perfect example of this dichotomy. Every major franchise or chain is represented here, along with a stunning century-old movie house with a classic art deco marquee. The trash containers that line Main Street feature whimsical quotes from famous authors and personalities. The one in front of Vidler's read, "Anyone who has never made a mistake has never tried anything (Albert Einstein)."

East Aurora is also well known as the home of three American legends. One was a movement, one was a president, and one is a beloved toy company

The Roycroft Arts and Crafts Movement was started here by Elbert Hubbard in 1895. Millard Fillmore, the thirteenth president of the United States, practiced law here, was married here, and lived in East Aurora for more than two decades. His home is the only house built by a U.S. president himself. And Fisher-Price Toy Company was founded here in 1930 and is still headquartered at 636 Girard Avenue.

All three have museums here in their honor.

Essentials

What: Vidler's Five & Dime

Where: 676 Main Street, East Aurora; Erie County

Contact

Vidler's: www.vidlers5and10.com

President Millard Fillmore presidential site: www.aurorahistoricalsociety.com

The Elbert Hubbard Roycroft Museum: www.roycrofter.com/museum

11

Parkside Whispering Pines Miniature Golf

Irondequoit
Monroe County

America's oldest miniature golf course.

Upstate New York has had a long and glorious love affair with the game of golf. No, I'm not talking about the professional sport. You, know. The other one.

With the clown's head and the windmills.

Miniature golf's roots run deep and strong down through the years in Upstate New York. In 1938, it was a duo from Binghamton who capitalized on the then-boring game of miniature golf by adding whirling obstacles, humps and bridges, cartoon characters, wishing wells, bells and buzzers, lighthouses, and, yes, the ubiquitous clown's head at the end of the course. Joseph and Robert Taylor built their own courses and then franchised them out all over the country, greatly expanding the cult nature of this fairly new fad.

Our region still has a lot of courses to play on. The Around the World Miniature Golf Course is located on the shores of Lake George. It is a magical seventeen-hole course that takes the player around the world, with each hole highlighted by a landmark from a different country. Think putting your ball through the legs of the Eiffel Tower or underneath the London Bridge and you get the idea. The Jungle Mini Golf in Fulton is the largest miniature golf course in the state. Don't expect to end up dry after your round of golf here. Animatronic jungle elephants have been known to soak the golfers as they play through.

Chuckster's Family Fun Park in Vestal has a course that features the longest miniature golf hole in the country, a mind-boggling 201 feet of green-turfed craziness that allows the player two ways to score a hole in one.

But one special little course holds a rare and distinct place in the annals of miniature golf royalty (if there is such a thing). The Parkside Whispering Pines Miniature Golf Course in Irondequoit, a northern suburb of Rochester, is the oldest continuously operating miniature golf course in the United States.

I had a fun day on my visit here. Irondequoit sits right on Lake Ontario, and in fact the area is called Seabreeze because of its oceanside ambiance. Whispering Pines is a small course cluttered with all sorts of things you'd be more apt to find at a mini course in Maine or Rhode Island.

Hole 1 has curious crabs watching your every move from piers. Hole 4 is the tried-and-true lighthouse. Hole 7 makes you shoot through a lobster trap. The rest of the course is whimsical, if not very challenging, and is very colorful with its red, white, and blue bunting and ever-present American flags.

The course is laid out under thick spruce trees and is a perfect setting for families with small children seeking refuge from the nearby crowded Lake Ontario beaches. The small pubs that surround the course have touristy names such as Shamrock Jack's, Margie's Lakeside Tavern, and Rochester's legendary Bill Gray's World's Greatest Cheeseburger stand.

The course opened in 1930 and has never shut down. It has earned a place on the Register of National Historic Places and is still the only miniature golf course so recognized. Attached to the course is the 1950s-themed Parkside Diner. I had a filling and inexpensive breakfast here, and noted that the wait staff was fully aware of the historic significance of the little course right outside their front door. Conducting my own unofficial survey I noticed on the day in August when I visited Whispering Pines to play a round, the cars in the parking lot sported license plates from New York, Pennsylvania, Ohio, and Kentucky, as well as several from Canada.

I think it is fair to say that today's kids will quickly become bored playing at Whispering Pines, especially when they hear the shrieks and laughter coming out of the huge Seabreeze Amusement Park just a block down the street. That park, built in 1879, is America's fourth-oldest amusement park, but unlike Whispering Pines, it has kept pace with the times and today features enough hair-curling, demonic high-speed rides to please any teenager looking for a summertime thrill.

This mini course is a real throwback to the day when Upstate New York was known to all as "Vacationland!" (as the ubiquitous bumper sticker on our station wagons declared). Many of our beloved little theme parks and entertainment destinations are long gone, whether they be the totally enchanting up-close-with-nature thrill of Catskill Game Farm or the memorable turn-of-the-century-themed Gaslight Village at Lake George.

But Whispering Pines plugs along steadily at its own pace, certain of its well-earned reputation. It is starting to show its age a little, adding a patina of preciousness to the whole experience. Sure, it may need a coat of paint here and there, and maybe the light on the lighthouse might not be blinking like it should, but for those of us of a certain age, this will be a wonderful visit back to that snow globe of our youth, when there was absolutely nothing more exciting that you could do than to putt a golf ball into a grinning clown's open mouth.

This place defines charm.

Other Nearby Attractions or Sites

After your rousing game of mini golf, a good place to relax is right around the corner at the Irondequoit Bay State Marine Park. In fact, drop the kids off at the big Seabreeze Amusement Park and stroll along here, just you and your sweetheart.

The bay is a deep, rich blue lagoon with bobbing sailboats, quaint beachside homes, sandy beaches, and small pubs and eateries. Located just a few miles from Rochester's center, the park is a busy spot on a warm summer afternoon. The history of the bay is described on several plaques and historical markers along the beach. One reads:"Irondequoit Bay Harbor. Home of the Seneca People, the Keepers of the Western Door." Walking trails here are clearly marked and easy to maneuver.

Essentials

What: Parkside Whispering Pines Miniature Golf Course

Where: 4353 Culver Road, Sea Breeze (Rochester); Monroe County

Contact

Parkside Whispering Pines Miniature Golf Course: http://parksidediner.com/miniature-golf

Seabreeze Amusement Park: www.seabreeze.com

Around the World Miniature Golf (Lake George): www.aroundtheworldgolf.com

Jungle Mini Golf Course (Fulton): http://www.thunder-island.com

Chuckster's Family Entertainment Center: http://www.chucksters-vestal

12

Lucille Ball's Grave

Jamestown
Chautauqua County

I love Lucy.

There is something fascinating about the grave of a celebrity. We really didn't know these people. Yet we loved them from afar. We enjoyed their work, followed their lives in the newspapers and tabloid magazines, and spent our money getting into their shows and concerts and buying tickets for their records, books, and movies. So it is right and natural that we would want to visit a star's final resting place to say thank you and pay our respects. We would never dare to go up to a Lucille Ball, for example, and talk to her. Well, most of us wouldn't. But it is so easy and comfortable to go to her grave and pay a visit with this legendary star who was a part of our lives for generations.

I know. I have done it.

When you go through the gates of the sprawling Lake View Cemetery on the north side of Jamestown, your first thought is, "How will I ever find her in here?" There are nearly fifty thousand people buried here (the first burial took place in 1859), and the cemetery stretches over seventy acres of hills, glens, hollows, and terraces. And then you notice a small "This way to Lucille Ball's grave" sign and the little red hearts inscribed in the pavement. These hearts lead you directly to the grave of the comedienne. Untold thousands of fans have visited her final resting place, and the cemetery has solved the problem of tourists wandering around aimlessly by just placing this simple, eloquent "heart road map" to her grave in the Highland Section.

Lucy died on April 26, 1989, at the age of seventy-seven. She was originally interred in Forest Lawn Cemetery in Hollywood, but was later brought home to rest in her family plot in her hometown of Jamestown. Her grave marker is unmistakable. Her last name, "Ball," is inscribed signature-style across the center of a large pink heart. It is evocative of the Lucy logo that opened her comedy *I Love Lucy* on television for so many years.

On the rear face of the stone is a list of Ball family members buried in the plot. She is listed below her parents, Fred and Desiree, and above her brother, also named Fred. Lucy's inscription reads: "Lucille Desiree Ball Morton, August 6, 1911–April 26, 1989. You've Come Home." There is no mention of the name Arnaz on the gravestone.

The one thing I noticed when visiting Lucy's grave (I have been there three times) is that it is not a forgotten place. Trinkets, dolls, cards, and notes have been sprinkled over the grave by admirers. Each time I have visited at a different time of the day, and I have not been alone. Once a couple wandered by while I was there and left a small bouquet of flowers

Lucille Ball and Desi Arnaz were the undisputed number-one stars of early television, when their child, Desi, Jr., was born on January 19, 1953, he was featured on the cover of TV Guide as "Lucy's $50,000,000 Baby."

at her grave. Another time a gaggle of young teenagers came by and stood around nervously, giggling in the presence of such a famous person. And the third time I was at Lucy's grave, a motor coach came up the road and emptied out fifty senior-citizen tourists who stood around the grave and shared stories and laughter about the comedy legend.

Would we have approached Lucy on the sidewalk to say hello? Not me—I would have been too nervous. But I found it very easy and comforting to come to this quiet place under the trees in her hometown and spend a minute to say thanks to this wonderful entertainer. Thousands of others have done so, too.

Ever since Lucy came home to Jamestown, the city has embraced her mystique with wholehearted enthusiasm. In fact, a whole weekend immersed in Lucymania is certainly well within the realm of possibility. Jamestown is dotted with historical markers and buildings attesting to its hometown girl's fame. Massive, multicolored murals cover empty building facades with humorous and immediately identifiable images of Lucy from her television shows. On one downtown wall is a giant three-story image of Lucy downing some buzz-inducing Vitameatavegamin. Another building depicts Lucy shoving chocolates into her mouth as her female superior hollers, "Speed it up!" at the end of the candy conveyor belt. My favorite, and the city's newest mural, depicts Lucy and Desi and their neighbors, Fred and Ethel Mertz, smiling and laughing as they motor along in a convertible on their way to California. This one is especially brightly colored and covers the entire length of a large building near the southern entrance to the business district. It is unabashedly smile-inducing.

These colorful Lucy murals speak volumes for the love that Jamestown has for their native daughter.

The Lucille Ball–Desi Arnaz Museum is packed with Lucy lore. From her original gowns, to awards, to scripts, and even her original luxury car with the monogram "M" on the doors (for her last husband, Gary Morton), the building fills thousands of square feet of pure Lucy. There are numerous videos of Lucy's greatest moments constantly showing throughout the museum. The center tells the story of Lucy's childhood in the area (Jamestown and neighboring Celeron) and gives some background on Desi's famous family in Cuba. The well-stocked gift shop is a collector's dream.

The museum and other activities all fall under the auspices of the Lucy-Desi Center for Comedy on West Third Street in downtown Jamestown. The center hosts live entertainment (with nationally known comedians), festivals, and Lucy tribute events on a fairly regular schedule. The Lucille Ball Comedy Festival is in fact one of western New York's largest attractions. Over the years tens of thousands of her fans have come to enjoy the likes of Bob Newhart, Joan Rivers, Jay Leno, and Ray Romano.

In 2011, the hundredth birthday of the comedienne, 915 fans gathered beneath the giant Vitameatavegamin mural to sing "Happy Birthday" to their star. Both men and women donned blue-and-white polka dotted dresses and T-shirts and held Lucy masks over their faces while they sang. Why did they do this strange thing?

To be officially certified by the Guinness Book of World Records as the "most Lucille Ball lookalikes in one place."

Other Nearby Attractions or Sites

Roger Tory Peterson (1908–1996), one of America's premier naturalists and artists and a founder of the American conservation movement, was born in Jamestown. An institution of learning in his name is located here, and they have events, exhibits, performances and seminars on a frequent basis.

Essentials

What: Grave of Lucille Ball

Where: Lake View Cemetery, 907 Lake View Avenue, Jamestown; Chautauqua County

Contact

Lake View Cemetery: www.lake-view-cemetery.com

Lucy-Desi Center for Comedy: 2 West Third Street; www.lucy-desi.com; this website gives you all information on museums and Lucy events.

Roger Tory Peterson Institute: 311 Curtis Street; www.rtpi.org

13

Our Lady of Victory Basilica

Lackawanna
Erie County

A church for Father Baker.

Father Nelson Baker never wandered far from home. He was born on February 16, 1842, in Buffalo and died nearly a century later on July 29, 1936, almost within sight of his birthplace. He is buried at "his" church, Our Lady of Victory Basilica in Lackawanna, a southern suburb of Buffalo.

Baker was the son of a small grocer in Buffalo. After a stint at college and service in the Civil War, Baker entered the seminary in 1869 and was ordained a priest on March 19, 1876. Father Baker organized the Association of Our Lady of Victory to help care for unwed mothers and operate an orphanage. These organizations grew to such a size in Buffalo that at one time Baker's various associations and groups comprised the largest private charitable organization in America. His home for wayward or truant boys changed how people thought of these street urchins. Baker took the bars off the windows, gave his charges plentiful nourishment and encouragement, and built them gyms and classrooms.

In the 1890s, the city of Buffalo was shocked when the news spread that reconstruction of the Erie Canal had revealed the skeletons of hundreds of babies dumped in the canal by unwed, shamed, or unknown mothers. Baker established a home for unwanted babies that immediately filled to overflowing. Baker's Infant Home had a revolving door on the sidewalk at the entrance. Women could come up, place their unwanted child in an empty crib, ring a bell, and then leave. The crib would then be brought inside the building while the mother remained anonymous to all. Some reports say that more than six hundred women availed themselves of the revolving door at Father Baker's Infant Home.

Thousands of babies, unwed mothers, and young boys all benefitted from the services of Baker, now known as "The Padre of the Poor." Lads who grew out of his St. John's Protectory, Working Boys' Home, and other services were forever known as Father Baker's Boys.

Father Nelson Baker's footprint is still a large one in the greater Buffalo area. It is said that Baker and his charitable organizations virtually kept Buffalo alive during the Great Depression. He served over a million free meals a year, clothed a half-million, cared for countless thousands of unwanted infants and children, and offered free medical care to over 250,000 people. Today there is a nationally ranked nursing home that bears his name, and several benevolent organizations are active in his honor under the umbrella of Baker Victory Services.

The priest was recently named "Buffalo's Most Outstanding Citizen of the Twentieth Century."

Many believe that Baker will be the first American male to be named a saint by the Roman Catholic Church. On January 14, 2011, Pope Benedict XVI elevated Baker to the status of "venerable."

In 1921, Father Baker embarked on one of the most ambitious church construction projects ever seen in the United States. He was determined to raise a church in tribute to Mary, Mother of God, right in his hometown. The resulting Our Lady of Victory Basilica is, in a word, jaw-dropping. Baker cajoled, prayed for, and worked for contributions to his church project on a national level. Donations ranged from thousands of dollars to as little as a quarter. He supervised much of the construction himself. The final cost of the church was three million dollars.

The church is built of white marble from Georgia. The flourishes and architectural embellishments all reflect the mighty cathedrals of Europe. Inside are countless statues, stained-glass windows, paintings, grottos and alcoves, tile mosaics, carpets, hundreds of pure African mahogany pews, and rare tapestries. Among the stand out marble figures inside the church is a nine-foot-tall marble statue of Mary, which was personally blessed by Pope Pius XI before it was shipped from Italy to Lackawanna. Each Apostle is represented with a life-sized statue.

The exterior of the church, which rises almost sixteen stories tall, is amazing. The copper dome is one of the largest in North America and is "guarded" on all four sides by eighteen-foot-tall trumpet-blowing copper angels. A massive twelve-foot eight-ton marble statue of Our Lady of Victory towers over the main entrance. Elaborate marble statues adorn each corner of the church. Look carefully at the figures residing atop the western colonnade. The marble tableau depicts Father Baker leading a large group of children!

Perhaps Father Baker's most precious area of the church is the exact replica of the Grotto of Lourdes, where a vision of the Blessed Virgin Mary was reported in France in 1858. He insisted that the grotto be constructed with materials that had never been touched by human hands. That material was ultimately found in the original lava rock that flowed down from Mount Vesuvius.

Father Baker's death plunged his native city into a period of mourning unlike any other before or after. An estimated 500,000 people witnessed

A life-size bronze statue of "The Priest of the Poor" stands directly across the street from the front entrance to "his" church.

his funeral, which was attended by seven hundred priests. He was buried in Holy Cross Cemetery adjacent to his massive church.

In 1999, the priest's remains were moved to the Lourdes Grotto inside the basilica. Six men, all former Father Baker Boys, carried the small casket inside. When the casket was unearthed from its original burial spot, everyone was perplexed to find another, separate smaller casket buried alongside Father Baker's. When opened it was discovered to hold vials of the priest's own blood. The blood was inexplicably still in liquid form after nearly a century. Some called it a miracle.

Baker's remains are today ensconced in a sarcophagus inside the church. Approximately three thousand people from all over the world make the pilgrimage here to Lackawanna every month to be awed by this incredible religious edifice and to pay tribute to "The Priest of the Poor."

Other Nearby Attractions or Sites

Lackawanna is blue-collar country. For decades it was one of America's leading steel-producing centers. That is all gone now, but a fascinating museum has opened that tells the gritty and prideful tale of this hard-working city and the generations who toiled in the steel mills in the area (mainly the long-gone Bethlehem Steel Company and Republic Steel).

Essentials

What: Our Lady of Victory Basilica

Where: 767 Ridge Road, Lackawanna; Erie County

Contact

Our Lady of Victory Basilica: www.ourladyofvictory.org (Tours are given and Father Baker's tomb is easily accessible to the public. Masses and holy days are held and open to the public. A new Father Baker Museum has recently opened here also.)

Baker Victory Services ("Continuing Father Baker's Legacy of Caring"): www.bakervictoryservices.org

The Steel Plant Museum of Western New York: www.steelpltmuseum.org

14

Erie Canal Locks

Lockport
Niagara County

The Flight of Five.

The Erie Canal is the great historical footprint which shadows Upstate New York from Albany to the Great Lakes. The routes of both the original canal and the later enlarged Barge Canal, laze along the New York State Thruway almost from border to border. Canal towns popped up and thrived along the entire route at the beginning of the canal era, and although very little travels on the canal now except for pleasure craft, the canal towns are still here.

Each of the towns along the way, many of them with a "port" in their name, remembers the significance of being a canal town in different ways. Canal museums proliferate, old locks are enshrined, walkways and bike paths accompany the canal on its route through town, and small harbors and marinas welcome the tour boats and private water craft that pass by. Towns such as Spencerport, Brockport, Middleport, and Gasport all mark their connection to Clinton's Ditch in various ways, big and small. Fairport, in Monroe County, hosts a Canal Days Festival every summer that attracts more than 200,000 visitors to this village of five thousand residents. Canal tour boat operators do a brisk business taking tourists along the route, and when all eyes focused on the two-hundredth anniversary of the beginning of construction of the canal in 1817, a lot of new national attention was given to America's most famous manmade waterway. When the diggers and planners of the canal began their Herculean march from the salt water to the fresh water, they encountered a plethora of harrowing obstacles. Mountains, labor strife, mosquitoes and disease, faulty equipment, and more all added to the woes of the project. A thousand workers died of malaria just trying to cross the Montezuma Marsh west of Syracuse. One of the most significant natural obstacles was found here in Lockport, just a few short miles from the western end of the Erie Canal.

The Niagara Escarpment loomed in front of the engineers, a formidable eighty-foot wall of solid limestone. After much discussion, the canal diggers realized that the only way around this barrier was up and over it. They constructed five stairstep locks on top of each other. This enabled a boat to enter at the bottom lock, lift up to the next lock, lift up to the next, and so on, five times. Eventually, at the top, the boat would sail on to the Great Lakes.

The "Flight of Five" was a difficult and costly construction challenge. Much of it was done by hunch and guess. A lot of the rock excavation had to be done with explosives, and many workers were either killed or injured in the process. When completed, the series of water steps up and over the escarpment was heralded as the greatest wonder of the Erie Canal. To see these locks today is awe inspiring. There are actually ten of them, five going up and five down on the other side. They are perfectly situated, one on top of the other. Water still cascades down through the locks, although the old wooden doors are long gone. As you stand at the bottom and look up at the precise construction of the locks, you can't help but be amazed at the thought of these being built in a time long before computers or electricity or even skillful construction techniques. In fact, there wasn't a single engineering school in America at the time, and only one engineer, Nathan Roberts of Canastota, who had any training in canal construction. Roberts designed the locks here.

The city of Lockport arose during the construction boom of the canal in the 1800s. Today it is an important stop for thousands who want to visit and celebrate the Erie Canal. The town has a busy main street and lots of tourist amenities, such as gift shops, museums, restaurants, and shopping venues. There are walking tours (including a fascinating cave tour that takes you inside the hillside that runs parallel to the canal and locks), and history abounds in downtown Lockport.

Despite all the cars and families and motor homes and hurly-burly along the canal site, everything still comes to a standstill when a boat approaches the Flight of Five. Everybody heads down to watch the spectacle of the boat lift, much as they did almost two centuries ago.

The approaching boat, usually a tour boat, blows its horn to announce its presence. The towering steel doors of today's Barge Canal slowly swing open. The ancient stairstep locks, five in a stack, are situated right next to this modern version. The boat slowly drifts into the lock and the doors swing shut with a loud slam. Water begins pouring into the lock from the bottom, and as it does the tour boat slowly rises almost to street level. There the mighty doors swing open, and the boat, its merry visitors all smiling, waving, and camera-clicking away, chugs on down the canal to its next stop.

And while this pageant takes place, the Flight of Five is right there to witness it in all its antique grandeur. The old meets the new. The stairstep locks, built with chalk lines and pickaxes and sticks of dynamite, is a testament to the grit and courage of the early builders of the Empire State.

For those looking for an introduction to the history and wonder of the Erie Canal, a visit to the historic and unique Flight of Five in Lockport is certain to satisfy. Better yet, take a ride along the canal yourself and experience real history as it passes by.

Other Nearby Attractions or Sites

Main Street has developed along with the interest in the locks in this city. There are many wonderful tourist options for the visitor, with the Lockport Underground Caves and Underground Boat Tour being the best.

For a glimpse of Lockport's historic past, visit the memorial plaza on Main Street, where many of the city's most famous native sons and daughters are remembered on inscribed pavers. Among them are author Joyce Carol Oates, Congressman William E. Miller (who ran for vice president on the ticket with Barry Goldwater in 1964), astronaut William Gregory, William Morgan (inventor of volleyball), and 1980s supermodel Kim Alexis.

Essentials

What: The Flight of Five

Where: Downtown Lockport; Niagara County

Contact

Lockport tourism, history, and events: www.elockport.com

Lockport Caves and Underground Boat Ride: www.lockportcave.com

15

The Sweet Spot

Mayville
Chautauqua County

Oh, if these walls could only talk.

In this book I have tried to chronicle a hundred unique and unusual places that a traveler "just passing through" might miss on a first visit. This is by no means a complete list, for sure. Even a book of 1,001 places couldn't come close to scratching the surface of the wonders of Upstate New York's little towns and villages. On this list you will find two restaurants. One of them is a legendary three-generation chicken barbecue eatery in central New York, Brooks House of BBQ in Oneonta. The other is this little "sweet spot" on the north end of Chautauqua Lake. It has a fascinating story.

The Sweet Spot, on the main road through Mayville, occupies a curious-looking brick building. "I have been in love with this building since I was fourteen years old," Darlene Wendell told me. "And to think that I own it now, well, it is just unbelievable," she gushed. The old brick building (actually two of them) sits on the corner right across the street from the huge Chautauqua County Courthouse. The sign over the front door of the Sweet Spot reads, "County Clerk, 1859."

"I have always wanted to own my own bake shop and restaurant, and to think I could do it in these buildings is just great. When my husband, Tim, and I bought these structures a few years ago we knew we had our work cut out for us. They needed a lot of cleaning up. The main building had been used for over a century to house all of the documents for Chautauqua County, and it was a mess. Records, lawyers' papers, deeds. All sorts of stuff. We knocked out a wall or two to enlarge the rooms and make them a dining room, but other than that we left as much as possible in its original 1850s configuration."

The building is a marvel. The floors are solid marble; the walls have exposed, original brick facing. In both this and the smaller (as yet unused) building, you can see the old vaults and safes. The building was one of the first certified fireproof buildings in the area.

"The only wood you will find here is on the window sills. Everything else is solid," she said. She even took me into the basement. Here, in a tall brick-lined room, you could see the arched metal ceilings above that are the actual floor foundations from the main room. Even the arches between the rooms were supported with, not wood, but metal bridge I-beams.

"Come and let me show you my favorite room," Darlene whispered as we approached a heavy door just in front of the kitchen area. "Go ahead, open it," she said.

I did. Barely. The solid metal door was laid into a twenty-four-inch cement wall. We stepped inside.

"This is our vault room. We use it for private parties and such. In fact, many people request this room. It is just so wonderful."

The vault room has soaring arches above and solid marble underfoot. Ceiling fans and high windows give the room an airy ambience. This room held the county's most important papers and records for well over a century.

"There was no money held here," Darlene was quick to tell me. "But the historic significance of this room cannot be denied. In fact, one of the most important men in our area, Albion Tourgee, had his office back here as he directed the legal prosecution of one of the most important Supreme Court cases of the nineteenth century right from this room."

Tourgee, a Mayville resident, was the lawyer who prosecuted the famous *Plessy v. Ferguson* Supreme Court case of 1896. He lost the case, which set the precedent for "separate but equal," but he gained a national reputation for his work in civil rights. Following this famous case President McKinley named him ambassador to France. His home is located two blocks from the Sweet Spot Café.

I asked Darlene if one of her biggest customers was the courthouse right across the street.

"Oh, definitely. Seasons come and go but the courthouse is busy all the time. And they all come over here, the lawyers, staff, judges, guards, just everybody. I know them all. And that has posed some tricky problems in the past."

How so? I asked.

"Well, for instance, we had a big murder trial here recently. When it came time to take a break in the court, everybody came over here for lunch or coffee or whatever. And I mean everybody," she laughed. "The prosecutors, the defense team, the jurors, the judge, the witnesses. They all came. And you can see, we are not the biggest restaurant in the world," she chuckled.

I said that must have been a pretty tense gathering.

"Well, I just separated everybody. They were certainly all welcome, but I just separated them. The defendant went over into the café, the prosecutors went to the other dining room. I put the jurors back in the vault room. And you know what, it all worked out just fine. They all know me at the courthouse and they trust me. A lot of important business gets done right here in this little café. But they all know my motto: 'I don't know. I don't care. We don't share.'"

The Sweet Spot is a lovely place for lunch and Darlene makes some of the, well, sweetest treats in town. She roasts her own turkey and makes her own soups. The café is decidedly retro in feel. Old advertising signs line the wall and an original 1950s 7-Up soft drink machine stands in one corner.

"That's my pride and joy. I brought that in here from my own home," she said.

Darlene Wendell is obviously in love with this historic old building. And has been since she was a kid. I asked her how it feels to own such a wonderful, unique piece of local history.

"I don't own this building. It owns me," she whispered.

Other Nearby Attractions or Sites

Mayville is one of western New York's prettiest little towns. With fewer than two thousand residents, it has all the prerequisites of a Norman Rockwell painting: grand courthouse, wide Main Street, quaint little mom-and-pop shops, American flags flying everywhere, and an old train depot (now the Mayville Museum). But Mayville also has an added attraction. The village sits high on a hill overlooking Chautauqua Lake, which gives this town that extra little waterfront bounce that so many other smaller communities would love to have.

And when you have finished eating in the Vault Room of the Sweet Spot, take a stroll around. Just cross the street and there in front of the courthouse is another famous vault (what is it about Mayville and old historic vaults?). Just a small, round stone room, this is the 1810 vault that held all of the papers of the famous Holland Land Patent Office, which was the original divvier-up of the land parcels back when western New York was founded. A bronze historic marker affixed to the front vine-covered room tells of its importance.

Essentials

What: The Sweet Spot Café and Bakery
Where: 4 North Erie Street, Mayville; Chautauqua County

Contact

The Sweet Spot Café and Bakery: www.mayvillesweetspot.com

16

The Lincoln-Bedell Statues

Westfield
Chautauqua County

The President's whiskers.

In a little park in the village of Westfield stands a whimsical double statue of President Abraham Lincoln and an eleven-year-old girl. The tableau depicts one of the most charming and sentimental presidential stories ever told.

On October 15, 1860, little Grace Bedell wrote a long letter to Abraham Lincoln telling him that she had seen a picture of him, clean shaven, and thought he might look better with a beard. She suggested to him that all the men would then vote for him and many of the ladies would look on approvingly also.

It is almost impossible to believe that this letter worked its magical way across the state lines and reached the office of Mr. Lincoln in Illinois, who was then a candidate for president. Somehow Mr. Lincoln came upon this letter, and for whatever reason, he decided to answer the girl, who was well under voting age.

Lincoln told Grace that he felt it would be a silly affectation for him to start wearing whiskers at this point in his career and that he was afraid people would find him silly if he did so. He made no promises but thanked her as "your sincere well-wisher" and sent his letter back to the child in Westfield.

And the rest, as they say, is history.

Abraham Lincoln did in fact grow a full beard, and he did in fact win the campaign for president. On the long ride from his home in Springfield, Illinois, to our nation's capital for his inauguration, Lincoln's train ended up stopping in Westfield. The word had gone out that the soon-to-be next president was coming to town, and thousands were on hand at the depot when the inaugural train pulled into town. Lincoln, tall, thin, and bearded, came out on the back balcony of the train and greeted the crowd with a wave of his stovepipe hat. Eventually he called for quiet and then addressed the throng.

Near the end, the president-elect reminded the crowd that a little girl from their town was responsible for his "new look" and he called out to see if a Grace Bedell was on hand.

As the crowd hushed, an elderly man accompanied a young girl up to the train. Mr. Lincoln came down and stood, towering in front of the little straw-hatted girl. She presented him with a small bouquet of flowers. Lincoln then bent down, took off his hat, and spoke to her quietly, saying, "I have been growing these whiskers for you, Gracie"; he then asked her to feel his face. She did, and then Mr. Lincoln gave her a little kiss on her cheek. The crowd roared with delight.

This whole scene, which probably took less than ten minutes in real time, now lives on forever in bronze in downtown Westfield. You can see the little girl timidly approaching the much taller Lincoln. You can clearly see the pleats in her dress, her flowers, her straw hat with a ribbon on it, and the apprehensive look on her face. Mr. Lincoln appears in a long formal coat and vest with one hand outstretched in greeting and the other holding his top hat. And yes, he obviously has a full beard!

The double statue, created by Westfield native Don Suttile, sits in Lincoln-Bedell Park at the main intersection in downtown Westfield. There are informational plaques and comfortable park benches surrounding the little plaza for you to sit and enjoy this delightful Upstate landmark.

Grace Bedell died in Kansas in 1936 at the age of eighty-eight. The two letters, obviously highly valuable, still exist. Grace's original letter to Lincoln is owned by the Detroit Public Library. Lincoln's responding correspondence is owned by a collector who remains anonymous.

Other Nearby Attractions or Sites

Westfield is like many of the little towns and villages throughout western New York. Several mom-and-pop stores line the small business district and a village green provides a bucolic backdrop to the community. A band gazebo, draped in red-white-and-blue bunting, adds to the historic ambience of the place. Farmers' markets (usually populated with Amish farm stands featuring produce, cheeses, and baked items) are popular here on weekends. The village green is anchored on the south end by the historic McClurg Museum, which is also the home of the Chautauqua County Historical Society. James McClurg patterned his 1818 mansion after his family's original residence in Pittsburgh. The Irish-manor-style home was one of the first brick homes built in the county. New York Governor William Seward (later to be Lincoln's secretary of state) lived and worked at the mansion in the 1830s.

The building directly across the street from Lincoln-Bedell Park was once the home of Welch's Grape Juice. Although now empty, the 1897 building was the center for grape-juice manufacturing in America. It is the last original building from the Welch's grape-juice company, and it was listed on the National Register of Historic Places in 1983. Thomas Welch and his son, Charles, began forming their grape-juice empire here in 1893.

Westfield is in the heart of grape-growing region of western New York. Just a mile outside of town, in either direction, vineyards carpet the landscape as far as the eye can see. One of New York's newest museums, the Lake Erie Grape Discovery Center, is the official visitor's headquarters for those exploring the region. They feature a gift shop, displays, audiovisual exhibits, and a comfortable tasting area nestled in an actual Concord grape vineyard for you to enjoy wines, cured meats, and artisanal cheeses. It is located just minutes from the statues.

Essentials

What: The Abraham Lincoln–Grace Bedell statues

Where: Intersection of US 20 and New York 394, downtown Westfield; Chautauqua County

Contact

Westfield: For information, history, and events, www.westfieldny.com

McClurg Mansion and Museum: Group tours are welcome with advance notice, www.mcclurgmuseum.org

Lake Erie Grape Discovery Center: Admission is free, www.grapediscovery center.com

REGION TWO

Finger Lakes

◆ ◆ ◆

Including parts of Cayuga, Chemung, Onondaga, Ontario, Seneca, Wayne, and Yates Counties

17

Harriet Tubman's Grave

Auburn
Cayuga County

The Moses of her people.

Harriet Tubman saw much in her ninety-one years.

She was born into slavery on a plantation in Maryland in 1822. As a child she was whipped by her owner for so many offenses that she took to wearing several layers of clothing to lessen the sting of the lash. She escaped from Maryland to Philadelphia in 1849 at the age of twenty-seven. She later went back to slave country to rescue members of her family. Over an eleven-year period, Tubman singlehandedly abetted the rescue and escape of possibly three hundred slaves. Slave catchers and owners put a forty-thousand-dollar reward on her head, dead or alive. She served in the Union Army in the Civil War as a nurse, advisor, and spy. On June 2, 1863, she became the first woman to lead an armed attack for the Union forces (during the Combahee River Raid). The tales of her courage in the face of slave hunters and nervous escapees who wanted to turn back are legendary.

Harriet Tubman is the most famous of all the conductors who worked the famous Underground Railroad. After emancipation, she continued to work for civil rights, a woman's right to vote, and other social causes. She lived in Auburn, N.Y., where her friend and powerful abolitionist colleague New York senator William Seward (a future U.S. secretary of state, New York governor, and the force behind the purchase of Alaska, "Seward's Folly") sold her a parcel of land, where she lived for the rest of her life.

The story of the Underground Railroad is one of the great threads that runs throughout Upstate New York. Because of the need for secrecy and anonymity in this dangerous and clandestine movement, many of the sites that were key to the escaping slaves remain unknown to this day. Several, however, are still around, identified as such and glorified for future generations. Auburn was a hotbed of the antislavery cause, as were many Upstate cities. Several museums in the region are dedicated to telling about this proud chapter in our history. Two best are the National Abolition Hall of Fame and Museum in Peterboro and the North Star Underground Railroad Museum at Ausable Chasm near Lake Champlain.

Harriet Tubman's funeral was attended by masses of mourners, both black and white. She is buried in Auburn's Fort Hill Cemetery. The name on the front of her grave is recorded as Harriet Tubman Davis (married name). On the rear of her simple stone it reads: "In memory of Harriet Tubman Davis. Heroine of the Underground Railroad, Nurse, Scout in the Civil War, Born About 1820 in Maryland, Died March 10, 1913 at Auburn, NY, Servant of God, Well Done."

Fort Hill Cemetery is located within the city limits of Auburn and is a very interesting place on its own. Built along a hilly landscape, it includes many interesting graves other than that of the famous lady buried in West Lawn C section. Tubman's mentor and benefactor, William Seward, is buried in the Glen Haven section. The Seward family plot is far different from Harriet Tubman's plain, weathered slate gravestone. Seward and his family are buried in elaborately carved above-ground sarcophagi adorned with fanciful carvings of Grecian urns. Legendary Civil War general Emory Upton is buried in the Mount Hope section. His grave is marked by a large bronze profile image of the general.

Perhaps the most famous landmark at Fort Hill Cemetery is Logan's Monument. This impressive fifty-six-foot-tall stone obelisk towers above the thousands of graves, and although it does not mark a final resting place, it does mark the site of the birthplaces of famed Cayuga Indian Chief Logan. After the Battle of Point Peasant on October 10, 1774, Chief Logan wrote a speech lamenting the bloodletting between the Indians and the white settlers. He wrote that his entire family had been killed and there was nobody left who carried a drop of his blood. If he were to die, he asked, "Who is there to mourn for Logan?" These became his most famous words and are inscribed on his monument at Fort Hill Cemetery.

Other Nearby Attractions or Sites

Auburn is one of central New York's most historic cities. One can visit many interesting places pertaining to the story of Harriet Tubman, William Seward, and the Underground Railroad. Tubman's home is now a museum, and tours are popular. William Seward's mansion is close by and is also a popular tourist destination. Seward's is perhaps the most magnificent residence in Auburn, befitting his international stature.

On a different note, Auburn is also home to one of the most famous prisons in New York. The Auburn Correctional Facility is the second-oldest prison in the state and one of the ten oldest working prisons in the nation. The prison is a grim landmark in the center of the city, with towering, blank concrete walls and turreted guard towers. Convicted murderer William Kemmler was the first person ever to die in the electric chair, at this prison on August 6, 1890.

Although prison tours are not offered, just a walk around the forbidding exterior walls will suffice to give the distinct impression that one might not want to see this place from the inside. On a lighter note, high atop the front edifice is a life-sized statue of "Copper John," a Revolutionary War soldier. Nobody knows why it was placed there, but it has been a "prison mascot" for nearly two centuries. The statue, constructed by inmates, has grown in fame and legend and has attracted visitors and admirers of his own. It was recently noticed that Copper John was constructed to be "overly" anatomically correct. Because of the number of visitors who come to photograph the statue, in 2004 the prison had him removed, made gender-neutral, and replaced.

Essentials

What: Harriet Tubman's grave

Where: Fort Hill Cemetery, 19 Fort Street, Auburn; Cayuga County

Contact

Harriet Tubman Home: www.harriethouse.org

Fort Hill Cemetery: www.forthillcemetery.net

William Seward Museum and Home: www.sewardhouse.org

National Abolition Museum (Peterboro): www.nationalabolitionhalloffame andmuseum.org

18

Boathouse Row

Canandaigua
Ontario County

The chosen spot.

The Seneca Indians called this village Kanadarque, which translates to "the chosen spot."

Present day Canandaigua prides itself on being the welcome mat to the Finger Lakes region. Although other towns claim to be the gateway to this fertile grape-growing outdoor playground (Skaneateles, for example calls itself the "Eastern Gateway to the Finger Lakes," and Hammondsport has used the moniker "Southern Gateway to the Finger Lakes"), the crown lies securely with the city of Canandaigua as the "official" gateway. It is also one of the largest of the Finger Lakes communities, with about eleven thousand residents.

Located at the northern tip of the lake of the same name, Canandaigua is a tourist mecca for those exploring the region. The New York Wine and Culinary Center, on the waterfront, is a multimillion-dollar facility that features wine tastings, culinary delights, a food demonstration theater, an extensive gift shop, and a cozy eatery on the second floor that affords the visitor a pleasurable experience wining, dining, and enjoying the view of the lake. Thousands pass through the doors of the center each year.

As you stroll along the waterfront you get a distinct sense of New England. The water is clear and dark blue; the vistas along both sides of the lake evoke the waterways of, say, New Hampshire or Connecticut. The few businesses along the largely undeveloped Lakefront Drive sell seafood and "boardwalk fare," and the gift shops stock everything from talking-fish wall plaques to T-shirts. It is just a short walk to the Main Street business district, where your options expand greatly with antique shops, cafés, jewelry stores, pubs, motels, restaurants, and clothing stores.

A long pier is the central focus for strollers, sightseers, artists, and nostalgia lovers. The Canandaigua City Pier was built in 1848 for fishermen to house their boats in side-by-side boathouses of different sizes and shapes. The pier was expanded in the early 1900s, and today more than eighty of these little boathouses crowd the sides of the three water alleys (called "finger piers") jutting out from the main pedestrian pier. The houses are quaint and gaily colored, each with its own inimitable style and personality. Owners can be seen relaxing on the tiny verandas above the boat bays underneath, or perhaps in hip waders standing in the water to fix a boat engine or paint a fishing boat hull. Living in the boathouses is prohibited, and the owners' association enforces strict rules and guidelines to preserve the antiquity and integrity of the pier. The whole atmosphere is "seaside" rather than "lakeside," and it is one of the most charming sights in the entire Finger Lakes region.

From the end of the pier, just beyond Boathouse Row, the pristine lake spreads out before you. The lake is the fourth largest of the Finger Lakes, only sixteen miles long and at no point even two miles wide. The village of Naples is at the south end of the lake. Regularly stocked with rainbow, brown, and lake trout, the lake is popular for pleasure craft and fishing. Locals spend much of the summer casting for "brownies" and "lakers."

At the end of the pier is a large historical marker that tells the story of Squaw Island, which sits just off the shore. The island has been called "The Smallest New York State Park" for as long as anyone can remember, but there is no official state governance over the island.

The whole city pier, the boathouses, the view of Squaw Island, and the vistas down the stunning lake all contribute to make this a most memorable place. There is one lone tree on the fishing pier, which sits in the middle of the parking area at the end. Below that sole tree is a bronze plaque affixed to a large boulder. The inscription on this marker sums up what many of the young men who left this beautiful little spot over the years to fight in wars far from home must have felt. The veterans' tribute reads:

> Look to the hills that cradle this beautiful lake,
> And remember those who served their country with honor,
> And those who gave their lives on sea, land and in the air.
> This is their Chosen Spot.

Other Nearby Attractions or Sites

Sonnenberg Gardens is a historic house and exquisite gardens famed for their grand architectural style. This was the summer home of Mary Clark Thompson, daughter of the New York governor Myron Clark. Thompson and her husband, banker Frederick Thompson, built fabulous gardens to surround their forty-room Queen Anne–style home. The house and grounds are open to the public, and thousands visit here each year. The gardens feature more than twenty-five hundred rose bushes, an extravagant Japanese tea garden, an Italian Garden built in 1903 that has plantings of fifteen thousand red and gold flowers, a Moonlight Garden of only white flowers, and a private greenhouse that has been called the finest in the country.

One of the most popular events at Sonnenberg is the Moonlight Stroll. This event takes place in the evening, under a silvery moon, and participants walk through the shimmering Moonlight Garden accompanied by strolling musicians. Hors d'oeuvres and wine are served during this event.

Canandaigua is also known for its beautiful churches. One significant church is the First Congregational Church on Main Street. The design is unique, combining the best of the Federal style with whimsical and unusual flourishes. The architect is unknown. A massive sweeping overhead arch is unlike anything else found in Upstate New York. The fancy froufrous on the edifice include round wheel windows, hand-hewn wooden beams fastened with pegs rather than nails, a long dramatic teakwood swag over the front door, and a golden feather for a weather vane that twirls around in the lake breeze from atop the church bell tower. A large stone chapel sits adjacent to the church. Money for the chapel was donated by Mary Clark Thomson. The church is over two hundred years old and was designated a National Landmark in 1958.

Essentials

What: Boathouse Row

Where: The City Pier, Canandaigua; Ontario County

Contact

City of Canandaigua: For history, information, and events, www.canandaigua chamber.com

New York Wine and Culinary Center: www.nywcc.com

Sonnenberg Gardens: www.sonnenberg.org

First Congregational Church of Canandaigua: www.canandaiguachurch.org

19

Teal Park Gazebo

Horseheads
Chemung County

Zim's Bandstand.

Eugene Zimmerman was one of the premier cartoonists of the late nineteenth century. One of the most prominent contributors to the wildly popular magazine Puck, he created more than forty thousand drawings and sketches. He left Puck in 1885 and went to another popular weekly magazine, Judge. Here he was known for his satirical political cartoons and sharp wit. He stayed with Judge until he retired in 1912. He was also a pioneer in cartoon correspondence courses, in which he offered advice garnered from thirty years in the business to the many aspiring artists who wished to follow in his footsteps.

Zimmerman was born in Basil, Switzerland, and came to the United States in 1868. He married Mabel Beard of Horseheads and moved to her small town in 1888. Zim continued to work in New York City periodically, making the trip to the city when his job called. He loved his time in Horseheads and built his Queen Anne–style home there in 1890. The house, an architectural gem now listed on the National Register of Historic Places, was the scene of lively social events. An adjacent park, which the village had owned since 1807, drew Zimmerman's eye, and he went to work creating a bandstand–gazebo for the whole community to use and enjoy.

"Zim's Bandstand" is a whimsical and attractive green, red, gold, and white octagon decorated with cartoon animals and musical symbols. The front cornice features two cartoon crickets blowing trumpets; a frog sitting on a red-and-white polka-dot mushroom sits between them. The eight columns are "held up" by gold musical lyres. The park is a popular summer gathering place, and concerts are held frequently in the bandstand. In fact the first band to play there was the Zim Band, made up of the cartoonist and some of his musical friends. The whole effect is fantastical and charming and endows Teal Park with a perfect reflection of Horseheads's most famous resident.

Zimmerman was a great neighbor to his adopted hometown. He served on many boards and helped the community financially in many endeavors. After he died (March 26, 1935) all the schools and businesses in Horseheads closed for the funeral. He was buried in the local Maple Grove Cemetery.

Zimmerman's home, now a museum operated by the Horseheads Historical Society, contains personal items of the famous cartoonist, including many original cartoons and sketches. The house and all of its contents were donated to the village in 1980 by Laura Zimmerman, the only child of Eugene and Mabel Zimmerman.

Other Nearby Attractions or Sites

Horseheads has to be one of the most unusually named places in all New York. And yet there is a clear, reasonable explanation for the name.

In 1779, the Sullivan-Clinton campaign was on the march carrying out a scorched-earth policy against Indian tribes and villages throughout western New York. Coming through an area near the present village, Maj. Gen. John Sullivan found that his patrol was burdened by a large number of sick and ailing pack horses. As many as three hundred were put down and buried in this area. Months later the returning Indians found the unearthed bleached white skulls of the horses and lined the road to the village with them as a reminder of the history that happened here. From that day to the present the village has been known as Horseheads.

A life-sized bronze statue of a military pack horse was unveiled in front of the village offices on the 175th anniversary of the Sullivan-Clinton Campaign. The village is recognized as "the first and only town and village in the United States dedicated to the service of the American Military Horse."

The "unofficial" logo of the village is a depiction of three horses, drawn by Eugene Zimmerman in his unique cartoonish style. One of the horses can be seen puffing on a corncob pipe. A large plaque of this cartoon adorns the front of the Horseheads Historical Museum at the Chemung Railway Depot.

Two major flight museums are located in Elmira, about ten miles from Horseheads. The National Soaring Museum is located on Harris Hill. This was the site of numerous glider competitions in the 1930s and 1940s, and one of the top glider manufacturers, Schweizer Aircraft Corporation, was located here. Elmira was the first site chosen to train glider pilots for World War II. Elmira is known as "The Soaring Capital of America."

"Wings of Eagles Discovery Center" is a wonderful museum that features dozens of military aircraft from World War II to the present day. This is a modern museum that maintains an active schedule of events and displays. In recent years the Wings of Eagles has hosted the annual reunion of the last surviving Tuskegee Airmen, the famed all-black pilot group from World War II.

Essentials

What: Zim's Bandstand

Where: Teal Park, Horseheads; Chemung County

Contact

Zim Home Museum: www.horseheadshistorical.com

Wings of Eagles Museum: http://www.wingsofeagles.com

20

Ohmann Theatre

Lyons
Wayne County

The oldest movie and stage theater in upstate.

Movie houses of one fashion or another have been around since they converted an old retail store on Canal Street in New Orleans and opened up the Vitascope Theatre for the exclusive purpose of showing movies. The year was 1896. A few years later some movie houses (now gone) opened in New York City, and less than twenty years later the Ohmann Theatre in Lyons showed its very first film.

That theatre is now the oldest continuously operating movie house and live stage theatre in Upstate New York. The Ohmann, owned by brothers Burt and Amos Ohmann, was a rarity when it first opened its doors. The few existing movie houses of the time were often located on second floors, and the Ohmann created quite a sensation when it opened at street level on Main Street, Lyons, on December 6, 1915. The first movie shown was *Vanity Fair*, which ran seven full reels and starred an actress who went by the name of "Mrs. Fiske." It was a silent movie with piano accompaniment. Early news reports of the theatre's grand opening hyped its amenities as among the finest in the state. The theatre could hold a thousand patrons and was thought to be fireproof (it was constructed out of concrete and steel). One great feature that the Ohmann crowed about was his and hers "retiring rooms." The ticket price on opening night was a dime.

The magnificent three-sided Ohmann marquee, which still hangs over the sidewalk on Main Street, featured 250 lights and could be seen from one end of town to the other. The theatre and marquee underwent a full renovation in 2006, and the Ohmann Theatre is still run by the founding family.

In a day when small-town movie houses have been turned into other businesses, closed, neglected, or even torn down, it is refreshing and satisfying to see an ancient old theatre still up, open, active, beautiful, and facing the future with confidence. The Ohmann is a marvel to see. What once was an old silent-movie theatre and later a vaudeville house and even a venue for boxing events is now a nostalgic showplace. At a cost of over a million dollars, the newest members of the Ohmann family have dragged the old theatre into the modern era without losing all of the wonderful, charming effects of the "good old days." When the seats were refurbished, the old, original seats were removed and placed in the balcony. The modern seats were constructed with an eye on the design of the old ones. And that is the magic of the theatre. You can still see a first-run movie at the Ohmann and sit in a hundred-year-old seat in the balcony that actually has a hat rack underneath it!

The box office was originally located at the Lyons National Bank and dates to the Civil War. The polished wood banisters and railings in the theatre are original to its opening in 1915.

Because the theatre is so old, there are references to its history in a host of sources, including archival newspapers, old advertisements, oral histories, and sepia-toned photographs. One interesting tidbit I uncovered in my research is the two top-grossing movies ever shown at the Ohmann. They are *Gone with the Wind* and *Jaws*. The latter is curious because the theatre couldn't get a print of the 1975 hit movie until 1977 because the Ohmann was located in such a small community. In 1988, the movie *Lady in White* held its premiere at the Ohmann. The cult horror film was made in Lyons, and the writer and director of the film, Frank LaLoggia, was raised in the vicinity of Lyons.

Even if you are not able to see a movie at the Ohmann, it is definitely worth a look. The old marquee is one of the finest in Upstate, particularly at night when the lights are twinkling. The deep red velvet curtain on the

Lyons is still known as the Peppermint Village.

stage harkens back to a time when all theatres had exquisite and exotic adornments.

Heck, the theatre still has its original organ from the silent movie days!

Other Nearby Attractions or Sites

For many years Lyons was famous for its peppermint production. In fact even today the signs at the village entrances proclaim, "Welcome to Lyons. The Peppermint Village!" The H. G. Hotchkiss International Prize Medal Essential Oil Company, founded in Lyons in 1841, was at one time the largest manufacturer of peppermint oil in the world. It was located in Lyons because of its proximity to the Erie Canal; visitors coming down the canal always said they knew they were getting near Lyons when they detected the sweet smell of peppermint on the air. The company moved out of Lyons in 1990. The village still celebrates its peppermint history with festivals and celebrations through the year.

Lyons is also known as the "Mural Village." Many wonderfully painted murals decorate the once-empty walls of business and public buildings throughout the downtown area. Many of these murals depict historical chapters in Lyons history.

Essentials

What: The Ohmann Theatre

Where: Main Street, Lyons; Wayne County

Contact

Ohmann Theatre: www.ohmanntheatre.com

Wayne County events, tourism, and history: www.waynecountytourism.com

Mural Trail Tour: There are dozens of painted murals in Lyons and the surrounding area, and mural tours are popular with tourists. For information about the tours, both guided and self-guided, visit www.fingerlakes.org.

21

Birkett Mills

Penn Yan
Yates County

The world's largest pancake griddle. Photograph courtesy of Birkett Mills.

What a funny (and startling) sight it is coming down Penn Yan's Main Street to see this giant pancake griddle attached to the side of the ancient Birkett Mills production facility. It begs for an explanation.

Birkett Mills is one of the oldest flour and grain mills in the country, having opened its doors in the same spot in 1767. They made pancake mixes long before other major companies got on board, and are now known for their buckwheat mixes. Many years ago, Birkett Mills began manufacturing buckwheat products, and still today they are considered to be the oldest and most successful buckwheat producer in the United States. Their products are now sold all over the world. The manufacturing facility is in the same structure as when it was founded, although the facility has been expanded several times over the years. The old buildings creak and groan, but they still retain their sturdy presence as one of the larger structures in downtown Penn Yan.

Many years ago the folks at Birkett Mills, along with the city fathers of Penn Yan, decided to pay tribute to the almighty pancake by attempting to set the record for the largest pancake ever made.

They were successful.

On September 27, 1987, hundreds gathered in the main business district for a giant Buckwheat Harvest Festival. The makings of the world's largest pancake were nothing short of heroic. A roaring fire set the stage for this herculean cook-off. A massive two-piece metal griddle was welded together by local mechanics. A large cement truck was brought to the scene, the buckwheat pancake mix was dumped inside, and the water was hosed in after it. Around and around it went until it was thoroughly mixed. A hush came over the throng as the cement mixer poured out its breakfast bounty into the red-hot griddle.

The easy part was concocting a pancake that could be poured over a fire. The hard part, and a part that was required to be considered for inclusion in the world record books, was the actual flapjack flipping. When it was ready to be turned over, a huge crane rolled up and hooked a chain to the griddle to finish the job. To the cheers of the crowd, the actual flipping went without problems. At the end, the massive pancake was served up to those attending to benefit a local church. A truck from nearby Batavia brought a large pat of butter over from a dairy farm, and local maple syrup providers slathered the cakes with their gooey sweetness poured out of five-gallon cans.

And yes, the *Guinness Book of World Records* was on hand to do the certification. A roar went up throughout the crowd of more than forty thousand when their homemade pancake monstrosity measured in at almost thirty feet in diameter!

The pancakes, butter, syrup, and other festival goodies were soon consumed, and all that was left of that day was the trophy, the original giant pancake griddle used in the record-achieving feat. Today it hangs on the side of the Birkett Mills company headquarters in the center of Pen Yan.

For those who are curious about the actual dynamics of this feat, the list is awesome. The pancake contained an estimated 1,728,000 calories, weighed more than two tons, measured twenty-eight feet one inch in diameter, and had a circumference of eighty-eight feet. It was covered with fifteen gallons of maple syrup and topped with a seventy-pound pat of fresh butter.

The Penn Yan Buckwheat Festival ended many years ago, once the record for the largest pancake was secured. It is bittersweet to note that the Penn Yan world record no longer stands. The community of Rochdale, Manchester, England, was crowned the king of the pancakes with their incredible feat in 1994. Their English pancake came in at over three tons, and was nearly fifty feet in diameter. It took two giant cranes to flip the monster concoction.

So, in fact, Penn Yan did hold the world record for about seven years and can now accurately be described as holding the record for making America's largest pancake. There is no evidence of where the British pancake griddle is today, if it even exists.

Other Nearby Attractions or Sites

Penn Yan (a portmanteau term referencing the earliest Pennsylvanian and Yankee settlers) lies at the northern end of Keuka Lake. This lake is one of the most beautiful of all the Finger Lakes. It has a sixty-mile shoreline and is very narrow, giving the lake area a small, comfortable feel. Both shores are easily in view of each other. This is the heart of New York's wine country, there are many wonderful wineries within a short drive of Penn Yan. A good source for "wineing" in the area is the Keuka Wine Trail.

Keuka Lake is also known as "Crooked Lake." Halfway up the lake it branches out into two separate "legs," each with its own personality. The

Esperanza Mansion is one of the most beautiful and historic old homes in the area. It sits high above the western branch of Keuka Lake. It is now a restaurant, inn, and destination resort and a popular spot for weddings, with the lake offering a shimmering backdrop to any gala affair.

Essentials

What: The world's largest pancake griddle

Where: Penn Yan; Yates County

Contact

Penn Yan tourism, history, and events: www.villageofpennyan.com

Birkett Mills (location of the record-setting pancake griddle): www.the birkettmills.com

Keuka Lake Wine Trail: www.keukawinetrail.com

Esperanza Mansion: www.esperanzamansion.com

22

Howe House

Phelps
Ontario County

America's only two-story brick outhouse.

Unlike other subjects covered in this book, this one is best described in just a few simple words rather than florid terminology.

It's a two-story outhouse. There.

The Howe House was built in 1869 by Moses Barlow, a successful physician in Phelps, N.Y. Thirty years later he expanded his home and made an unusual addition to it. The two-story outhouse features local bricks, four-paned windows, and a flared-slate, hipped mansard roof. For easy access there are separate entrances to each floor of this unusual privy.

It is the only two-story brick outhouse in New York. For those more curious about this Upstate oddity, it is a six-holer! Three up and three down.

The two-story outhouse is owned by the Phelps Community Historical Center, which occupies the Victorian mansion attached to it in the front. The construction of a two-story outhouse had to take into consideration the proper "evacuation flow" of the top floor to the bottom. Suffice to say, somehow it worked. The Phelps two-story brick outhouse is the only one of its kind in the United States. There are a few other wooden ones, however. Believe it or not, there is actually a three-story outhouse in Bryant Pond, Maine. How that "evacuation flow" works is anybody's guess, but it is still in use!

The Howe House is one of the architecturally remarkable buildings in Phelps. Besides the intricate brickwork and the two-story oddity hanging off the back porch, the house has one of the first three-story bay windows of its era. Today, the historical group acts as the caretaker of the house and the museum within. More than two thousand items of Phelps history are on display at any one time at the museum. And, yes, you can view the two-story outhouse from within the museum.

In recent years, members of the Phelps Community Center have reported strange goings-on in the mansion, and many believe it is haunted. Strange noises (no, not flushing sounds) and apparitions have been sensed by several members of the group, and several paranormal groups have come to investigate. They found that ghostly happenings are possible but unverified in this historic home.

Outhouses were common sights around Upstate New York as recently as the 1940s. A common two-holer was not meant to be used by two people at once. Instead a small hole was built in for children to use while the adults accommodated themselves on the larger opening. The famous

Phelps celebrates its heritage as the one time "Sauerkraut Capital of the World" by holding a sauerkraut festival each year.

crescent-moon cutout on the door may have signified that it was a "ladies facility"; others suggest it was used to let in moonlight for nighttime bathroom reading!

Other Nearby Attractions or Sites

For many years, Phelps was the world center of sauerkraut manufacturing. Several major kraut factories sprang up in the mid-twentieth century, and the industry was once the largest employer in the region. Among the top sauerkraut producers here were the Silver Floss–Empire State Pickling Company (closed in 1985) and the Seneca Sauerkraut Factory (closed in 1994).

Today, the self-proclaimed "Sauerkraut Capital of the World" remembers its long-time "golden egg" with a giant community-wide Sauerkraut Festival. Thousands attend each year.

Among the hallmarks of this, perhaps the most unique food festival in the state, are the crowning of the Kraut King and Kraut Queen and a sauerkraut parade. Other weekend events held in the past have included cabbage bowling and a cabbage food court. If you are daring, you simply must try the festival's legendary sauerkraut cake. It really is pretty good!

Another interesting side trip to take while visiting Phelps is to the Scythe Tree near Waterloo. The tree is approximately ten miles southwest of Phelps.

A rare Balm of Gilead tree stands in front of a farm along the Waterloo-Geneva Road. Protruding from it is an ever diminishing farmer's scythe. A sign tells the story (remember, although you are welcome to observe this unique spot, this is private property).

The story goes that in October, 1861, twenty-six-year-old farmer Wyman Johnson hung his scythe in the tree, telling his distraught mother that it would remain there until the Civil War was over, and that when he came home he would take it out of the tree and go back to working his parents' fields. Sadly, he never came home. He was wounded in battle in North Carolina and died of his injuries on May 22, 1864. He was buried in an unmarked grave somewhere in the South.

Over the years the Scythe Tree has been a poignant memorial to this young man's unfulfilled promise to his dear mother. More than a century and a half later, the tree has almost wholly swallowed up the farmer's scythe, but it is still there, and you can still see the blade end glistening in the sun. Over the decades, other owners have left scythes in the tree during wartime. Two of them, the Schaffer brothers, did this when they went off to fight in World War II. Unlike Wyman Johnson, they both returned safely from the war and removed the scythe handles from the tree, leaving only the blades. All three blades have been painted so the visitor can find them on the tree. An American flag flies in front of the Scythe Tree and a historical monument has been erected telling of its story.

Essentials

What: Two-story brick outhouse

Where: Howe House Museum, 66 Main Street, Phelps; Ontario County

Contact

Two-story outhouse: http://phelpsny.com/historical-society. This website tells the history of the mansion as well as the story of the outhouse

Sauerkraut Festival: The festival is traditionally held the last weekend in July: http://phelpsny.com/sauerkraut-weekend

Scythe Tree: There is no website for the tree. It can be seen at 842 Geneva-Waterloo Road, two miles west of Waterloo on US 20.

23

Canal Bridge

Seneca Falls
Seneca County

It's a wonderful life.

Seneca Falls is known around the world as the "Birthplace of the Women's Rights Movement."

In July of 1848, many of the most important women in America converged on this village in Upstate New York to hammer out the basic foundations of the national women's rights agenda. Thousands of visitors come to this Finger Lakes community every year to visit the hallowed grounds of the famed Wesleyan Chapel where the convention was held. Although very little is left of the original 1843 structure, that which does remain is as close to a national shrine as it gets in America.

The chapel suffered through years of use, abuse, renovations, disrepair, neglect, and disinterest. By the time the National Parks Service got their hands on the chapel, there was little left but a few old stone walls. Still, one can feel the power and importance of this place by just strolling through the grounds and reading the texts provided. The NPS has overseen the restoration of what was left of the Wesleyan Chapel. The site, the Women's Rights National Historical Park, is now in good hands to welcome visitors far into the future.

The National Women's Hall of Fame, the nation's oldest membership organization dedicated to recognizing the achievements of women, is the most popular destination in Seneca Falls. It is a modern museum and hall of fame with many interesting exhibits and displays telling the stories of the famous (and unknown) women inducted into the shrine. Since the Hall began in 1969, the list of inductees has included athlete Althea Gibson (class of 2001), Congresswoman Bella Abzug (1994), First Lady Eleanor Roosevelt (1973), Sesame Street creator Joan Ganz Cooney (1998), chef Julia Child (2007), writer Zora Neale Hurston (1994), Saint Katherine Drexel (2011), and blues singer Bessie Smith (1984).

And although the local chamber of commerce will no doubt tell you that the majority of visitors who come to Seneca Falls are here for the women's rights landmarks, I have a sneaking suspicion that many are also here to see the similarities between this quaint little Upstate community and one of the most familiar celluloid towns ever depicted in a Hollywood movie.

Is Seneca Falls, New York, the model for Bedford Falls, New York, as seen in *It's a Wonderful Life*?

Well, here is the story.

When telling the tale of the Bedford Falls–Seneca Falls connection, it is important to separate fact from fiction. And one of the most important facts that we know for certain is that Frank Capra, who produced and directed the film, did visit Seneca Falls in the latter part of 1945 (the movie was released a year later). He was in the area visiting a relative in the nearby town of Auburn. Capra stopped in Seneca Falls to get a haircut at Tommy Bellissima's shop. Tommy had no idea who the famous director was, but made the connection when the movie came out a year later. He remembered that a guy named "Capra" had come in, and he had joked with the customer about his last name meaning "goat" in Italian.

There are many movie references to local place names in the film. Perhaps the most famous is when the cranky old bank examiner tells George Bailey to hurry up because he has to catch a train to Elmira. Elmira, clearly a little-known name to almost anybody in Hollywood, is just an hour south of Seneca Falls. Conspiracy lovers will go on to tell you that both Bedford Falls and Seneca Falls were mill towns. A prominent street in the fictitious movie town was Genesee Street, and the Upstate community sits along what was once known as the Genesee Turnpike. The architecture of both communities is strikingly similar, and both towns had wealthy old civic lions who held sway over the comings and goings of the community and its inhabitants. The movie had "old man Potter" and Seneca Falls had Norman J. Gould, the powerful manufacturer of America's most popular water pumps and one of the town's wealthiest residents.

And then there is the bridge.

The steel truss bridge in *It's a Wonderful Life* plays a pivotal role at both the beginning and the end of the film. We first see it covered in snow as a desperate George Bailey, having lost everything, jumps from it in a failed suicide attempt. We, of course, all know now that George's life is saved when an unlikely angel named Clarence jumps in to rescue him from the freezing waters. So much for the script. In real life, there is a mirror image of the movie bridge in Seneca Falls today. That bridge straddles the canal that runs through town. And it is here, on this old steel bridge, that one can easily be convinced that *It's a Wonderful Life* was born.

In 1945, director Frank Capra would have left Tommy Bellissima's barber shop and crossed this very bridge to get to Main Street. One would assume that a man in the business Capra was in, an occupation that relies heavily on imagination and creativity, would have been looking around as he crossed the bridge. If so, he would have certainly noticed an old plaque affixed to the bridge. The plaque is dedicated to the memory of a real-life Seneca Falls resident, Antonio Varacalli, who in 1917 jumped into the water below to save a woman from drowning. Varacalli died while attempting this heroic act.

It would be a small leap of faith to assume that a creative genius like Frank Capra would have been compelled by this real-life story to configure it into a movie he was planning to make.

And that, at least in my mind, is the clincher.

The bridge in the movie is almost identical to the one in Seneca Falls. And so, while thousands visit the shrine to America's famous women just three blocks away, many others walk down the hill from Main Street and stand on this bridge to pay their respects at a shrine to one of the greatest American movies ever made.

Today, the plaque in memory of Antonia Varacalli is joined by another bronze tablet, which reads "The village of Seneca Falls may have inspired the hometown look of Frank Capra's 1946 holiday film classic *It's a Wonderful Life*. Mr. Capra is known to have visited here in the mid-1940s at the time the screenplay was being developed. Many similarities exist between Seneca Falls and the fictional Bedford Falls. Among these are the design of Bridge Street bridge, the use of several place and personal names, and the village's geographic location."

There are four road signs on the short span that goes over the bridge. They say "George Bailey Lane," "Bedford Falls Boulevard," "Angel Avenue," and "Clarence Street."

Other Nearby Attractions or Sites

Of course no visit to Seneca Falls would be complete without spending some time at the very interesting and historic National Women's Rights Hall of Fame. The hall, the women's rights park area, Main Street, and the historic district of the village are all an easy walk from one another as well as from the It's a Wonderful Life bridge.

Essentials

What: The It's a Wonderful Life bridge

Where: Bridge Street, Seneca Falls; Seneca County

Contact

Seneca Falls: Check here for events, links, and information: www.seneca-falls.com; the village has held It's a Wonderful Life celebrations in the past.

National Women's Hall of Fame: www.greatwomen.org

24

The Dickens Christmas Stroll

Skaneateles
Onondaga County

A Jolly Olde Tyme.

A Dickens Stroll, sometimes called a Victorian Stroll, is a common sight throughout New York and New England during the holiday season. These events let tourists and townsfolk enjoy interaction in a setting of Merry Olde England where caroling is a must, elaborate Victorian attire is suggested, and centuries-old traditions should be adhered to.

It all adds up to a unique Upstate New York holiday hallmark.

Strolls can be found in several communities across Upstate. The Victorian Stroll in Troy, now over three decades old, takes place in the downtown district, where many original buildings harken back to the late 1800s. In fact, this River Street area has such a distinct London air to it that is has been featured in several major British-themed Hollywood films, including Martin Scorsese's *Age of Innocence*. More than twenty thousand visitors come to enjoy the stroll, walk along the historic streets of the Antique Row, marvel at the Victorian decorations, interact with the costumed strollers, and enjoy street vendor foods. It is a great place for a Victorian Stroll, especially since it all takes place basically right outside the front door of the building where the *Troy Sentinel* newspaper first published a new poem, "A Visit from St, Nicholas ('Twas the Night Before Christmas)," on December 23, 1823.

Little Sharon Springs triples in population during their annual Victorian Stroll. They hold a parade that features many ladies in full satin finery and outrageously feathered hats, who join a small army of men in long coats and top hats to march into town to kick off the festivities. Josh Kilmer-Purcell and Dr. Brent Ridge, known to millions as the television stars *The Fabulous Beekman Boys*, are a major presence at this celebration (they have a store on Main Street). No need to get a brochure to tell you the times of the many happenings all day long. A leather-lunged town crier, in vest, gold-braided coat, and black buckle shoes, goes up and down the tiny main street ringing his large brass bell and announcing at the top of his voice the series of musical events, theatrical presentations, and Christmas events taking place.

The Athens Victorian Stroll, one of the best along the Hudson River, brings out many in Victorian garb and features wine tasting, live performances, family events, a Christmas-tree-lighting ceremony, and an old-fashioned Victorian singalong.

There are many others across the Upstate region, and I suspect that more and more will pop up as the tradition grows. The one I would like to feature is the Skaneateles Dickens Christmas Stroll.

I have been to it several times and it certainly qualities as an Upstate landmark. A holiday one to be sure, but a landmark nonetheless.

Every weekend between Thanksgiving and Christmas, the streets of this little Finger Lakes village appear as if they have come from the pages of a Christmas fairy tale. More than fifty performers stroll the streets, mingling with the tourists and locals as if it were just another day in town, circa 1890. The costumes are elaborate and extravagant, from the dazzling red-and-white fur-bedecked St. Nicholas holding court on a Main Street front porch, down to the knickers-wearing lads darting about in the lakeside park. Women wrapped in antique furs and wearing gigantic lace bonnets, men in bright red vests and satin pants, gaily costumed carolers singing in the old Victorian band gazebo, and garlanded horse carriages slowly loping by all add to this wondrous Christmas tableaux. And everyone and everything you see is resplendent in an array of elegant Victorian finery worthy of Hollywood's Edith Head.

What separates this stroll from others I have attended is the remarkable way the "players" stay in character. Listen in on three elderly spinsters gossiping on the corner and you are likely to hear a conversation laced with British accents. Even St. Nicholas sounds like he came from London's East End. Maybe the most remarkable player, perhaps even the star of the day's production, is old Scrooge himself.

A friend and I attended the stroll recently, and he spied this legendary miser hobbling down the street leaning heavily on a cane, suspiciously surveying the surroundings near the carolers' gazebo. He was dressed in a top hat, wrap-around scarf, green jodhpurs, and a brown vest and was sporting a heroic pair of muttonchops. He was observing the goings on while peering over his wire-rimmed spectacles. We approached with caution.

"Hello, Ebenezer. Top of the morning to you," my friend Dan offered in his most cheery faux British accent.

The old man whirled around and looked directly into his face. He scowled, "Ebenezer? It is Mr. Scrooge to you, sonny boy." Dan pardoned himself for the indiscretion but plowed on with the conversation undaunted. "What a lovely day, sir." "Lovely you say? I don't think so. Say, don't I know you?" he said as he leaned closer to Dan's face and took off his glasses. "Yes, it is you," he positively shouted. "You owe me rent, boy!" I could barely contain my laugh as this hambone of an actor carried on completely absorbed in the Scrooge character. "Why, yes, I think I do," Dan sheepishly replied as he reached into his pocket and pulled out a handful of assorted coins. Scrooge dived right into the change and pulled out a quarter. "There that'll do," he said as he turned and walked away. We yelled, "Nice meeting you, Ebenezer," to him. He whirled around, took out the quarter and put it into his mouth and bit down on it. "Um, good. And it is real," he said with a wink and disappeared into a crowd of laughing revelers.

That did it for me. The Skaneateles Dickens Stroll had me at Scrooge!

Other Nearby Attractions or Sites

The Sherwood Inn is one of Upstate New York's oldest fine-dining establishments. It first opened its doors in 1807 and is still one of the most popular restaurants in the region. The old blue clapboard building with the tall windows overlooking Skaneateles Lake sits at the end of Main Street across from the waterfront park. It has a comfortable tavern, several beautiful dining rooms, and twenty-five antique-appointed overnight accommodations.

Essentials

What: Dickens Christmas Stroll

Where: Skaneateles (throughout the village); Onondaga County

Contact

Skaneateles Dickens Stroll: www.skaneateles.com/visit/events-a-attractions/dickens-christmas

Sherwood Inn: www.thesherwoodinn.com

Troy Victorian Stroll: www.victorianstroll.com

Sharon Springs Dickens Christmas Festival: www.enjoysharonsprings.com

Athens Victorian Stroll: www.athensculturalcenter.org

25

Mail Boat Cruise

Skaneateles

Onondaga County

The mail must go through.

Skaneateles Lake is one of the prettiest lakes in Upstate New York. Located in the Finger Lakes, it is the lake at the highest elevation, giving it the moniker of "The Roof Garden of Lakes." The lake is clean. And we mean clean. Always ranked among the top three cleanest lakes in the state, Skaneateles Lake provides much of the water for Syracuse and many other surrounding communities, and it is not even treated! Filtered, yes. But they use the lake water untreated.

Like I said, that is one clean lake.

The lake is also historic in that it is one of the last lakes which provide daily U.S. mail by boat.

"We really do not know of many other lakes that have mail service," Sarah Wiles told me. She runs the family business, Mid-Lakes Navigation, out of Skaneateles. "My family secured the U.S. mail delivery contract in 1968. We have been doing it ever since."

I asked Sarah how many homes she serves and what a typical day is alike.

"Well, with the weather and the tourists there really is no typical day," she laughed. "We load up the mail boat in the morning at ten and it takes us about three hours to make the whole lake circuit. We have thirty-four homes presently that get mail from our boat. We usually slowly sidle right up to the dock and either hand the mail to the owners or place it in the boxes they have out for us. It really is a lot of fun, and most owners come out. It is like a daily ritual for them. Something fun and unusual to do."

I told her that if I had a camp I would never miss going out to greet the mail boat.

"Most people really do, and that is great. We give a little blast of the horn first to let them know we are coming. The dogs are usually the first ones to run down to the dock. We always keep the mail boat well-stocked with doggie treats for obvious reasons," she smiled. "Some people hold out a long fishing net with their mail for us in it. Others toss it in. There is a large summer camp along the lake, Lourdes Camp, and we usually have many sacks of mail for them, from the parents of the children."

Is that a big hassle having to drop so much mail off at one dock?

"Oh, no. In fact, that is our favorite stop. The camp counselors always come down to the dock and greet us with a song and dance. The call it the 'Mail Boat Dance.' It is a hoot. Our boat guests love it."

You mean you take guests on the boat?

"Yes, it is one of our most popular tours. We load up with people and mail and start making the rounds. Sometimes we even provide a box lunch for them. It is a nice, leisurely cruise and they get to see all the fabulous mansions along the lake. And they get to help deliver the mail."

I had to ask. What happens in the winter?

"Well, that gets a little rough for some. Since this is a seasonal lake, we only have the mail contract from June to Labor Day. After that, those who stay are on their own. Then, it is just like it is when we have a storm coming in and we can't take the boat out. The residents have to get in their cars and drive a long way out to the road or into town to the mailbox. Believe me, they much rather the boat come to them."

Mail has been delivered on Skaneateles Lake since the mid-1800s. It was by steamboat then. The first boat used by Sarah's family is now in the Finger Lakes Boating Museum. The current mail boat, the *Barbara S.*, started as a delivery boat in Canada and then spent decades as a tour boat on Lake George. Mid-Lakes bought it in 1981.

"We had our big seventy-fifth anniversary a while back. Everybody came out. We had cake and balloons and a great celebration. The *Barbara S.* was built in 1937 and is a classic, old-fashioned mahogany tour boat. We get real sentimental when we talk about our boats," she said softly. "It's just been such a wonderful life on the lake here. We feel so connected to our surroundings. We have been a part of the community ever since, well, ever since I was a little girl," she chuckled.

Has anyone ever dropped any mail in the lake?

"Oh, sure! We have had our little mistakes over the years. But everybody takes it in stride. Yes, we have dropped a couple of pieces in the lake before, but we have never lost a single piece of mail. We go in after it, dry it out, and deliver it again."

Taking a ride on the mail boat in Skaneateles is about as fun and unusual a cruise as you can take in Upstate New York. There are ten boats in the Mid-Lakes fleet and they do all kinds of custom boat tours, including multiday tours along the Erie Canal.

Sarah Wiles can trace her roots back through several generations here in the Skaneateles area.

"My great-great grandfather was a very famous man, Gustav Stickley. He was one of America's most famous furniture designers. He spent a lot of time here in Skaneateles."

"Did he get his mail by boat," I asked?

"No, I don't think so. He lived a ways away from the lake," she said.

Other Nearby Attractions or Sites

Skaneateles is a thirty-minute drive from Syracuse. The picturesque community of eight thousand residents hugs its namesake lake, and the lakefront park is the center of many community events.

One of the village's legendary eateries is Doug's Fish Fry. Doug Clark has been serving up a memorable fish dinner here since 1982. He gained a little national notoriety in 1999 when he said if the president and Mrs. Clinton visited Skaneateles, he would not serve them, based on "principles." Sure enough the president and his wife showed up, enjoyed a summer vacation at a friend's mansion along the lake, and stayed far away from Doug's Fish Fry!

Essentials

What: The Mail Boat Cruise

Where: 11 Jordan Street, Skaneateles; Onondaga County

Contact

Mid-Lakes Navigation: www.midlakesnav.com

Skaneateles Tourism and Events: www.skaneateles.com

Doug's Fish Fry: www.dougsfishfry.com

26

The Birthplace of Memorial Day

Waterloo
Seneca County

We will never forget.

At the very end of the hostilities of the Civil War, which left almost 600,000 dead both in the North and South, the widows of Southern soldiers began a movement to decorate the graves of the dead from both sides who were buried in the South. This was an unorganized act of reconciliation that soon caught on in the North. On May 5, 1868, Union general John A. Logan issued a proclamation, General Order 11, which called for a "Decoration Day" to honor the war dead that "lie in almost every city, village and hamlet churchyard in the land." Logan was a revered general and was one of the founders of the Grand Army of the Republic, a Union Army veteran's organization. Even today "Logan's Order" is read or recited at many Memorial Day observances around the nation.

So where does the little Upstate village of Waterloo come into the picture?

It all started in 1865 with a local druggist, Henry C. Welles, who believed the time was right for everyone to seek out the graves of the fallen from the Civil War and decorate them with fresh flowers. Locals liked the idea, but Welles's idea that it should become a national effort failed to catch on. Waterloo went ahead with decorating of graves and with a celebration commemorating the dead and honoring the survivors. Later, Welles enlisted the support of a local Civil War hero, General John B. Murray, in the cause.

With this prominent military officer lending his considerable support, the idea of a day to memorialize the dead gained further traction. One year later, on May 5, 1866 the village of Waterloo had the first fully realized Memorial Day celebration in the land. Parades and speeches were the order of the day, and the village was decorated with mourning flags, bunting, and fresh flowers. General Murray gave a fiery keynote speech and led the entire village in a procession to the cemetery where the graves were decorated. The festivities were held the next year, too, and the one following. By that time, many communities across the land were holding ceremonies in response to General John A Logan's "orders."

But Waterloo was the first.

Or was it?

Many other communities across the America have stepped forward and proclaimed themselves as the "Birthplace of Memorial Day." Each time, Waterloo has aggressively defended her honor. According to the United

States Department of Veteran's Affairs, nearly thirty communities lay claim to being the birthplace of Memorial Day. Among them are Columbus, Mississippi; Boalsburg, Pennsylvania; Carbondale, Illinois; and Charleston, South Carolina. And while these other communities can legitimate their claims with brown and brittle newspaper articles and ancient proclamations from city fathers, they all lack that one thing that Waterloo has.

An official presidential decree.

The road to certification initially took Waterloo through Albany, where Governor Nelson Rockefeller signed an official state document attesting to Waterloo's historic claim on March 7, 1966. This further buttressed the village's efforts to get a national stamp of approval on their effort to claim their rightful place in history. That came when Congress passed a House resolution on May 17 and 19, 1966, the hundredth anniversary of the first commemoration in Waterloo, designating the city as the holiday's birthplace. One week later the bill was signed into law by President Lyndon B. Johnson. That year's centennial celebration was one of the largest, and national recognition having been received with the presidential proclamation, many dignitaries came for the festivities, including descendants of the founders of the original Memorial Day in 1866.

Today, Memorial Day is celebrated in grand fashion in Waterloo. A long banner is strung over Main Street broadcasting to all who travel through that they are indeed visiting the birthplace of Memorial Day. The annual holiday celebration sees one of the largest parades in Upstate New York and a full weekend of civic ceremonies and community activities.

Other Nearby Attractions or Sites

At the east end of Waterloo's Main Street sits a regal 1850 brick mansion that has been turned into the Memorial Day Museum. Inside the former William H. Burton home are many rooms decorated in the 1860s style with much of Waterloo's history on display. Of course there are many exhibits and artifacts pertaining to the founding of Memorial Day.

Waterloo is the largest village in Seneca County. Now it is the county seat, but formerly the center of the government was in Ovid fifteen miles to the south. The seat was moved to Waterloo in 1819. To alleviate hard feelings between the two communities, New York State has allowed Seneca

County to be the only county in the state with two official county seats, in Waterloo and Ovid. (Waterloo is the primary location of administrative offices.)

When the county commissioners meet in Ovid they generally meet in one of the most unique sets of government buildings in Upstate New York. "The Three Bears" are three similar-looking columned buildings constructed in the mid-nineteenth century. They occupy a unique place on the National Register of Historic Places (1976). These buildings are the only set of three intact adjacent public buildings with Greek Revival architecture still standing anywhere in the United States today.

Essentials

What: The birthplace of Memorial Day

Where: Waterloo, New York; Seneca County

Contact

Waterloo history, events, tourism: www.waterloony.com. This website lists the details of the annual Waterloo Memorial Day celebrations. Because of the historic nature of the holiday in this village, thousands attend, and it is wise to secure your travel places, including hotel and camping reservations, well in advance. This website also serves the Waterloo Memorial Day Museum and lists all activities, events, hours, and other pertinent information.

27

Chimney Bluffs

Wolcott
Wayne County

An eerie moonscape along Sodus Bay.

Of the hundred unique and unusual Upstate New York landmarks chronicled in this book, just a small handful are natural ones. This eerie outcropping of sand and rock spikes along the coast of Lake Ontario is certainly the most unusual. I had to go and see them for myself, and since I did I have struggled with how to describe them.

In a word they are . . . awesome.

Chimney Bluffs State Park is located at the end of a long country road that parallels Sodus Bay. On the day I arrived at 8:00 a.m., I was the only car in the unattended parking lot. The temperature changes dramatically the closer you get to our ocean-sized Great Lakes, and it was cool and brisk with a bit of a chill in the early morning air.

A small park is your welcoming point to Chimney Bluffs. It is very well maintained and features park benches, beautiful landscaping, and picnic facilities. Grills are provided for family get-togethers. From the edge of this park, you can scan the shore and lake, and you will no doubt glimpse either a ship passing on the horizon or a seaplane floating by overhead. From this recreation area, you can look east along the shore and get a distant and enticing first view of the bluffs.

To see the actual natural oddity known as the Chimney Bluffs you must walk off to your right and follow a path about a mile into the woods. This forested area hugs the high cliffs overlooking Lake Ontario, and great care and caution should be taken while hiking the trail. I wouldn't call the trail an easy hike, but it certainly should be doable for most adults and teenagers. I would strongly caution you not to take young children on the hike.

After about a twenty-five-minute walk through the woods, a path that swerves from deep into the forest to areas where you are literally walking on the cliff's edge, you will begin to see the Chimney Bluffs ahead of you. You cross several wooden bridges spanning creeks and streams along the way.

The bluffs were created over ten thousand years through the constant beating of rain, waves, snow, and high winds. Called drumlins, these phenomena were formed by glacial activity, and when the glaciers retreated, these unusual-looking formations remained. Drumlins can be found throughout the country, but the ones here near Sodus Bay certainly must be the most dramatic.

As you inch closer to the bluffs, you struggle to identify what you are seeing up ahead. To me, the landscape looks like something I saw years ago in the High Atlas Mountains of Morocco. Tall, razor-sharp spikes of beige rock stab out from the ground, some of them hundreds of feet into the air. They are an eerie sight for sure and create a backdrop reminiscent of movie sets in science fiction films (the original *Planet of the Apes* film could definitely have been shot here).

As I sat on a tree stump and observed for about an hour, the constantly rising morning sun caused the spires to cast ever-changing, dramatically dancing shadows throughout the deep stone canyon where the bluffs are located. The setting was peaceful and isolated, and the crashing waves below added a distinct solitariness to the experience. It was beautiful, odd, a bit scary, and one of the most surprising natural landmarks I have encountered in all my travels throughout Upstate New York.

I only observed the Chimney Bluffs from the top, but there is also a shoreline trail that leads you to the rocky moonscape from the bottom.

This area became Chimney Bluffs State Park in 1963. It had previously been operated as a recreational area by private owners. With the state's acquisition also came heated restroom facilities and service buildings. To try to describe the indescribable to the average park visitor, there are informational signs, diagrams, and exhibits. One of them reads, "10,000 years ago a vast Ice Age glacier melted and retreated from New York State, leaving behind Lake Ontario. South of the lake the glacier packed clay, sand, and boulders into thousands of long, rounded hills called 'drumlins.' Chimney Bluffs is the most spectacular remaining drumlin in the state."

Chimney Bluffs State Park is open year round. In winter it is a destination for snowmobilers and snowshoe hikers. The trail from the park entrance to the actual bluffs is not maintained in the winter months.

Other Nearby Attractions or Sites

Across Sodus Bay, just to the west of Chimney Bluffs State Park, is the little waterfront community of Sodus Point. Here a visitor will find an assortment of restaurants, cafés, gift shops, and other amenities. The village, with fewer than a thousand year-round residents, sits right on Lake Ontario at the mouth of Sodus Bay, and like so many other communities along the vast Great Lakes shoreline, it exudes an oceanside ambiance.

The Sodus Bay Lighthouse (first founded in 1825), with its original limestone keeper's home attached, is a popular tourist destination. A museum inside tells the history of the lighthouse and the community.

Essentials

What: Chimney Bluffs natural formation

Where: Chimney Bluffs State Park; 8105 Gardner Road, Wolcott; Wayne County

Contact

Chimney Bluffs State Park: http://nysparks.com/parks/43/details. As I mentioned in this chapter, when I arrived at the park in the early morning hours I was the only one there. But as I left about three hours later, the park was beginning to fill up with families, hikers, and tourists. Even though this is a remote state park, it was obvious to me that it was a popular one.

Sodus Bay Lighthouse and Museum: http://www.sodusbaylighthouse.org

REGION THREE

Central New York

◆ ◆ ◆

*Including parts of Chemung, Chenango, Cortland, Delaware,
Fulton, Herkimer, Madison, Montgomery, Oneida,
Onondaga, Otsego, and Schoharie Counties*

28

Kirk Douglas Park

Amsterdam
Montgomery County

The ragman's son.

Many famous people have come from this city located along the Mohawk River. Politicians, artists, writers, and athletes. But none has ever reached the level of fame and familiarity of one Issur Danielovich Demsky.

Kirk Douglas.

Douglas was born in 1916 on Eagle Street in this blue-collar city of eighteen thousand. His father was an Eastern European immigrant who couldn't speak English and collected and sold rags to provide for his family. Issur chafed under the stifling conditions of his family's poverty as a youth in Amsterdam, and using all of his inchoate acting wiles, he talked his way in to St. Lawrence University, about seventy-five miles north of his hometown.

He later enlisted in the Navy where he suffered an injury, and after his discharge went to New York City, where he began acting in radio and in workshops. Within a couple of years, an also young Lauren Bacall gave him a tip about a role in an upcoming film. Douglas made his film debut in *The Strange Love of Martha Ivers* in 1946, costarring with screen legend Barbara Stanwyck. He had just turned thirty years old.

Douglas soon became a Hollywood favorite and embarked on one of the most storied careers in Hollywood history.

He may have left Amsterdam, but Amsterdam never really left him. Totally.

"Old timers around here say that even well into his nineties if you listen closely to Kirk Douglas you can still hear that familiar Amsterdam twang," Rob von Hasseln told me. He is the Amsterdam city historian.

"Kirk Douglas surely left our Mohawk Valley many decades ago, but no matter where he lived or how famous he got he always kept a little bit of his hometown with him. Not all of his memories were good ones, of course. He was dirt poor; his parents didn't speak English. His father was a rag picker, and he was Jewish. But the actor still called longtime friends once in a while to ask how they were doing, to find out if they had seen his latest movie or to ask them a favor, like making a short trip to Schenectady to check on an ailing relative."

The Great Depression years in Amsterdam oddly were good times for many of the young people. The mills were humming, churning out brooms, caskets, pearl buttons, metal springs, and of course carpets. Some of the largest carpet mills in the nation were located right here along the Chuctanunda Creek.

"Issur Demsky wanted out of Amsterdam. His best friend, Pete, decided that they were going to go to college at St. Lawrence University, north of us. Of course they had no money. So they hitchhiked to the college on the back of a manure wagon. When they arrived, the school admission officer was horrified at the sight (and smell) of the two young men, but they talked their way in. Again, the fact that he was just a ragman's son was not a plus when it came time for him to enroll at St. Lawrence. Still, he was accepted and it was a turning point in his life. The two young adventurers would remain close friends for many years after that little trip on the back of the wagon."

The actor would slip in and out of Amsterdam over the decades, always trying to visit without fanfare. In 1985, he came and visited with three of his sisters who lived here: Marianne, Ida, and Fritzi. He was known to contribute monetarily to local charities such as the area American Heart Fund.

"Of course our city is proud to call Kirk Douglas a native son. We carved out a beautiful little park in our downtown area and dedicated it to him back in 1988. We held a Kirk Douglas Day. The streets were packed with excited onlookers as the actor and his wife rode in an open car waving to the crowd. His manure wagon–riding best friend, Pete, was sitting right next to him fifty years after their escapade to St. Lawrence University. At the park we dedicated a monument to the actor. A large boulder was placed prominently for all to see. On its face is a bronze plaque featuring the actor's famously handsome chiseled features. The inscription reads: "Kirk Douglas Park. Named in Honor of Our Native Son, Distinguished Actor and Recipient of the U.S. Medal of Freedom for his Example to the People of Amsterdam.""

The park is situated along the banks of the roaring Chuctanunda Creek, Amsterdam's most famous and important waterway.

"This creek and the falls near the park were vital to Amsterdam's growth," von Hasseln told me. "At one time there was no park and you could barely even see the creek. Giant mills stood shoulder to shoulder along either side, harnessing the rushing water to power their machines and giant knitting looms. It was the heartbeat of Amsterdam and a place of incredible activity. It is said that all you had to do was look at the color of the water to know what color fabric was being made at the mills that day. As the mills dumped their waste into the creek, the water would run red one day, green the next, then blue. Of course, that was a long time ago."

The last of the giant mills stopped churning out carpets and other products in the 1960s. "The work left Amsterdam and went overseas. We really took a hit," he said.

Amsterdam's population was around thirty-thousand in 1950. Today it is about eighteen thousand.

So what is in store for Kirk Douglas's old hometown?

"We like to look forward. I think in terms of a 'Rule of 14.' In 1714, if you predicted that in sixty years the pristine wilderness would be gone, with no Mohawk villages to be found, people would say you were crazy. In 1814, if you predicted that in sixty years the little village would grow so big you couldn't even see the Chuctanunda anymore, people wouldn't believe you. In 1914, if you said in sixty years that all the mills would be closed and gone and you could see the creek again, you would be laughed at. So now it is 2014. And we think Amsterdam's future is bright. With the growth of Upstate's high-tech triangle (Malta to Schenectady to Albany), we are perfectly positioned for a rebirth. People seeking high wages in those locales can live here, just a half hour away, and enjoy all the urban amenities while living in the center of the most beautiful area of Upstate. I like to say, 'You don't have to get out of our city to get into the country.' We really are excited about our future."

And what about Kirk Douglas's memory in the future?

"As the old timers fade away, including many locals who actually knew him, we will continue to hold his memory dear. We have the park, and once in a while organizations have exhibits and displays of his career. The house he was born in is still over on Eagle Street (a private residence) and certainly his legend as a Hollywood superstar will never fade away. And if you really want to see a lasting memory of Kirk Douglas's time here as a kid, you can go over to his old high school and see for yourself," he told me.

What is there?

"If you go over to Wilbur Lynch Middle School [then his high school], inside you can see an old wooden beam with the name 'Izzy Demsky' scratched into it."

Other Nearby Attractions or Sites

Amsterdam is a fascinating little city with several interesting stops for a weekend trip. The Walter Elwood Museum tells the story of the Mohawk

Kirk Douglas posted some pretty remarkable figures over the century he graced us with his presence: a sixty-year career, more than ninety movies, three best actor nominations, one Academy Award for Lifetime Achievement, and a marriage of over sixty years to his wife, Anne.

Valley against the backdrop of a thousand unusual items from the collection of Mr. Elwood, one of the city's great pack rats. Elwood, an esteemed educator in the city school district in around 1900, traipsed around the world trying to satiate his desire for gathering things. Victoriana, ethnographic treasures, art, oddities, nature rarities, photographs, military memorabilia, and rooms full of Mohawk Valley history all add up to make this a highly entertaining and enlightening destination.

Perhaps the most exciting news concerning Amsterdam's future is the creation of the Mohawk Valley Gateway Overlook. This attractive park-like pedestrian bridge over the Mohawk River is bringing new tourists to this area (including waterway travelers). It connects the historic north and south sides of the city and affords a rare overhead vista of the old Erie Canal waterway. Governor Andrew Cuomo authorized construction of the sixteen-million-dollar "Park-over-the River" in 2014.

Essentials

What: Kirk Douglas Park

Where: Amsterdam, on Guy Park Avenue across the street from the back of the Amsterdam Public Safety Building; Montgomery County

Contact

Amsterdam history, tourism, and events: www.Amsterdamny.gov (city)

Walter Elwood Museum: www.walterelwoodmuseum.org (museum)

Kirk Douglas Foundation: www.douglasfoundation.org (Kirk Douglas Family Foundation)

29

The Shrine of the
North American Martyrs

Auriesville
Montgomery County

The church of seventy-two doors.

In the 1600s, the Mohawk Nation built an outpost high on a bluff over-looking the Mohawk River in what is now Montgomery County. Between 1642 and 1646, three French Jesuit missionaries came to their village, named Ossernenon (now Auriesville). Within a short period, their mission-ary work turned deadly and all three were savagely killed by the Indians. Rene Goupil, Isaac Joques, and Jean LaLande were later canonized by the Roman Catholic Church. Goupil was the first canonized North American martyr.

The site of the ancient Mohawk village of Ossernenon is now known as the Shrine of the North American Martyrs. It is a unique place in Upstate New York and one of the most holy places for Catholics in North America. Tens of thousands of pilgrims visit here each year to honor and worship at this revered place where four saints actually walked. Blessed Kateri Tekakwitha, who was canonized and elevated to sainthood by Pope Benedict XVI in 2012, was born in Auriesville in 1657.

The shrine is spread over four hundred acres of Mohawk Valley splen-dor. Walking paths, secluded resting areas, dozens of religious statues, small chapels to pray in, and abundant landscaping all contribute to make this parklike place unlike any other Upstate religious site. At a precipice on the property you stand in the middle of Teresa's Rosary. A vast "rosary" of large white stones is laid out over a field; some have called it the largest rosary in the United States. It symbolizes a small set of rosary beads made from tiny pebbles secretly used by a captured Huron maiden who was imprisoned here by the Mohawks (Teresa Chihwatenha). From this rosary, the view out and over the Mohawk Valley is one of the best in the state.

Reliquaries can be found throughout the grounds holding relics and artifacts from the original martyrs. There is also a beautiful replica of Michelangelo's *Pieta*. A wooded glen, known as the Ravine, surrounds the stream where some of the martyrs were killed. It is one of the holiest places at Auriesville.

The magnificent centerpiece of this religious shrine is the Coliseum. Thousands have visited this enormous church for services over the decades (it was built in 1930, from donations from worshipers). I happened to visit Auriesville and the Coliseum on a day when there were no other visitors. On a sunny weekday afternoon, I pulled into the massive, empty parking lot. I literally had the place to myself.

Religious music was piped throughout the grounds from loudspeakers hidden on poles and in trees. It set an appropriately reverential mood. I strolled to the Ravine and out to Teresa's Rosary and even stopped to pray at a couple of the little chapels along the path. But none of this prepared me for the stunning awesomeness of the Coliseum.

This round church (257 feet in diameter) is cavernous. And yes, it does have seventy-two doors. The motif inside is of a rustic palisade. There are four altars, each surrounded by wooden stockade posts to evoke the wilderness fort that Auriesville once was. A soaring two-ton, nine-foot wooden crucifix hangs over the religious tableaux. The carved image of Christ is suspended from a giant hemlock log taken from a tree in the Ravine.

Again, as there was not a single visitor with me this day, I spent a great deal of time up close to the special areas in this church. Nearly two thousand electronic votive candles guided my path around the seventy-two-foot communion rail, with special stations marked along the way. One station was a reliquary holding bone fragments from the original martyrs. Special statues commemorated the lives of a number of saints, including the Mohawk maiden, Kateri. As one of the most popular religious figures of the Upstate region, her statue always has notes and cards and blessing requests surrounding it. A warm light filtered in from the hundreds of single-pane windows around the rotunda roof.

One very interesting station held an old carved statue of the Virgin Mary that came from a shrine in Rouen, France. Since the three Jesuits who were martyred here in Upstate New York made their novitiate in Rouen, it is especially notable that an item that they would certainly have seen and perhaps touched is still "near them" in Auriesville. Hundreds of handwritten special wishes and pleas for divine intervention were strewn about this small shrine to Mary. Paper and pencils for this purpose are provided.

The round church can hold more than six thousand for a service on any given Sunday. Many times a mass takes place at each of the four altars, sometimes in different languages. One of the two largest crowds to fill the Coliseum was at the time of Kateri Tekakwitha's canonization, when more than six thousand filled the pews and thirty-seven hundred cars and buses jammed the parking lot. The largest crowd came when Richard Cardinal Cushing of Boston presided over a mass from the high altar above the four

Three crosses here pay tribute to the lives and deaths of the three North American martyrs.

commonly used altars. His mass was attended by a shoulder-to-shoulder crowd of ten thousand worshippers. The service, on August 29, 1959, was the only time the high altar has been used.

The Shrine of the North American Martyrs is fully equipped to handle large crowds. There is designated motor coach parking, all areas are handicap accessible, there are several clean restrooms, and a cafeteria provides drinks and snacks for tourists. Self-guided tours around the grounds are suggested. Many informational signs and plaques explain what you are seeing along the way.

There is also a gift shop at the visitor's center. I always thought this must be a tricky job to have—souvenir buyer at a revered religious shrine. Well, you can almost guess what they sell here. Everything from expensive high-end religious items and art, to the usual mugs, hats, and T-shirts all emblazoned with images of the saints. You can even buy a small bottle of Ravine holy water for a dollar.

Other Nearby Attractions or Sites

Just five miles west of Auriesville is Fonda, N.Y. Here you will find the Kateri Tekakwitha Shrine. Kateri lived in this village (then known as Caughnawaga) most of her life. The chapel, buildings, and grounds are beautiful and much visited by admirers of this new saint. A small stream, used to baptize the infant Kateri, still flows on the grounds, and many believe it has healing powers. (Fonda, by the way, is named after actor Henry Fonda's family, who were early settlers to the area.)

Essentials

What: "The Church of Seventy-Two Doors," the Coliseum Church

Where: Shrine of the North American Martyrs, 136 Shrine Road, Auriesville, Montgomery County

Contact

Shrine of the North American Martyrs: www.martyrshrine.org

Kateri Tekakwitha Shrine: www.katerishrine.com

30

Birthplace of Elmer's Glue

Bainbridge
Chenango County

Stick with us.

For as long as anyone can remember, the sign at the outskirts of town read "Welcome to Bainbridge. Home of Elmer's Glue. Stick With Us." The sign is still there, even though the glue is gone.

In 1904, the good folks in Bainbridge realized the potential of an often cast-off by product of milk called casein. One of the first products to come out of the Casein Manufacturing Company was an early type of glue. In 1929 the Borden Company perfected the product, called it Elmer's Glue, and a legend was born. This was the first nonfood product produced by the Borden milk company based in Bainbridge.

Elmer's Glue was an instant success. After many variations, they hit on the school-supply-standard Elmer's Glue-All, and the company's fortunes skyrocketed. Many baby boomers remember the classic glass bottle of white glue with the "popsicle-stick" applicator attached to the side with a rubber band. And with the invention of Elmer's School Glue, parents and teachers alike no longer had to worry about curious tykes taste-testing the glue (it was nontoxic and not harmful to consume).

For many years the mascot of the Borden's Milk Company was Elsie the Cow. The real-live Elsie was the picture of bovine beauty and made hundreds of appearances around the country. In 2000, *Advertising Age* magazine named Elsie the Cow one of the top ten most recognizable advertising icons of the twentieth century. With the popularity of Elmer's Glue soaring, the company decided to come up with a male counterpart to Elsie. Elmer the Bull was created in 1940, and the pair were wildly popular at fairs, in parades, at theme parks, in print ads, and even at world expositions such as the 1939 World's Fair.

Borden's was the major employer in Bainbridge for decades. Inventor Gail Borden was born just fifteen miles over the hill from Bainbridge in Norwich, N.Y., on November 9, 1801. The most famous product that carried his name was Borden's Condensed Milk. Borden witnessed women and children dying aboard ship as he was returning from a trip to England. They had consumed contaminated milk from sick cows on the ship. This invigorated his inventive mind and he came up with the first successful canned (or condensed) milk in 1856. During the Civil War, thousands of his little cans of milk accompanied Union soldiers on their march to victory. At one point, the demand from the army was so great that Borden's couldn't come close to keeping up with it.

Borden's vacuum process for condensing milk had made him rich and famous. His original equipment for the initial processing of condensed milk is now enshrined in the Smithsonian Institution in Washington, D. C.

The Borden Company in Bainbridge closed at the turn of the twenty-first century and is no more. However, the village's glorious past, famed as the birthplace of Elmer's Glue and so much more, is still heralded on the signs at the edge of town with the saying it was famous for over a half century, "Stick with us."

Other Nearby Attractions or Sites

Bainbridge is a surprising little community. It has a whole museum's worth of famous men, famous products, and famous events in its annals.

Jedediah Smith (1799–1831) was born in Bainbridge. He was one of America's legendary explorers in the 1800s and the first American to explore the California coast from the south all the way up to Oregon. He was also the first man to trek over the Sierra Nevada Mountains from west to east. His charts, notebooks, and maps aided immeasurably in the exploration of the American West. His life has been depicted in Hollywood movies and in books and paintings. He was killed at the age of thirty-two by a Comanche war party in Kansas.

The American Plastics Company was also formed in Bainbridge. Again using the casein byproduct, its plastic items were showcased as early as 1936 at the New York State Fair. The exhibit displayed buttons, hard hats, buckles, and more. Later, the company would invent one of the 1950s' most popular children's toys: Fisher-Price Pop Beads!

The American Separator Company, founded here in 1895, produced an early machine that separated whole milk from cream and was designed to be used easily by farm families in remote areas.

Irving Ives, a U.S. senator who served from 1947 to 1959, was born in Bainbridge. As a member of the New York State Legislature, he authored the first state law in the land to prohibit employment discrimination based on sex, color, or creed. He is buried at Greenlawn Cemetery in his hometown.

Hansmann's Pancake Mix began manufacturing in neighboring Smithville in 1832; it moved its manufacturing to Bainbridge in 1971 where it stayed for another twenty-four years. It is widely recognized as the first American instant breakfast item ("Just add water!").

The General Clinton Canoe Regatta was established in Bainbridge in 1943. The sixty-mile flat-water canoe race, from Cooperstown to the finish line in Bainbridge, is the longest in the nation. In 1963, the race had forty-three entries. Today that number is in the hundreds.

So you can see, for a sleepy little village of about three thousand, this place has a real story to tell!

Essentials

What: Birthplace of Elmer's Glue

Where: Bainbridge; Chenango County

Contact

Bainbridge Museum: The website for the Bainbridge Museum was under construction at the time of this book's publication. At this small museum you can see many items and historical artifacts pertaining to the subjects of this chapter. The museum has examples of the many Elmer's Glue products dating back to the founding of the company. You can also see early products from the American Plastics Company, a whole grocery shelf full of the various Hansmann's pancake products made down through the years, as well as an original milk-separator machine. The museum is located at 136 Main Street. For information, you may phone the museum director Mary Drachler at (607) 967-8546.

31

The Rod Serling Carousel

Binghamton
Broome County

Walking distance.

Rod Serling (1924–1975), who grew up on Binghamton's West Side, was one of the great pioneers of television. His anthology show The Twilight Zone is, was, and perhaps always will be the quintessential science fiction TV show.

On October 30, 1959, in the show's fifth episode, Serling took a dark turn into the past. The episode, titled "Walking Distance," depicts a grown man seeking answers to his adult life and then finding those answers, and many more questions, when he steps through the mirror and goes back to his childhood. The show stars Academy Award–winner Gig Young; his costars are actors whose faces are more familiar than their names—performers such as Pat O'Malley, Frank Overton, Irene Tedrow, and Byron Foulger, who between them appeared in nearly five hundred television shows and movies. Five-year-old child actor and future Academy Award winner Ronnie Howard plays the Gig Young character as a small child.

In the episode, Martin Sloan (Young) finds himself back in Homewood confronting a town that doesn't want him, parents who do not recognize him, and a young boy (himself) who is afraid of him. Sloan ends up in a park with a carousel in it. He finds his young self there, and while Sloan is trying to help him at the carousel the young boy injures his leg. The episode is grim, and filled with Serling's famous touches—when grown-up Martin walks out of Homewood, he is limping from the injury he received from falling off the imaginary carousel as a boy.

This is perhaps his most autobiographical story. Serling was born in Syracuse, but his family moved to Binghamton before he was three. He is a 1943 graduate of Binghamton High School, where a historical marker on the front lawn tells of the school's most famous alum. There is a Rod Serling School for the Arts here as well. In "Walking Distance," the key scene takes place when the main character returns to a familiar childhood haunt, a carousel in a neighborhood park.

There really was such a place, and it is still in Binghamton.

George F. Johnson's Recreation Park is one of the city's largest neighborhood recreational areas. Johnson (1857–1948), the founder of Endicott Johnson Shoes, once the city's largest employer, built several of these parks around the city for use by his thousands of employees. Johnson was a bit of a carousel nut, and in the 1920s and 1930s he placed an extravagant, gaily-colored working carousel in each park. They are still there, justifying Binghamton's title as the Carousel City.

For this episode, Serling recreated an exact replica of the Recreation Park carousel that he would have visited as a child. The Hollywood setting of the program also mirrors the park's surroundings. The carousel, erected in 1925 and open from Memorial Day to Labor Day, is still amazing to behold. Majestic steeds, resplendent in brilliant red, white, blue, and gold, prance regally around the carousel as if they were Royal Lipizzaner statues come to life. There are sixty of them all lined up, four in a row, as if in a fanciful stampede. A mighty Wurlitzer Band Organ pumps out gay calliope sounds as the horses march in perfect precision around the mirrored center. It is all housed in a giant sixteen-sided wooden round house to protect it from the elements.

The top of the carousel is adorned with several lengthy paintings by artist Cortlandt Hull. It is fun to view these scenes and see how many are familiar to you. Hull has paid homage to the TV writer by including several vignettes from different *Twilight Zone* episodes, including "Walking Distance." I actually felt a jolt of excitement as I hurried around the carousel, looking up for my own personal favorite *Twilight Zone* show. And there it was!

The episode was "Time Enough to Last," starring Burgess Meredith, who played the bank employee bookworm who survives a nuclear blast because he was hiding out (and reading) in the bank's vault. He then finds himself surrounded by thousands of books at the ruined library, and while exalting his good fortune breaks his eyeglasses, condemning himself to eternal myopia. It aired four weeks after "Walking Distance," on November 29, 1959. I was glad to see it among the colorful carousel panels.

Near the carousel is a white Greek-style bandstand supported by fourteen columns. This is where the band gazebo of the TV episode would have been located. In the center of the floor of the bandstand is a large bronze medallion. It reads: "Rod Serling. Creator of the Twilight Zone. 'Walking Distance.'"

The park also features a ball field, swimming pool, children's playground, and picnic areas. "Walking Distance" has a patina of black-and-white nostalgia and sentimentality, which are still evident in this park today. The rules posted on the carousel include "No Horsing Around," "Be Courteous to Others," and "Be Polite." A sign at the entrance to the carousel admonished one and all to remember, "No Profanity, Please! Young Ears Are Listening!"

Rod Serling remains a beloved figure in Binghamton. A bronze bust honors him at Binghamton Central High School, where he graduated in 1943. A Rod Serling School for the Arts is also located here.

Other Nearby Attractions or Sites

While you are revisiting your youth here, it would be fun to make your way to all six working carousels in the area. None are more than a mile or so away from each other. And each has its own special feature.

One of them is located at Binghamton's Ross Park Zoo, the fifth-oldest zoo in America. The carousel at C. Fred Johnson Park is the largest of all of them. This enormous carved herd consists of seventy-two animals, all of them horses and all of them "jumpers." C. Fred was George F.'s brother. The carousel at Highland Park consists of jumping pigs and dogs and was originally situated in En-Joie Park. The park was the city's premier outdoor recreation venue for years (the name En-Joie leans heavily on the "E" and the "J" of the Endicott Johnson Shoe Company). The

George W. Johnson Park carousel includes several chariots. George was the founder's son.

The carousels have all been restored over the years. There is no charge to ride them. It is estimated that more than a million rides have been taken on George F. Johnson's gift to his city.

Essentials

What: The Rod Serling Carousel

Where: Recreation Park, Binghamton, Beethoven Street at Jefferson Avenue; Broome County

Contact

Carousel information: www.gobroomecounty.com/community/carousels

Binghamton tourism and events: www.visitbinghamton.org

32

Last of the Pedestal Traffic Lights

Canajoharie
Montgomery County

The last of the dummy lights.

When people hear that Canajoharie has the one of the last "dummy lights" left in New York State, they seem befuddled. "You mean a traffic signal on the ground in the middle of an intersection," they ask, "not hanging from wires or a pole overhead, right?" Yes, that is what we mean. And, no, you don't see them anymore. Still, people will swear that they see them all the time.

Sorry, folks, this is one of the last ones left.

This pedestal light was put in service in 1928 at the intersection of three of the city's main streets; Washington, Church, and Mohawk Avenues. All converge at the end of the main business district in Canajoharie in an area called Wagner Square, and when you approach this mishmash of traffic, don't scan the sky above the street for traffic instructions. No. The light is right there in front of you, on the ground in the middle of it all.

Dummy lights were put in place during the early era of automobile driving. As more and more cars hit the road, intersections were increasingly dangerous places to find yourself. Originally a traffic officer would be in the center of the intersection keeping the flow going smoothly and safely. As electronic devices became more sophisticated, the officers were replaced by these pedestal lights with all the traffic beacons located on a single pole. Before long they too were the focus of errant drivers and the cost of replacing them became prohibitive. To the sky they went, hanging above the fray, safely out of harm's way. The pedestal lights, dummy lights, quickly faded from the scene.

Today, there are fewer than a handful of them standing sentinel in the middle of busy intersections across America. The few communities that have these relics from the early days of motoring hold tight to their sentimental attraction. Efforts have been made to eliminate the lights in some of the communities, but many locals have risen up to vociferously defend these souvenirs of the past.

Between 1900 and 1940, thousands of pedestal traffic lights were produced and they were the norm at almost every highway intersection, urban or rural. Today these traffic lights are historically important and a curious attraction for those seeking out vestiges of yesteryear. If a community still has an operating dummy light at an intersection, you can be certain that camera-wielding tourists will be lurking around the sidewalks trying to capture on film this oddity from the "good old days."

I know this is true, because I even felt it myself as I skulked around the bushes and sidewalks in Canajoharie trying to get a photo of the dummy light for this chapter.

New York State has three of these traffic relics, more than any other state. All of them are fully operational. They are located in Croton-on-Hudson, Beacon, and Canajoharie. Most states cannot claim a single remaining pedestal traffic light from all of the thousands used over the years. The two thousand residents of Smackover, Arkansas, saved the last one standing in their state. It was destined for removal, but the state came to their rescue and placed it under the care and protection of the Arkansas State Historic Preservation Office.

There are many reasons to visit the Mohawk Valley and Canajoharie, but any trip would be incomplete without a stop at that odd little blinking thing standing right in the middle of the hubbub at Wagner Square.

Oh, and for those who are interested, Canajoharie, one of the most mispronounced and misspelled place names in New York State, is Iroquois for "the pot that washed itself." It refers to an active water channel that pours through a nearby gorge.

Other Nearby Attractions or Sites

Canajoharie is the town that Bartlett Arkell (1862–1946) built. He was the founder of the Beech-Nut Packing Company, which was located here for over a century. The sprawling white factory that once produced millions of bottles of baby food now lies empty. Arkell made millions in his food-packaging endeavors and was extremely generous to the community he lived in for so long.

The Arkell Museum, attached to the village's library, is an absolute gem of a museum. It is located just two blocks from the dummy light and sits directly across the street from the now-empty Beech-Nut factory. This museum is top shelf and has an extensive collection of Arkell's American and European paintings. Among the artists are Mary Cassatt, Childe Hassam, and Gilbert Stuart, and there are nearly two dozen paintings by Winslow Homer. Arkell opened the museum in 1927 as a unique cultural outlet to be enjoyed by the hundreds of employees who worked just steps from the front door.

The most popular object at the museum is a copy of Rembrandt's 1642 painting *The Night Watch*. Bartlett Arkell was used to getting what he wanted. On a trip to Amsterdam, he fell in love with this giant, muscular painting hanging in the Rijksmuseum and wanted to share his love of it with the folks back home. He commissioned an exact replica of the painting, which hangs in his museum in Canajoharie today. The magnificent replica dominates an entire gallery wall.

The grounds of the museum are lushly landscaped and feature reflecting pools and statues. An added bonus to the museum is a separate collection of Beech-Nut food memorabilia tracing the history of one of America's most popular products.

Essentials

What: Canajoharie's "dummy light"

Where: Wagner Square, Canajoharie; Montgomery County

Contact

Canajoharie tourism, events, and history: http://villageofcanajoharie.org

Arkell Museum: www.arkellmuseum.org

33

The Cardiff Giant

Cardiff
Onondaga County

America's greatest hoax.

First of all . . . no!

The Cardiff Giant is not here. He lies in a hole in the ground under a roof in Cooperstown for all to see at the Farmers' Museum. But it was here at this tiny map-dot off of US 20 that the story of the mystery man made of stone began. This is the birthplace of the Cardiff Giant.

On October 16, 1869, men working on the Stub Newell farm here uncovered a giant petrified man. The men had been digging a well for the farm's owner when they hit something hard. They hit something odd. And, ultimately, they hit pay dirt.

George Hull, a tobacconist and a self-described huckster from Binghamton, came up with the idea of creating a giant stone man to mock the Bible-thumpers of the time who told of giants once walking the earth. Hull hired some artisans to carve an enormous man and then to age the gypsum statue with acids, and poke knitting needles in the body to recreate skin pores. They made the ten-foot naked man physically correct right down to his rather impressive man parts. The statue weighed 2,990 pounds.

He then hired workers to transport the giant to his cousin Newell's farm and bury him. They were all sworn to secrecy, and a year went by before they pulled the trigger on their hoax. The giant was dug up with great fanfare, and word of the "Cardiff Giant" spread far and wide. People even paid to see this wonder. Hundreds came by wagons and oxcarts over the dirt roads of Upstate New York to pay a quarter to walk into a striped tent and view the mysterious man reposing in a hole in the ground. The sign outside read, "The single most valuable exhibit in the world today!" Soon the crowd grew so large that the giant was moved to a larger venue, an exhibition hall in Syracuse. There, attendance swelled into the thousands.

Even P. T. Barnum knew the value of this great attraction and offered thirty-five thousand dollars to buy him. When he was turned down, Barnum went right ahead and created his own stone giant, so then two Cardiff Giants toured the land. The proprietors of each giant accused the others of fakery, and the charges flew back and forth. The legal case ended up in court, and it was here that George Hull stepped forward and announced his hoax to the world. From there interest obviously waned, and the giant started on a peripatetic journey that lasted nearly a century. While the whereabouts of Barnum's fake man has been lost to history, the New York State Historical Association bought the original giant for thirty-thousand dollars and brought him to the Farmers' Museum in Cooperstown, where he currently resides in stony slumber.

An interesting sidebar to this phenomenon is a saying still used today. When David Hannum, one of the entrepreneurs who originally bought the giant and took it to Syracuse, learned that P. T. Barnum had duplicated the stone statue and was touring to great crowds with his copycat giant, Hannum proclaimed, "There is a sucker born every minute."

Thousands of visitors come to the Farmers' Museum along the shores of Otsego Lake in Cooperstown every year. It is one of Upstate New York's greatest traditions. I first visited the museum in 1959 with my elementary school class on a field trip. I vividly remember slowly approaching the silent giant, who was in a tent all by himself. A tour guide quietly told us wide-eyed schoolchildren the story of the hoax. A sign overhead told of the giant's huge proportions. And then the guide, with great fanfare, said,

An annual apple festival on the grounds where the Cardiff Giant was "found" is one of the most popular autumn festivals in the state.

147

"And now children, behold! The Cardiff Giant!" With that he threw back a curtain, and there he was.

We saw a stone-white, crudely etched cartoonish statue of a very large man. His body was twisted, his arms and hands were folded in front of him (but not quite hiding his private parts), and his eyes were closed in slumber. It was the least scary thing you can imagine. My lasting impression of the Cardiff Giant was that he looked a little sad, a little lonely. Even for a ten-year-old it was hard to imagine how many thousands of "suckers," adults no less, had been caught up in this hoax.

The Cardiff Giant remains by far the most popular attraction at the Farmers' Museum.

Other Nearby Attractions or Sites

The location of the Stub Newell farm, the birthplace of the Cardiff Giant, is now the home of one of the largest food festivals in New York State. The LaFayette Apple Festival is held every year at a sprawling farm with a red barn on US 20 in Cardiff. Over a hundred thousand tourists descend on the farm over the weekend before Columbus Day weekend. Tour buses fill the fields disgorging happy festival goers from all over the Northeast to enjoy one of the legendary apple festivals in New York. Hundreds of juried artisans and crafters (and bakers) compete for prizes, live music fills the air, and the scent of freshly baked apple pies wafts over the hollow that is the site of the festival.

Just a mile west of the festival site on US 20 you begin to see miles of apple orchards on both sides of the highway for as far as the eyes can see. This fertile apple farming goes on all the way to the next community, Skaneateles.

I'm sure that many happy festival-goers arrive at the Lafayette Apple Festival every year without realizing the significance of the location. But all visitors pass a New York State historical marker at the entrance, which describes the events of 1869 and the spectacular hoax that was born just up the hill from the festival grounds.

Essentials

What: The Cardiff Giant

Where: US 20, Cardiff; Onondaga County

Contact

The Cardiff Giant: www.farmersmuseum.org; information and photos about the giant from its present home, the Farmers' Museum in Cooperstown

The LaFayette Apple Festival: www.lafayetteapplefest.org

34

The Tepee

Cherry Valley
Otsego County

Drums along the Mohawk.

This is a place where the dreams of your youth come alive.

More than four generations of travelers have stopped at the venerable Tepee in Cherry Valley to buy Indian drums, toys, candy, clothing, and moccasins. This unique gift shop sits on a knoll alongside US 20 three miles east of the village of Cherry Valley. The view from the Tepee is a stunning hundred-mile sweep across the Mohawk Valley right up and into the foothills of the Adirondacks.

"When you are looking for a landmark in Upstate New York, well, we are it," laughed Dale Latella. She and her sister, Donna, are the co-owners of this one-of-a-kind gem. "The original tepee was torn down in 1950 and was reborn right here when the Cherry Valley bypass came through. Thousands of visitors have stopped by over the years. Our tepee is fifty feet tall and we are open all year long. We have thousands of unusual items for sale. We have sold thousands of children's Indian drums over the years. But the Minnetonka moccasins are by far our biggest seller. Some people even stop by to get a new pair every year," she said.

The Tepee is a wonderful glimpse back to a time when US 20 was the main east-west thoroughfare across the state. The route used to be dotted with motels, ice cream stands, miniature golf courses, odd tourist attractions, and small but thriving towns and villages. That was before the New York State Thruway came along and most of the traffic, tourist and otherwise, moved just a few miles north.

"We are one of the last ones from that nostalgic era," Dale told me. "We see grandmothers coming in here with their grandchildren telling them stories of how it was when they visited back here in the 1950s. And really, not much has changed."

The Tepee is chocked with items, including many Native American crafts made by the Sioux, Mohawk, Pawnee, Navajo, and Onondaga tribes. Other items include toys and children's musical instruments, T-shirts, jewelry, and greeting cards, among many others. It is one of the only gift shops left along the highway, which, at 375 miles, is the longest surface road in the state.

"Our dad bought the place back in 1994 and immediately started refurbishing it to what it is today. He decided early on that we needed to be open year round. Dad always listened to what our customers were saying, and they wanted to be able to stop by and purchase some of our unique items for Christmas, so we decided to be open all the time. It has been very successful. My sister and I feel very strongly that we are the keepers of the memories for our large customer base. We don't make a lot of changes here. People love the old-time, nostalgic 1950s, 1960s feel of the place. We cherish our 'regulars' and welcome all newcomers. In fact, we have had people stop by the Tepee from as far away as Russia and New Zealand," she laughed.

The family connection here even extends to brother Pete.

"Pete runs the Chow Wagon outside. We added it in 2000. Many of our customers asked us for a bite to eat over the years, and like our dad always did, we listened to them. Our Chow Wagon serves up all types of hot and cold sandwiches and makes a nice place to take a break while traveling our area of Upstate. And every 'newbie' gets to have a free chili shot from Pete. Some say he makes the best chili around."

Well, since I was a newbie I asked for my chili shot. Pete made me sign a release form before I tried it. This tongue-in-cheek guestbook had hundreds of pages of signatures from tourists who had stopped at the Tepee and had a free chili shot. The two names before mine were tourists from Brooklyn, New York, and Tucson, Arizona.

"Here you go," Tepee Pete said as he ladled up a small paper cup of chili for me. "After this you won't be a newbie anymore." The meat-based chili was spicy, hot, and definitely delicious. I said as much in the guest book.

So what does the future hold for this snow globe of nostalgia?

"Well, we think our future is bright. As we like to say, we used to be a stopping-off place on the way to a destination. Now we are the destination," Dale said with a wink.

As I drove away from the Tepee, I had the distinct feeling that I had just left an old and wonderful memory behind me.

Other Nearby Attractions or Sites

The hamlet of Cherry Valley is a quiet respite from the hurly-burly of its neighbor, the "just over the mountain" tourist magnet of Cooperstown. The community has beautiful old homes and some fine niche restaurants, which attract a discriminating clientele. Many downstate residents have second homes in the area. Cherry Valley's history is steeped in Revolutionary War lore. In 1778, the village, then known as Fort Alden, was raided by British Loyalists and their Indian supporters. The resulting massacre was one of the war's most infamous bloodlettings. At the edge of town is the Cherry Valley cemetery. Just inside the entrance gate is a large, impressive monument to the tragedy. It reads: "Sacred to the memory of those who died by massacre in the destruction of this village at the hands of the Indians under Brant and Butler, November 11, 1778." The giant tombstone marks the common grave of the men, women, children, and servants slaughtered during the attack.

Essentials

What: The Tepee Gift and Souvenir Shop
Where: US Rt. 20, Cherry Valley; Otsego County

Contact

The Tepee: www.thetepee.biz

35

Birthplace of L. Frank Baum

Chittenango
Madison County

Follow the yellow brick road.

What a perfect chamber of commerce–worthy gift to the village of Chittenango. It is the birthplace of the author of one of the most beloved tales in American history. The possibilities for promotion are endless. And Chittenango knows that.

The first thing you notice here are the sidewalks. Yes, they are made out of yellow bricks (or regular bricks painted yellow). That tells you that a visit here is going to be fun. Baum was born here on May 15, 1856. His parents were local business people who owned a barrel-making factory. Baum wrote dozens of books, and many of them were fantastical children's stories centering around his imaginary Oz. Of course, his most famous book was *The Wonderful Wizard of Oz*. The Hollywood film of the book, made in 1939, insured that this fable would be treasured forever. If ever there was an American book that became immortal, this is it.

There are vestiges of the Oz story almost everywhere in Chittenango. From murals to plaques to signs in store windows and to the banners hanging from the lampposts along Main Street, Baum (and Oz) are everywhere. Over the years you could shop at the Oz and Ends Antique Store, Auntie Em's Ice Cream Parlor, the Tin Man Construction Company, or even the Emerald City Café. But it is the sidewalks that are the great eye-catchers here.

With a glance toward tourism, the village installed the yellow brick sidewalks in 1982. After the weather (and souvenir hunters) took their toll on the original sidewalks, newer ones were installed. They were replaced with concrete sidewalks that are painted yellow and stamped to look like bricks. It is almost impossible to wander through Chittenango on any day and not see a giggling family taking a selfie on the "yellow brick road" here in Madison County.

In summer, the sleepy community of about five thousand literally explodes in a cavalcade of Ozmania. A three-day festival attracts tens of thousands here for Wizard of Oz–themed parades, plays, musicals, costume contests, and celebrity appearances. A full carnival with a midway is there to entertain all ages. The whole village gets behind this key fundraiser for their not-for-profits and community organizations. The parade, which routinely lasts well over an hour, features almost every resident in the village, and all of them are costumed to the hilt.

Over the years, many celebrities have been invited to take part in this Oz explosion of fun. Actors, writers, authors, historians, film experts, and more have all enjoyed a visit to the festival, which is officially called "Oz-stravaganza."

I have been to this festival a couple of times, and it is great fun. Of course several years back the highlight of the weekend was the appearance of a group of the surviving Munchkins from the movie. One year, I stood in line with over two hundred people to get an autograph from Meinhardt Raabe, the diminutive actor who played the coroner in the film and declared the Wicked Witch to be "not just merely dead, but most sincerely dead!" Raabe was fully costumed in his iconic coroner's outfit from the movie, including a black cape and his recognizable rolled-brim top hat. He was a rock star that day, for sure.

Other Munchkins have made appearances in the parade in Chittenango over the years, including film actors who portrayed soldiers, flowerpot

Some have called The Wizard of Oz one of the most perfectly cast movies of all time. Besides the immortal foursome pictured above (left to right, Bert Lahr, Judy Garland, Ray Bolger, and Jack Haley), who could forget Frank Morgan in several key roles, including the Wizard, and perhaps moviedom's quintessential witch, Margaret Hamilton.

children, and even one of the boys from the Lollipop Guild. Sadly, they have all passed away now. Frequent and popular guests at the festival are Bob and Roger Baum, the great-grandsons of the famous author. They are also children's book authors and Oz researchers, and their presentations and book signings are always a highlight of the weekend event.

To further solidify Chittenango as a tourist destination for fans of the book and movie, a new gaming house, the Yellow Brick Road Casino, opened in June of 2015.

So the next time you are looking to travel a well-beaten path in Upstate New York, make it the gold-colored path that goes right through the center of town in Chittenango!

Other Nearby Attractions or Sites

The entrance to the village is marked by one of Upstate's most dramatic waterfalls. The Chittenango Falls State Park is a cooling respite from the Upstate summers, and the park is very popular with locals and visitors. Chittenango Falls roars over a 167-foot cliff of ancient bedrock. Bridges and overlooks allow you to get as close as possible to this mini (very mini) Niagara. It is a lovely spot.

The Chittenango Landing Canal Boat Museum is an interesting venue that tells the story of the village and its connection to the Erie Canal. The displays are very well done and the museum is a popular canal must-see. You can view a very rare sight: actual restored canal-boat dry-docks. These wooden "pens" are where the canal boats would lay up out of water to be repaired and restored. It is a very unusual sight to see.

Essentials

What: Birthplace of L. Frank Baum

Where: Chittenango; Madison County

Contact

Chittenango history, tourism, and events: www.chittenango.org

Oz-stravagana (festival): http://www.oz-stravaganza.com. Remember that this is a very little town that holds a very big festival. If you plan to visit for the Oz festival, make your arrangements well in advance. If you don't, you will most likely find that the nearest available hotel room is in Syracuse some twenty miles away.

Chittenango Canal Boat Museum: http://clcbm.org. Be sure and contact them in advance because the museum is only open seasonally.

Chittenango Falls State Park: A full array of activities is available at the park, but overnight camping is not allowed. http://nysparks.com/parks/130/details.aspx

36

Hyde Hall Bridge

Cooperstown
Otsego County

America's oldest covered bridge.

In the "Land of the Leatherstockings" at the north end of James Fenimore Cooper's fabled Glimmerglass stands one of America's finest homes.

Cooperstown boasts many fine and unusual landmarks. Although well known as the home of the National Baseball Hall of Fame and Museum, Cooperstown hosts many other fine museums, a world-class opera house, and one of the nation's top rural hospitals. The small, winding streets of Cooperstown (population less than two thousand) can teem with tens of thousands of tourists during the summer. Most of them, clad in shirts with iconic sports emblems and toting bags of souvenirs from the Main Street baseball shops, never meander far from town.

And that is too bad.

Hyde Hall is a pristine example of an extravagant neoclassical country mansion of the type built in the 1600s. It was the home of George Clarke (1768–1835), heir to George Clarke (1676–1760), one of the last colonial governors of New York State. The younger Clarke married Ann Low Cary Cooper in 1813, forever wedding two of the legendary families of this area (Ann was the widow of James Fenimore Cooper's brother, Richard.)

The fifty-room mansion took seventeen years to build. It is located at the north end of Otsego Lake at the base of Mount Wellington. Today the rooms are filled with period furnishings, original family artifacts, antiques, and colorful portraits of the Clarke family down through the years. The home (which is open for tours) has dozens of rooms, including bedrooms for adults and children, a billiard room in the attic reached by climbing a curved staircase, a library, and a kitchen with all the necessary accoutrements for cooking, butchering, and baking for the mansion's residents. The magnificent grounds offer sweeping views of the lake.

This famous home has two more amazing highlights. One is the massive limestone ballroom, thirty-four by twenty-six feet, with soaring nineteen-foot ceilings. The other highlight is the first working flush toilet in the county!

Hyde Hall is now located at Glimmerglass State Park. The park offers swimming, picnic areas, and a sandy beach. Since there is no public access in the village for swimming in the lake, this park can become very busy during the summer months.

On entering the park grounds, and before you reach the mansion, you will notice a small wooden covered bridge on your right. The bridge spans the Shadow Brook. Hyde Hall Bridge was built in 1823. It is the oldest bridge of any kind in New York State and the oldest covered bridge in the entire country. The bridge, a Burr arch truss design, consists of a single fifty-three-foot span. It was listed on the National Registry of Historic Places in 1998. The bridge is a popular site for photos. It sits just out of sight of the main road in a little tree-shaded glen. In the blaze of an Upstate autumn, it can be a nostalgic and unforgettable sight.

Some might say that a small, rural covered bridge tucked away in a wooded glen might not rise to the level of historic landmark, but it is when you consider the history of covered bridges in New York State. At one time there were over three hundred wooden spans over waterways of all sizes, in locations from just north of metropolitan New York to the St. Lawrence River. Today there are fewer than thirty left. Bridges, especially very old wooden bridges, are susceptible to all kinds of enemies, not the

This historic covered bridge is one of the area's most popular photo ops, especially in autumn.

least of which is flooding. Even here at the Hyde Hall Bridge, the usually sleepy, slow-moving Shadow Brook can turn violent and dangerous in a moment. This little bridge has survived all kinds of challenges over the centuries.

Just fifty miles from Cooperstown once stood another historic covered bridge. The Old Blenheim Bridge opened in 1855. An engineering marvel of its day, it spanned Schoharie Creek in the town of North Blenheim. At 210 feet, nearly four times the length of the Hyde Hall Bridge, it was the longest single-span covered bridge in the world. That all changed when Tropical Storm Irene came stomping through central New York in 2011, sending streams and creeks over their banks and causing some of the worst weather-related damage the state has ever seen. On the night of August 28, 2011, Schoharie Creek swallowed up this giant bridge with a mighty roar and sent her crashing downriver and into the history books. Even today, volunteers continue to search the riverbank for miles looking for pieces of the old bridge in hopes of someday rebuilding it.

And that is why the Hyde Hall Bridge and all the others should be treasured for their craftsmanship, beauty, and history. Like the Old Blenheim Bridge, they can be gone in the blink of an eye.

Other Nearby Attractions or Sites

A leisurely stroll from the mansion down to the lakefront will take you by several interesting features. Tin Top is the name given to the original domed gatehouse, which acted as the entrance to the mansion. It was repurposed and refurbished in 2012. And don't forget to keep your eye open as you wind your way to the lake. Just after leaving the main property of the home, you will notice a distinct opening in the small mound on your left. Upon further investigation you will see that this is the original and very creepy old crypt in which the Clarke family remains were buried in for generations.

Essentials

What: The oldest covered bridge in the country

Where: Hyde Hall, Glimmerglass State Park, Cooperstown; Otsego County (Note: The bridge, home, and park are actually located in the hamlet of

Springfield, N.Y., which is eight miles north of Cooperstown. For obvious reasons, they list their address as the more famous Cooperstown, and in fact they are only separated from the village of Cooperstown by Otsego Lake.)

Contact

Hyde Hall: www.hydehall.org

Glimmerglass State Park: http://nysparks.com/parks/28/details

37

American Indian Totem Pole

Cooperstown
Otsego County

A mighty fine guy.

You'll be hard pressed to find another original, hand-carved totem pole in Upstate New York. Whether through personal journeys or searching online, there just aren't many left. Back in the 1950s and 1960s, when small mom-and-pop amusement parks dotted the Upstate area, many totem poles could be found at Indian villages, Western theme parks, and even miniature golf courses. Today they are hard to find. Which makes this one in Cooperstown so rare.

"We love this totem pole," Eva Fognell told me. She is the curator of the Eugene and Clare Thaw Collection of American Indian Art at the Fenimore Museum in Cooperstown. "Mr. Thaw is perhaps the most famous collector of American Indian art today. He lives nearby in Cherry Valley, and he and his wife have provided us with an absolutely marvelous exhibit of wonderful art. It is housed in its own wing at the Fenimore Museum and consists of nearly nine hundred priceless, beautiful pieces of Indian art. So when Mr. Thaw told us he wanted us to have a totem pole, we were thrilled."

The totem pole is a towering signature piece in the Thaw collection. It sits regally on the front lawn of the Fenimore Museum, a structure built in 1930 by members of one of Cooperstown's founding families and leading benefactors, the Clark family (of Singer Sewing Machine fame and fortune). The former mansion, now a museum, occupies a stunning promontory overlooking the blue waters of what author James Fenimore Cooper referred to as "the Glimmerglass," Otsego Lake.

"The artist who created our totem pole is Reg Davidson, from Haida Gwaii (Queen Charlotte Islands, British Columbia); he is one of the world's leading totem-pole carvers and researchers. The reason you don't see many totem poles anymore is because there just aren't that many big, tall trees capable of handling all the carving. Mr. Davidson found a sturdy thirty-foot-tall cedar tree that was perfect for his project. It was thick, over four feet wide, and had deep rich colors. He carved out a whimsical Indian tale from bottom to top. The carvings are intricate and beautiful."

At the bottom of the totem pole we find a beaver with his tail curled up, and then the raven holding the beaver's houses, and above that a large eagle. The top figure is a black finned whale, which is the artist's family crest. These central figures are surrounded by other supporting images. The whole piece tells a well-known Indian tale of the raven stealing a beaver's lodge to teach them how to fish. The colors, mostly black and red, are vivid and really make this piece come to life.

"The totem pole came to us via a very circuitous route," Ms. Fognell told me. "It came from the forests of western Canada, to the carving shop, to a ferry boat, and then by tractor trailer to Cooperstown. It was problematic trying to figure out how to install this thirty-foot carved tree trunk. We couldn't just dig a hole, for obvious reasons, and we were afraid the bottom would rot during the Upstate winters. Eventually an engineering firm came up with a unique design for the base, which allows the totem pole to stand erect, out of harm's way, and provides proper drainage at its base. It was quite a procedure," she laughed. "We had work crews, bucket lifts, and workmen everywhere. Once it was up, we kept it covered for a month."

So what is the reaction to this unusual sight along the shore of Otsego Lake?

"On the day of the dedication of the totem pole, Memorial Day weekend of 2010, we had a large crowd, maybe a thousand people, here to see it. We had speeches and an unveiling. Mr. Thaw looked on quite proudly. The artist, Reg Davidson, came with an Indian dance troupe from Canada. It was a day of celebration and joy. There just isn't anything quite like it anywhere."

The totem pole has become a popular photo opportunity in a village with no shortage of photo opportunities. It is dramatically lit at night, and there is an informational plaque nearby to describe what you are looking at, what the story means as well as the sculptor's biography.

"Over the years the totem pole has aged beautifully," the curator said. "It has weathered a bit for sure, but this is a unique experiment for us at the museum. By nature our mission is to preserve things. Under normal circumstances we would have taken this totem pole inside, surrounded it with glass, and kept it pristine forever. But instead it is outside, in the elements, for all to see. It has a life of its own. It is now part of us, part of the landscape. It has aged with grace and dignity. It is the beautiful face of what is inside this museum."

As Ms. Fognell and I stood in silence for a few minutes absorbing the grandeur of this unique landmark, I could tell she was moved just being in its presence.

"Yes," she whispered. "He is a mighty fine guy."

Other Nearby Attractions or Sites

Cooperstown is known as "The Village of Museums," and of course the National Baseball Hall of Fame and Museum is its major drawing card. But for an interesting side trip from the Fenimore Art Museum's totem pole, you don't even have to get in your car. Just walk across the road and you are at the Farmers' Museum. Here, James Fenimore Cooper's actual farm has been transformed into a stunning rural campus with more than two dozen historic buildings, which have been moved here from all across Upstate New York. Among them are a blacksmith shop, a printer's shop, a tavern, a schoolhouse, a church, a pharmacy, and more. The Farmer's Museum is also the home of the Cardiff Giant (see chapter 19). This ten-foot stone giant became the biggest sensation of its day (even P. T. Barnum got involved). Known as "The Great Hoax," this sad-looking giant has been the biggest attraction at the museum since it arrived here in 1947.

Also, be sure and take a spin on the Empire State Carousel here. It is a vintage (1947) working merry-go-round covered in colorful carvings of icons from New York State. Kids and adults alike enjoy riding the carousel while keeping their eye out for Grandma Moses, a rose, a bluebird, Jackie Robinson, Eleanor Roosevelt, a brook trout, Uncle Sam, and many more.

Essentials

What: Indian Totem Pole

Where: Fenimore Art Museum (front lawn), Rt. 80, Cooperstown; (Otsego County)

Contact

Fenimore Art Museum: www.fenimoreartmuseum.org

Farmers' Museum: www.farmersmuseum.org

Otsego County tourism and events: www.otsegocounty.com

38

Cortland Country Music Park
and Hall of Fame

Cortland
Cortland County

Upstate's "Nashville of the North."

In 1984, a group of central New York country music lovers got together and bought a bankrupt campground park just east of Cortland. Here they envisioned building a "Nashville of the North" where regional country music bands would find a showcase and national country music artists would have a place to play when they swung through the Empire State. They also envisioned a New York State Country Music Hall of Fame, where each year local country music stalwarts could be enshrined forever in recognition of their contributions to preserving hillbilly music for those of us who actually lived up here in the hills.

The result is the Cortland Country Music Park and Hall of Fame. Certainly nobody would ever confuse this with Nashville or the historic Grand Ole Opry. The music park is just an open field with a large outdoor stage for performers to entertain from. Later an Opry Barn was built, which allows shows and concerts to be performed year round. It has a fifty-by-thirty-foot wooden dance floor, a full kitchen, and seating for several hundred. When the founders originally bought the property, it came with a well-worn 1960s style A-frame residence that was the previous owner's home. That has been kept, renovated, and expanded into the Hall of Fame.

In an attempt at full disclosure, I can tell you that I have been a country music broadcaster in central New York for more than a quarter of a century. So I have attended many shows at the Music Park and have emceed a couple of them too. In fact, somewhere in the crowded jumble of wall plaques in the Hall of Fame is one honoring me for my years of promoting country music on the airwaves. It was a great thrill for me.

This place is not without a small dose of hokum and a large dose of charm.

First, the Music Park. Hundreds of local bands and singers have performed here over the years, some for the first time, some for the fiftieth. Many have disappeared from the music business, and many others can still be found strumming and singing in roadside bars and dance clubs throughout central New York. On a hot summer day, it is hard to beat sitting in your beach chair on the great lawn here listening to some pure old-fashioned live country music coming from the stage.

Over the years, many legendary artists have also graced the stage. I have attended some of these shows, and believe me, the people in this part of the state love their country music! Crowds numbering several thousand have stood and cheered Charley Pride, Loretta Lynn, George Jones, the

Statler Brothers, and many more. I had the opportunity to interview some of these legends before their concerts, and one and all praised the park for providing a place for them to come and perform up close and personal for their many loyal fans.

The Hall of Fame has hundreds of plaques and citations honoring a whole array of local acts over the years for their contributions to the industry, and the annual induction ceremony is a highlight of the year. Inside the Hall of Fame is a large exhibit room filled with memorabilia that has been doggedly pursued by the park's owners over the years. And the collection is pretty impressive.

A large assortment of musical instruments, publicity photos, concert posters, autographed items, and other memorabilia is scattered throughout the large hall. But the real attraction here are the actual performance out-fits that stars have donated over the years. There are more beads, spangles, belt buckles, and stitched birds-of-paradise designs in here than you can shake a stick at.

An exquisite white suit worn by singer Kenny Rogers is displayed right next to an album cover that features him wearing it. Grand Ole Opry member (the one in Nashville) Jack Greene, "The Jolly Greene Giant," donated a fancy suit he wore on a television show, and other stars have ponied up stage costumes on their own, too. Country Music Hall of Famer Porter Wagoner has donated one of his famous bright-yellow Nudie suits, and Jeannie C. Riley ("Harper Valley PTA") contributed a short and sexy turquoise stage outfit. One of country music's greatest legends, Ernest Tubb, is represented by one of his denim-and-gold outfits. And there are too many donated Stetsons and cowgirl hats on display here to even count.

The star attraction is an elaborately hand-stitched, beaded stage gown worn by "the Queen of Country Music," Tammy Wynette. It is jet black and sparkles under the fluorescent lights in the hall. Nearby is a pair of white cowboy boots donated by "the King of Country Music," Roy Acuff. Many of these artists have at one time or another performed on stage here at the park.

So, yes, this place has some pretty sturdy country music credentials. But it does suffer from a lack of funds, and relies mostly on a large and avid volunteer base. The items on display in the Hall of Fame are substantial and quite expensive (Tammy Wynette's dress alone is valued at more than ten thousand dollars). But without significant financial backing, these items can only be awkwardly draped in heavy, unattractive plastic for safe keeping, and they are usually identified only by hand-printed signs or cards.

The number of items relating to local country music history can be numbing, but you have to give the Cortland Country Music Park credit. They are the true keepers of the flame who have nurtured and showcased great entertainment down through the years for all of those kicking, stomping, yodeling, two-stepping, square dancing, high-lonesome-sounding pickers and grinners who have boot-scooted their way to this little "Nashville of the North" over the years from as far away as Fly Creek and Fishs Eddy!

Other Nearby Attractions or Sites

The CNY Living History Center in Cortland is one of Upstate's more recent additions to the Empire State museum family. Its three buildings house thousands of items stemming from the region's history and lore, including a Brockway Truck Museum. The famous truck brand was made in Cortland from 1912 to 1977.

Essentials

What: The Nashville of the North

Where: Cortland Country Music Park, Hall of Fame, Campground, Cortland; Cortland County

Contact

Cortland Country Music Park: Note that this is also a full-service campground featuring 107 camp sites, fishing, swimming, and other activities right on the grounds of the park and Hall of Fame; www.cortlandmusic park.org.

CNY Living History Center: www.cnylivinghistory.org

39

Indian Castle Church

Danube
Herkimer County

The oldest missionary church in New York.

They just don't come much older than this little white church in the pines overlooking the Mohawk Valley. It was built be Sir William Johnson in 1769 during his endeavor to bring Christianity to the Indians. Johnson was the Superintendent of Indian Affairs in New York and lived in nearby Johnstown.

"Johnson had a very big impact on this area," Eileen Warner told me. She is the president of the Restoration and Preservation Society of the Indian Castle Church. "Johnson was on the church premises many times and actually lived across the road from the church. Nothing is left of his home except the foundation, but his barn is still up. Johnson married Molly Brant, sister of Mohawk chief Joseph Brant, in that house."

Indian Castle Church is a small but heroic white structure nestled in a pine grove at the foot of a small hill. The building is tall, topped by a steeple, and banked on either side by towering windows. Each of the six windows has seventy panes of glass, so the church interior is flooded with sunlight. Indian Castle Church was named to the National Register of Historic Places in 1971.

"Our little church has stood strong and steady since 1769. It is the last Indian missionary church in New York and is one of the oldest active churches anywhere. We have withstood Indian raids, Revolutionary war battles, harsh Upstate weather conditions, and even vandalism, but we are still here," Warner said.

I asked her about the vandalism.

"Well, in 1979, we were almost done in for. Vandals broke a window late at night and threw some gasoline into the church and set fire to it. Praise God that the neighbor across the road saw it and called in the alarm. It was a terrible fire but the steeple stood and the roof didn't collapse in on us. There was tremendous damage, from which we are still trying to recover to this day. The vandals, probably some idle teenagers, were never caught," she said quietly.

The church recovered with the hard work and dedication of a small band of volunteers who are committed to keeping the mission and spirit of this historic building alive. They raise funds whenever they can through such small-town events as bake sales, dances, and raffles.

"One of our main sources of revenue is weddings. The church is so beautiful that we are a popular place for wedding ceremonies. And that income sure helps."

The inside of the Indian Castle Church is quite revealing. It has a small anteroom and a single large main room. The large room is spare and high-ceilinged and contains thirty-four old pews. Evidence of the 1979 arson is obvious. The upper ceiling consists of a grid of charred beams. A small section of the wall is encased in glass so a visitor can actually see the 1769 construction of the original prefire church. A small room leads to the belfry.

"The bell has an interesting story to it," Warren said. "It was purchased by Sir William Johnson and has hung in the belfry since day one. Even the fire couldn't take it out. But on a couple of occasions we almost lost it. Many years ago some Indians came to steal the bell, which would have been worth a lot of money to them. They actually managed to remove it from the steeple and hung it from a log and then two Indians carried it off into the woods. Unfortunately for them, they forgot to tie down the clapper and that darn bell rang and rang throughout the night as they

A fascinating and historic little cemetery is directly behind and next to the church.

ran through the woods with it. The neighbors heard the racket and chased the Indians down and brought the bell back to the church," she laughed.

In the rear of the church grounds is a tiny overgrown cemetery. I walked through it and was amazed at a series of iron crosses. Beneath each cross you could see small stones sticking up from the earth.

"The Mohawks buried a lot of their people in that little cemetery. Over time, the markers wore away, but it is such a special place to all of us. Years ago one of our church members, Ralph Horender, took it upon himself to fashion homemade iron crosses to mark each Indian grave for history."

The combination of age, history, beauty, spirituality, and remoteness all add up to give Indian Castle Church a unique place in Upstate history.

"I used to ride my bicycle up here to the church when I was a little girl. I have always loved this place and now as an adult, I continue to try and preserve this special little church. We do struggle. We have no heat, so we must close down in the winter, but we leave the door open from dawn to dusk during the summer. I come by at night and empty the donation box and look at the guest book. People have come here from everywhere just to see the church. We don't do regular services anymore; the population is just too small. But in the summer, we invite other churches to come and hold services each weekend. They are very popular."

So, what is next for the oldest Indian missionary church in the state?

"We have a lot of work to do. It never ends on a building this old. But we make do. We have a small but dedicated group of volunteers who, like me, adore this church. Recently a person left us some money in her will. I did not even know her but this church meant so much to her she left us a generous donation. We put that to good use, praise the Lord. She was an angel, for sure."

As I left, I hugged this woman on the front steps of this ancient place. You could feel her passion and dedication to the church. She mentioned that not many people have heard of the remarkable history here. She thanked me for putting the Indian Castle Church in this book.

I told her it was my pleasure.

As I drove off, Eileen Warren shouted to me, "Maybe someone will read about us and send another angel our way!"

I hope so.

Other Nearby Attractions or Sites

Rt. 5S follows the New York State Thruway running just a mile or less south of it. It is here, along the Erie Canal, that much of Upstate's history was written. Many remnants of the Erie Canal and the later Barge Canal, can be found along this east-west route. Signs and markers point out canal locks for you, which are always fascinating and fun. Canal Lock 16 is a good place to visit Clinton's Ditch.

Canal Lock 16 is located off Rt. 5S just three miles east of Indian Castle Church at Mindenville Road. It is clearly marked. You wind your way down to the canal through the old waterway hamlet of Mindenville, and to the lock itself. The grounds are meticulously maintained with benches and picnic tables, and the lock and all its pertinent buildings are easily viewed. A covered kiosk displays some informative maps, architect's drawings, and old photographs of the building of Lock 16. This lock was built for the "second canal," the widened Barge Canal, in 1908.

Of course a ship passing through the lock is always an eye-opening experience!

Essentials

What: Indian Castle Church

Where: Town of Danube; Little Falls, N.Y.; Herkimer County; corner of Rt. 5S and Dillenbeck Road

Contact

Indian Castle Church (includes information to make a donation): www. indiancastle.com

Old Fort Johnson (located nearby and also built by Sir. William Johnson): http://www.oldfortjohnson.org

Erie Canal (includes maps of all lock locations along the canal route): www.eriecanal.org/locks

40

The Newtown Battlefield State Park

Elmira
Chemung County

The Battle at Sullivan's Mountain.

The Revolutionary War battle that took place here is a forgotten chapter in our nation's fight for independence. But what took place here on August 29, 1779, was not insignificant.

In the wake of increasing restlessness among the Six Nations tribes in the Northeast, General Washington felt compelled to act. While he initially considered engaging in defensive acts against the Loyalists and Indians, he was pushed toward a more decisive operation by the massacre at Cherry Valley, where dozens of civilians, including children, were murdered, scalped, or taken hostage. Washington ordered a major offensive in the region led by Maj. Gen. John Sullivan and Gen. James Clinton. Word of the Clinton-Sullivan scorched-earth campaign raced ahead of the American armies on the march, and the Indians fled their villages. Few, if any, combat skirmishes took place; the Clinton and Sullivan pincer movement (Sullivan from the south and Clinton from the north) marched mainly into empty villages. But one battle did take place—the only one of the campaign. It happened at the Newtown Battlefield in Elmira.

The Sullivan and Clinton armies met at Tioga Point just south of Elmira and marched on the Iroquois settlement of New Town. A thousand Indians and a small contingent of British forces here made their only stand of the operation, on August 29, 1779. It did not go well for them.

Word of an enemy ambush reached the two American generals, and they planned accordingly. They attacked New Town full force, with five thousand men and artillery. Faced with overwhelming odds the Iroquois gave a spirited fight but soon gathered their people and retreated to the northwest part of the state. Unimpeded now, the Clinton-Sullivan Campaign chased the fleeing enemy and began systematically wiping out dozens of Indian villages along the route, burning them to the ground and destroying as much as 150,000 bushels of corn and other foods.

The campaign is considered to be either the largest or one of the largest military offensives of the Revolutionary War. The victory of the Continental Army over the Loyalists, British soldiers, and Indian combatants is remembered here high atop the mountain where the battle was fought.

Now a state park, the Newtown Battlefield is oddly one of the most serene and beautiful locales in the Southern Tier. A winding road, over a mile long, takes you up to the peak of the mountain, where military monuments, plaques, and flags mark the spot where the battle took place. Two features stand out.

The General Clinton Monument, a magnificent towering obelisk near the center of the park, was erected here in 1879. It collapsed during a fierce storm in 1911 and was rebuilt a year later. On August 29, 1929, more than ten thousand visitors came for a rededication of the monument on the 150th anniversary of the battle. The massive naval airship *Los Angeles*, all 660 feet of her, hovered overhead, giving the ceremony an air of excitement. The Civilian Conservation Corps built the park facilities in 1930.

The second great feature of the battlefield park is the observation deck. A large patio-like structure juts out from the mountaintop, affording a spectacular, unobstructed fifty-mile view. Informative plaques and photographic exhibits allow you to follow the routes of Clinton, Sullivan, and the enemy as the day unfolded below on August 29, 1779.

In 1973 the battlefield was listed on the National Register of Historic Places. The National Park Service recently gave Newtown their highest-priority ranking for historical significance and preservation.

Every year a major re-enactment takes place at the battlefield. Hundreds of military buffs, in the full uniform of the time, join in for a commemoration of the famous engagement. The weekend-long event includes historic musket firings, Colonial encampments, and performances of music from the pioneer days. Thousands come to watch this exciting spectacle.

Other Nearby Attractions or Sites

The city of Corning, "The Glass Capital of the World," is just ten miles east of the Newtown Battlefield State Park. The Corning Museum of Glass is one of the most popular museums in Upstate. It displays, with dazzling effect, more than forty-five thousand pieces of glass. Among the fascinating exhibits are those that describe the art of glass blowing. Visitors can not only watch artisans at work at this ancient art form, but can participate as well. Each spring a major GlassFest brings thousands to downtown Corning for a festival and celebration of the glass industry.

In 1972, a freak central New York storm, Hurricane Agnes, wreaked incredible havoc on the city's pride and joy. The swollen Chemung River came crashing through the museum, soaking priceless artifacts, breaking thousands of pieces of priceless glass, and causing what experts referred to as "the greatest single catastrophe ever borne by a single American museum."

The museum reopened later that year, and state-of-the-art flood-prevention measures have been employed in new construction of the damaged museum.

Corning is also home to the Rockwell Museum of Art, which showcases some of the finest examples of Western art found east of the Mississippi. It is located in the historic 1893 former city hall. You can't miss this building—a life-size buffalo head is crashing through the wall over the front entrance, as if to escape the museum!

Essentials

What: The Newtown Battlefield Park

Where: County Road 60, Elmira; Chemung County

Contact

Newtown Battlefield: www.nysparks.com/parks. This is a fully appointed New York State Park with overnight cabins, walking trails, restrooms, and a rustic lodge used for large gatherings.

Newtown Battle Reenactment: Chemung Valley Living History Center: 607-733-0950

Chemung County history: www.chemungvalleymuseum.org

Corning GlassFest: www.glassfest.org

Corning Museum of Glass: www.comg.org

Rockwell Museum of Art: www.rockwellmuseum.org

41

Mark Twain's Writing Study

Elmira
Chemung County

The birthplace of Huckleberry Finn.

It has been called one of the most famous literary landmarks in America. And it is tucked away in the middle of a rural college campus here in Upstate New York!

We so associate beloved American author Mark Twain with riverboats, jumping frogs, and the mighty Mississippi that it is actually quite jarring to come upon so many wonderful Twain artifacts in this Chemung County city of thirty thousand.

Twain spent a great deal of his time at his Quarry Farm home just outside of Elmira with its contemplative ambience and panoramic splendor. His family erected an octagonal writing gazebo for him, placing it about a hundred yards away from the main house. It was here, surrounded by the magic of Mother Nature, that Twain wrote all (or major portions of) his many classics, including *A Connecticut Yankee in King Arthur's Court*, *The Adventures of Tom Sawyer*, *The Prince and the Pauper* and, of course, *The Adventures of Huckleberry Finn*.

The study was moved intact to Elmira College in 1952, along with many of his personal items. Twain's wife, Olivia, graduated here in the class of 1864.

The study is staffed by volunteer students dubbed Twain Ambassadors.

"My favorite Twain quote is, 'I don't let schools get in the way of education,'" laughed Kashfi Ahmed, an international student and Twain Ambassador. "I first read Tom Sawyer in my village in Bangladesh when I was in fourth grade. And I was hooked," the charming young docent told me.

The study is small but perfect for writing, thinking, and quiet times. "Twain was the socialite, the entertainer, back at his big mansion in Hartford, Connecticut. Here he was the writer," she told me. Windows in the eight walls all open up, making the small space seem larger. There is a fireplace to warm it in the cold winters, and just room enough for a small writing table, a bookshelf, a couple of chairs, and perhaps a napping couch.

"I love the openness of this little space. Of course, try and imagine what this room would be like during a day when Twain smoked dozens of cigars, one right after the other. Thank goodness for the open windows, "Ahmed said. "Even the little children who come in here are intrigued by the place. The author was known for his fondness of cats and any number would be running around the study. He even constructed little doorways for his cats here to come and go as they please."

Mark Twain once referred to Elmira as a "foretaste of Heaven." He is buried in the city's Woodlawn Cemetery. Many people visit his grave throughout the year. It is marked by a twelve-foot granite monument featuring a bronze image of the writer at the top. It is not uncommon to find a cigar placed reverently at the foot of his monument in his honor.

The college also has a Mark Twain exhibit in one of the main halls, as well as two imposing statues of the writer and his wife. "For obvious reasons, we cannot leave the Twains' personal items out here in the writing study," she said, "but inside Cowles Hall we have original photographs of the Twain family, some of his furniture, and many priceless items. Scholars come from all over the world to visit the campus and absorb the special relationship he had with Elmira College."

There are statues of Twain and his wife located on the campus. The one to Olivia Langdon Clemens weighs over six hundred pounds and is situated near the one of her husband. Both are the work of sculptor Gary Weisman.

For literary trivia fans, it is fun to note that the writer's statue stands exactly twelve feet high. In riverboat parlance that is known as two fathoms or "mark twain." Sam Clemens would be proud of that clever tribute.

Other Nearby Attractions or Sites

While in Elmira, you may want to visit a tribute to another famous resident of the city. Ernie Davis, "The Elmira Express," was the first African-American Heisman Trophy winner. Davis was a star athlete at Syracuse University and was signed by the NFL Cleveland Browns in December 1961. Tragically, he contracted leukemia in 1962 and never got to play a professional football game. He died on May 18, 1963, at the age of twenty-three.

A life-sized bronze statue of the footballer stands in front of Davis's high school, Elmira Free Academy (renamed Ernie Davis Middle School), at 610 Lake Street, a few blocks from the campus of Elmira College.

Both Mark Twain and Ernie Davis are buried in Elmira's Woodlawn Cemetery at 1200 Walnut Street. The cemetery is famous in its own right. It is the resting place of former prisoners of war held at Elmira's infamous prison camp (known as Hellmira) during the Civil War. Each of the dead was buried with dignity and respect, with their heads facing south. They are buried in a ten-acre section of the cemetery, an area now designated as a National Cemetery. Even today, descendants of these Confederate soldiers visit Woodlawn to search for buried relatives. About three thousand Confederate soldiers are buried here.

Essentials

What: The Mark Twain Study

Where: On the campus of Elmira College, Elmira, N.Y.; Chemung County (open mid-June through August and by appointment at other times)

Contact

Elmira tourism and events: www.marktwaincountry.com

Elmira College: www.elmira.edu. This website also provides information on Twain's Elmira home, Quarry Farm. It is now a home for visiting Mark Twain scholars and it is owned by the college.

Elmira tourism and events: www.cityofelmira.net

Woodlawn Cemetery: www.friendsofwoodlawnelmira.org

Syracuse University: www.syr.edu. There is a statue on the grounds of Davis's college alma mater, and his original Heisman Trophy, the first ever won by an African-American athlete, is also on display inside the Syracuse Dome.

42

The Spirit House

Georgetown
Madison County

Built by spiritual hands.

There was a time when the Spiritualism movement found a welcome home in Central New York. Here in tiny Georgetown is a lasting testament to those times, and to one man in particular who made a pact with God (or at least to heavenly spirits) to help him build a home.

The result is the Spirit House, and it is a sight to see.

Formerly known as the Brown's Hall, it was built by Timothy Brown in 1869 using only Spiritual guidance. It took him a full decade to finish the house. Now, we cannot assume that God actually handed Mr. Brown hammers and nails or even that he held a chalk line once or twice. But the back story on the constructions of this residence is incredible.

It was built by Mr. Brown. He had never built anything in his life before. He was no carpenter at all.

To all who asked why and how he was able to do this, he simply replied that he was being guided by divine spirits. His purpose was to build a hall to be used by the growing members of the Spiritualism movement. He cut lumber, framed to windows, built porches, erected perfectly lined-up stairways, and built an entire kitchen without ever having done any of this before. People would come and watch him work and marveled at the detail of his finished product.

The Spirit House is a showstopper. Yes, it is slowly falling into severe disrepair, but just to stand at the sidewalk and view this architectural oddity is quite an experience. No frill was spared by those who "guided" Mr. Brown's hands. Intricate lattice work covers the entire buildings. Several rows of fancy woodwork ring the top of the structure, and many have commented that the building looks like a giant, white-frosted wedding cake.

Acknowledging the future residents of his hall, Brown made sure to include secret closets so that the spirits could have privacy; he also created a windowless room for them to congregate in. Spiritualist meetings were eventually held here, but many of the mystical rappings and moanings and visions that took place were proven to be fraudulent and members stopped coming.

The Spirit House is now in private hands, and you are discouraged from entering the property. Still, it sits near the sidewalk, and a historical marker in front helps flag down those coming through this rural hamlet in search of this unusual roadside site.

Other Nearby Attractions or Sites

Georgetown is located in a remote agricultural corner of Madison County without many other things to see and do. There is, however, a nice little country restaurant and tavern just a block away from the Spirit House. The Georgetown Inn also dates back more than a hundred years. The tap room is spare and comfortable with none of the fanciness of its more famous neighbor. It is the kind of place frequented by snowmobilers, hunters, and locals who stop off after a day's work. The dining room, however, is quite a surprise. They serve full meals, including prime rib and fish, and there are daily specials on the weekend. They are known for serving some of the best Buffalo chicken wings in the county.

Essentials

What: The Spirit House

Where: Rt. 80, Georgetown (Madison County)

Contact

There is a Spirit House Society which maintains an interest in the history and condition of the Spirit House: www.spirithousesociety.blogspot.com

43

Gilboa Fossil Forest

Gilboa
Schoharie County

The oldest trees on earth.

This is perhaps the most curious fact uncovered in the writing of this book. The remains of the oldest forest on earth are in rural Schoharie County in little Gilboa, N.Y. Granted there is not much to see, but when you consider the tropical rain forests of South America, the densely forested inlands of Indonesia, the dark confines of the jungles of Africa, the biblical backwoods of Jordan and Israel, the ancient timbers in the tundra of Siberia—well, how on earth could the oldest known forest be here in Schoharie County?

If you dig just under the surface in this area you are likely to hit solid rock. The bedrock is pervasive in this part of the Catskills, and that has been both good and bad. It has made farming tricky at times, but on the other hand it produced a great boon in the stone quarry business in the nineteenth century. It was the blasting of a stone quarry that uncovered some curious fossilized trees near the hamlet of Gilboa in 1869. This and later revelations brought archeologists and paleobotanists scrambling to this remote map-dot with shovels and pickaxes at the ready. Later, more careful diggings and a perfectly timed flash flood a century ago cleared away the area around treetops, leaf fronds, and tree trunks. All were fossilized and all were big news for little Gilboa.

Scientists have now declared that these petrified remains are the remains of a forest from the Devonian period. This era, at least 370 million years ago, sometimes called the Age of Fish, saw the first seed-bearing trees. Between 1915 and 1925, excavation and blasting began for the massive Gilboa Dam, which unearthed several exquisite tree stumps, standing upright and fossilized in their natural forest location.

And what is there to see? Like I said, not much.

In front of a building jointly used by the historical society, the town hall, and the Gilboa post office is an outdoor exhibit of the ancient fossils. There is a little automobile pull-off and an area to walk around these giant fossils to see what all the fuss is about. They look like clumpy, hardened ant hills. They are older than you can imagine. A permanent exhibit gives the visitor much history about these anonymous, rather boring-looking geological wonders.

Samuel Lockwood (1819–1894), a local minister and amateur archeologist, was the first one to stub his toe on history. He found the first fossilized Devonian tree stump ever recorded in North America, right here in the Schoharie Creek. In 1869, a torrent spilled over from the creek in a massive flash flood, washing away houses, stores, and more. It basically erased tiny Gilboa, but it uncovered many more historic in situ tree stumps from three hundred million years ago. In 1917, in response to the flash-flooding problem, construction started on the massive Gilboa Dam across the road from where this exhibit is today. Even more historic fossilized trees surfaced. It was an archeologist's dream come true.

Enter one Winifred Goldring (1888–1971). When the state wanted to ship off all of these prehistoric natural heirlooms to parts unknown, Ms. Goldring, a formidable force of nature herself and the first woman to ever hold the title of New York State Paleontologist, stepped in and said no, they were to remain where they were found. Right here in Gilboa. The entire exhibit is dedicated to Ms. Goldring for her efforts.

When peering down on these silent, chunky pieces of petrified wood older than time itself, you can't help but say to yourself, "That's it?"The text on the display above the stumps simply and eloquently explains why these are of global significance:"This exhibit is the only visible proof of the other ancient world that lies deep beneath the landscape."

Across the road from the Gilboa Historical Society stands the mighty Gilboa Dam. This dam, which blocks Schoharie Creek and forms the six-mile-long Schoharie Reservoir, was an engineering marvel when it was completed. The original hamlet of Gilboa was evacuated and razed to build the dam. The community of Gilboa that later rose a short distance away is the one that exists today. The reservoir is massive and holds 15 percent of New York City's drinking water. From this manmade lake the water travels through an eighteen-mile underground tunnel before spilling out in neighboring Ulster County. From there the water flows through creeks and rivers to New York City. The tunnel, eleven feet high and ten feet wide, carries six hundred million gallons of water every day.

Other Nearby Attractions or Sites

Five miles west of the Gilboa fossil exhibit, on Rt. 23, is the small village of Grand Gorge. Just south of the lone traffic signal you will see a curious mix of rusted old military vehicles. This, believe it or not, is a museum in the making. Mike Kulak, a Vietnam-era veteran, has been collecting military vehicles for decades. He hopes someday to formalize his collection in a museum. In the meantime, feel free to stop here at Mike's Army-Navy surplus store and ask him for "the dime tour." He tells a great story. Vehicles of all descriptions dot his ever-expanding lot, including troop transports from Desert Storm, artillery haulers from Vietnam, and an abundance of World War II vehicles that would make a historian smile with delight. Oh and ask Mike to name some of the movies that have called him up for some vehicles to use. It's quite a list!

Essentials

What: The oldest trees on earth

Where: The Gilboa Fossils, Gilboa, County Rt. 990V; Schoharie County

Contact

Gilboa Museum: www.gilboafossils.org; Stryker Road. This museum is about a mile from the fossils themselves. They have an abundance of information about the relics.

Gilboa Historical Society: www.northerncatskillshistory.com/societies/gilboa. This website provides information about the area and has archives of past historical newsletters and photographs of the area.

Grand Gorge Military Vehicle Museum: 37336 Rt. 23, Grand Gorge 12434; phone 607-588-7002

44

The Chocolate Train Wreck Festival

Hamilton
Madison County

A sweet commemoration.

First of all . . . nobody got hurt.

Having said that, this is one of the oddest-named festivals in the state. The Chocolate Train Wreck Festival in Hamilton commemorates an actual event that happened in this little Madison County village.

On September 27, 1955, a freight train was on its normal route along the Ontario and Western (O&W) rails in Upstate New York when it entered Hamilton. It wasn't supposed to stop here. But stop it did. The fifty-car train inexplicably got diverted from its main line and sped on down a little-used track, smashing through a coal shed at the end of the line and then crashing. Train derailments are not uncommon in the rail history of Central New York, and this one on the "Old and Weary" was fairly unspectacular as crashes go. But what made this event so memorable was the cargo the train was carrying.

Chocolates.

A couple of boxcars carrying Nestlé's chocolate bars, Nestlé's Quik, and other assorted chocolate treats rocked and rolled along the errant track as the train sped along. As the giant two-hundred-ton blue-and-white locomotive ground to a halt in the grassy scrub beyond the demolished coal shed, several of the boxcars split open. It was going so fast at the time of the crash that some eyewitnesses reported that they saw the locomotive actually go airborne for a few seconds.

As word (and sound) of the crash diffused throughout this small, tight-knit community, a strange thing happened. Young children, running, on bikes, and in large groups headed to the crash site to harvest some of the goodies. Stories tell of kids racing up to the train carrying baskets and boxes, loading them up with chocolate bars, and hurrying home with their treasures. I met a man once who told me he was one of those little "chocolate liberators"; he was actually was able to make four trips to the crash site before authorities cordoned it off.

So how do we remember a train crash in the proper, appropriate way? A train crash that could have been a lot worse, actually. In fact, it was reported that the parent company of the O&W gave a banquet for the train crew to honor them for coming through such an event with nobody getting injured.

Well, in Hamilton they remember "their" train wreck with a party.

Today the village of Hamilton is the classic example of making lemonade out of lemons. They commemorate this odd event by holding a festival in the village square. The Chocolate Train Wreck Festival (usually just shortened to the Chocolate Festival) honors the memory of the wreck in several unusual and fun ways.

I went to this festival recently. I had to—who could skip an event with a name like the Chocolate Train Wreck Festival? The green in the center of the pretty village of Hamilton was packed with vendors selling all kinds of foods and handicrafts. Live music wafted out of the Victorian gazebo located in the center of the park. Chocolate (in all varieties) is the star of this unique festival. You can buy more than a dozen chocolate concoctions, including handmade tiny chocolate locomotives. An exhibition tent shows archival newsreels and photos of the actual 1955 crash. Several adult residents who were the "children chocolate pirates" more than six decades ago are on hand to share their personal stories of the day. T-shirts and other train wreck memorabilia are also for sale.

Walking tours of the wreck site are organized for this day. Starting at the festival itself, a guide takes you about a mile to where the train wreck occurred. The festival began in 2008 and grows in popularity each year.

Hamilton boasts a lovely village green that is the location of many community events, including the Chocolate Train Wreck Festival.

Other Nearby Attractions or Sites

Hamilton is a beautiful little village of fewer than five thousand residents. It has many great shops, cafés, boutiques, and bookstores located along its very walkable downtown area. The massive Dutch-colonial style Colgate Inn anchors one end of the village green. It was built in 1925 and is one of the leading inns and meeting places in the region.

Of course, the reason that Hamilton is on the map at all is because it is home to Colgate University. The college is located downtown, just four blocks from where the Chocolate Train Wreck Festival is held. The campus is well worth a drive or walk through.

Colgate was founded in 1819, with soap and toothpaste magnate William Colgate on its board of trustees. Later, his son James donated a one-million-dollar endowment to the college, and the school was soon renamed Colgate University to recognize his benevolence.

In 2014, the prestigious *Princeton Review* magazine named Colgate University as having the most beautiful campus in the United States. The college sits on a hillside at the south end of Hamilton. Its sweeping 575-acre campus is dotted with dozens of species of trees, lagoons, arched bridges, and buildings displaying classic architectural flourishes. Swans and Canada geese float along the ponds, students stroll or jog along the campus's ten miles of roads and paths, and in the Upstate autumn when Colgate's twenty-three-hundred trees turn from green to red and brown and yellow, the view from atop "Cardiac Hill" can be breathtaking.

Pratt's Hollow is located ten miles north of Hamilton. This country back-road community is the official geographic center of New York State.

Essentials

What: The Chocolate Train Wreck Festival

Where: Hamilton village green, Hamilton; Madison County

Contact

The Chocolate Train Wreck Festival (also known as the Chocolate Festival): www.thegreatchocolatefestival.com

Colgate University: www.colgate.edu

Madison County history, events, and tourism: www.madisontourism.com

45

Homer Men's and Boy's Store

Homer
Cortland County

New York's biggest pair of pants.

There are very few men's clothing stores older than Homer Men's and Boy's. Roland "Frog" Fragnoli and his wife Margaret opened the store on Homer's Main Street in 1951. Fragnoli was an Italian immigrant who spent his youth working in a clothing store in nearby Cortland and opened up this store after he left the army.

"Originally it was an Army-Navy surplus store," Rob Garrison said. He is the new owner and Frog's son-in-law. "They sold tents, uniforms, ammunition, canteens, and just about everything. Later, military supplies became harder to get so he switched over to a men's and boy's shop. And yes, we do have a ladies section, too," he laughed.

The store is a shopper's dream. More like a bazaar than a clothing store, items are piled high on shelves, on racks, and along the walls. They carry all the top brands, including Carhartt, Levis, and North Face. And all at substantially lower prices than you'd find at stores in the bigger cities.

"We get an item in, crunch the numbers, figure out what the lowest possible price is we can ask for, and go with it. People know they can expect to save a lot of money with us. We sell everything from three-hundred-dollar winter coats down to a dollar fifty for a pair of socks."

I asked Rob what it is like to be the second generation running such a beloved store.

"It is quite a responsibility. My father-in-law, and the whole family, really poured their hearts and souls into this place, and it is now up to us to carry it forward to the future. We have grandparents coming in with their grandchildren telling them how they shopped here forty, fifty, and even sixty years ago. It is really is a special place."

They have hundreds of pairs of jeans in stock here. But one pair in particular caught my eye. It was a gigantic pair of blue jean pants standing tall on the landing of the stairs going to the second floor.

"Ah, the Big Pants," he chuckled. "Thirty years or so ago, Wrangler jeans gave us that big pair of pants. They stand more than eight feet tall. They were having a contest. We put the jeans on our main floor and asked our customers to try and guess how many stitches it took to sew the pants. The closest one to the right answer got a nice prize. Frankly, I don't remember what the prize was. All I do know is that we got to keep these pants that would fit a giant. People love the pants, like to get their photo taken with them, and we even put them in parades and on floats."

For its age, Homer Men's and Boys seems to be a pretty modern store—that is, for a shop packed with camo shirts, wool hats, and hiking boots. "Yes, even though Frog came to this country not speaking a word of English, and barely finishing school, he was always a guy with an eye for the future. In 2000, I was working as a manager at IBM in Endicott. Now, that seems recent, but most people still did not have a computer at home or work. Well, Frog told me we had to get the store on the Internet. I thought he was crazy. But he went ahead, researched it, and got us online. It was a smart move, and one that was way ahead of its time for a store like this. Today, we sell online to customers as far away as Germany and Hawaii. He is one smart guy."

Homer is as neat as a pin, with a grand and glorious historic district. Fancy Victorian homes with spacious verandas and sweeping, manicured lawns dot the Main Street, and old brick churches, nursing homes, and village office buildings stand gracefully among the homes and business. Small cafés and pubs give the shopping district the air of a boulevard. It is a lovely place.

"Homer has been wonderful for us, and in turn we try and give back to the community as much as we can. People are real friendly here; they keep the village clean and beautiful and the folks are real loyal to all the local businesses. I hope we are in Homer for another fifty years, God willing," he said.

I asked Rob if, after so many decades in business, the walls could talk and tell a good story what would they say.

He was ready with his answer.

"I love to tell this story," he began. "About thirty years ago the comedian Bill Murray was performing in Syracuse. After his show he was driving south on Interstate 81 and saw a sign for our exit, Homer. Well, Murray had a small son named Homer, so he wanted to get off the highway and look around. He found our store and came in. Everybody was excited to have this famous actor in our store. I went upstairs to get Frog. He said, 'Who the hell is Bill Murray?' I told him he was a famous actor and that he had to come down.

"Begrudgingly, he came down and met Murray. The actor proceeded to buy up every single shirt and hat we had in the store that said 'Homer' on it. It cost him about four hundred dollars. That made Frog real happy, even if he didn't know him. Well, fast forward thirty years, and Bill Murray comes back into our store. He and some friends were coming to our area to watch a Cornell football game. He brought his friends in and again bought everything in the store that said 'Homer' on it. Again, another four-hundred-dollar or so sale. Frog was here that day too. You'd have thought it was old home day. The two hugged and smiled for pictures. It was fun. After, the actor said goodbye to us all and drove on down the road to Ithaca.

"Frog started back upstairs to his office. I called after him and said, 'How about that. Bill Murray in here twice. What do you think of that?' The old man turned around in midstep and hollered down to me and said, 'It was nice. But I still don't know who the hell Bill Murray is.'"

A color photograph of Frog Fragnoli and Bill Murray now graces the sales floor. The actor is wearing a sweatshirt that says "Homer."

Other Nearby Attractions or Sites

Just a mile south of Homer on Rt. 11 you come to one of New York State's newest museums. The Central New York Living Museum holds vast collections related to Upstate history. The museum is technically in Cortland, the city that was once the home of Brockway trucks. Many vintage trucks and vehicles are on display here, as well as old tractors, World War II memorabilia, and an odd and fascinating assortment of artifacts pertaining to life in central New York. You can't miss the museum. A World War II armored tank welcomes you in the parking lot.

It is well worth a stop.

Essentials

What: Homer Men's and Boy's Store
Where: Main Street, Homer; Cortland County

Contact

Homer Men's and Boy's Store: www.homermenandboysstore.com
Central New York Living Museum: www.cnylivinghistory.org
Homer events and history: www.homerny.org

46

Howe Caverns

Howe's Cave
Schoharie County

New York's favorite hole in the ground.

The story goes that local farmer Lester Howe one day noticed his cows hovering around a certain spot on his property in the sizzling Upstate summer heat. When he explored, he found cool air coming from a hole in the ground. Ever the intrepid adventurer, Howe climbed into the hole to inspect it. The rest, as they say, is history.

Now, almost two centuries later, Howe Caverns is the largest cave in the Northeast that is open to the public. More than two hundred thousand visitors come to this Schoharie County landmark every year to ride an elevator several stories into the center of the earth (alright, so it is only 155 feet down) to revel in the wonders of the treasures below. Taking a guided tour here is a longtime tradition for locals and a must for any traveler in Upstate New York.

The tours include walking, a little gentle climbing, and an underground boat ride. For the first-time visitor, the experience can be thrilling. Various rock formations, some of them over eight million years old, are highlighted by dramatic backlighting and music. Among the most popular points are the Witch's Hat, the Titanic, and the Praying Hands, which are named for their appearance. The Chinese Pagoda is an astonishing twelve-foot stalagmite. Another curiosity is the Pipe Organ. When the tour guide or a tourist sings or hums into this twenty-foot conglomeration of rocks and glacial stones, the sound is reflected and thrown back at the participant in an eerie musical form.

The highlight of the tour is a stop at the Love Stone. Some refer to it as the Wedding Rock or the Altar. It consists of a brilliant calcite stone in the shape of a heart. Over the years many folk legends about this stone have popped up. For example, some say that if a married couple both step on the stone with a single foot each, it ensures many more years of marriage. Or if anyone places his or her left foot only on the stone and makes a wish, it is guaranteed to come true. These are all fun traditions and add a bit of whimsy to the hour-long subterranean tour.

More than five hundred couples have held their marriage ceremonies underground at the Love Stone. The first vows to be exchanged here took place on September 27, 1854, when farmer Howe's own daughter, Harriet, married Hiram S. Dewey on the rock.

The most intimidating section of the underground tour is the Winding Way. This natural passageway, almost six hundred feet long, twists and turns along its prehistoric eroded route, which dramatically expands and diminishes in width. Some parts of the Winding Way are large enough for several people to walk through at once. Other sections are a mere two feet wide, prohibiting a big guy (like myself) from entering for fear of getting stuck!

The underground boat ride along the Lake of Venus is one of the most unusual things a visitor to Upstate can do. Approximately a dozen or so tourists clamber aboard a flat boat together, and the tour guide poles you along, continuing his narrative about what you are witnessing. Without doubt, the "wow factor" of any trip to Howe Caverns is near the end of this boat ride. At this point, where you can go no farther yet you clearly hear rushing water ahead of you, the guide reminds you that you are nearly 160 feet underground and that all of the illumination along the tour is provided by electricity from above. To emphasize this, the guide dramatically says, "Why don't we all see what it is like to be fifteen stories underground in the total absence of light." At that point he throws a switch and all of the lights go out. All of them. You literally cannot see your hand in front of your face. It is brief, maybe twenty seconds, but in the total blackness, listening to the sounds of the unseen torrent of water just inches ahead of you—well, it can be a truly unforgettable Upstate moment!

In 2015, a new stretch of underground passageways was opened to the public for the first time in a century.

There is much to see and do above ground at Howe Caverns, too. A large and eclectic gift shop sells everything from regional history books to jewelry made from local gemstones to the usual Indian tom-tom drums and souvenir trinkets. You can buy a geode in the rock-and-fossil section, and the shop will split it into sparkly pieces for you. A full-service restaurant caters to the needs of the many tourists, which on any day may include several travel motor coaches from out of state. A mountaintop motel offers comfortable rooms for those wishing to make this a destination experience.

A perennial above-ground favorite is an area where young and old alike can "pan for gems" in a sluice in front of the Main Lodge. This fun activity pays tribute to the immediate area's history as a mining center (it was also a leading manufacturer of cement). There is also an indoor sluice so visitors can pan for their gems during the winter months.

Yes, Niagara Falls remains the most popular natural attraction not only in New York but in the eastern United States. But Lester Howe's discovery still remains New York's most famous hole in the ground.

Other Nearby Attractions or Sites

A recent addition at Howe Caverns is the Cave House Museum of Mining and Geology. The museum is located in a stunning 1872 pure limestone mansion built as the attraction's first overnight hotel. The exhibits inside tell an interesting story of the mining that took place in this area, and in fact still takes place. The mansion is located near the original site of the mouth of the cave, discovered by Lester Howe. The museum is also located on the grounds of an active stone quarry.

Essentials

What: The largest publicly accessible cave in the Northeast

Where: Howe Caverns, Howe's Cave, N.Y.; Schoharie County

Contact

Howe Caverns: This website also give details about the Cave House Museum of Mining and Geology and about motel reservation information; www. howecaverns.com

Schoharie County tourism, events, and history: upstatevacation.com

47

Fulton County Courthouse

Johnstown
Fulton County

The oldest active courthouse in New York State.

I don't know what size shoes Sir William Johnson wore, but he sure left giant footprints throughout Upstate New York. Johnson, born in Ireland, came to America in the late 1730s and immediately made his presence known in the Mohawk Valley. He came to this territory to help manage the large land estate of his uncle, Admiral Peter Warren. In a short time, Johnson was a trusted ally of his Indian neighbors; he would eventually be appointed the "Superintendent of all the affairs of the Six Nations and other Northern Indians."

Johnson built himself a magnificent home along the Mohawk River (it is still there) and helped nurture the growth and development of the village of Johnstown.

Johnson came up with the plan to create a new courthouse in 1769, when a request went out from the provincial government to erect a court building in the westernmost part of Albany County. In 1772, the area was separated from Albany County, and a new county, Tryon, was formed. In 1784, the county name was changed again, to Montgomery, in homage to Continental Army General Richard Montgomery, killed in the Battle of Quebec. In 1838, the named was changed to its present one, Fulton County.

The construction of the courthouse was overseen by Sir William personally. Stories tell of him supplying slaves to help build the structure and of his funding much of the construction. He even supplied more than twenty-five gallons of rum to keep the workers happy during the long hot summer of 1772.

The brick building is one-and-a-half stories high, with a large copper-sheathed cupola and bell tower. The original bell is actually a large iron triangle. It was used to ring in the first session of the court in 1772. It was also rung when word of Cornwallis's surrender at Yorktown reached the village, when the signing of the Declaration of Independence was announced, and when the signing of the U.S. Constitution was completed. It is interesting to note that the courthouse bell in Johnstown is one of only a handful of bells in the United States that rang in the Constitution's signing as well as the two-hundredth anniversary of the same event. The triangle bell is struck by a large hammer when a rope, which descends down from the cupola, is pulled. It is still used today.

The interior of the courthouse is simple and spare. Several large hanging chandeliers provide lighting for the court sessions, which continue today. It is recognized as the oldest Colonial courthouse still in use in New York State as well as one of the oldest in the country.

The courthouse is located on West Main Street in downtown Johnstown. Many commemorative tributes to the legendary Sir William Johnson are found right along the sidewalk across from the court building. Plaques tell of him as a friend of the Indians, a land baron, a businessman, a patriot, and more. His grave is a block east of the county courthouse.

It is interesting that this man, so famous throughout the region, would be resting eternally right in the middle of downtown. Not in an elaborate, landscaped plot in a rural cemetery. Not under a towering, heroic monument. No, he is buried here surrounded by retail stores, offices, and pubs. His grave marker is located on the grounds of the historic St. John's Episcopal Church. Sir William founded this church in 1760 and provided it with a real bell, which was reported to be the first bell installed in a church west of Albany. He also painted a wide red stripe around the exterior of the church to indicate to area Indians that they were welcome.

The epitaph on Sir William Johnson's grave uses his Indian name and reads "Warraghiyagey. He Who Does Much Business."

For a town of its size, Johnstown has much historical significance. Elizabeth Cady Stanton, who with Susan B. Anthony was one of our country's leading women's rights pioneers, was born at West Main and Market Street, just a block from Sir William's grave!

Other Nearby Attractions or Sites

You can easily make side trips from here to places that figure in the life of this giant figure. His home, known as Fort Johnson, is a massive, elegant three-story stone structure that he designed. It is a popular tourist attraction a few miles south of Johnstown.

For the more curious adventurer, and on a much different note, I would suggest a three-mile trip north of Johnstown to the city of Gloversville. Here, where 90 percent of all gloves were made in America at one time, you will find a real gem of historic value. It is a movie theatre.

The Glove Theatre, on Main Street, was the jewel of the Schine movie empire, which eventually grew to 150 movie houses throughout central New York. Junius Schine and his brother Louis were also land developers and hotel magnates. Their power was so great in filmdom that they were able to hold major motion picture premieres at the Glove before Hollywood even got the films. The Schines sold off many of their properties just before the Great Depression set in, but always held on to the Glove, which was their favorite.

The theatre is now used for live productions and concerts. It has been renovated over the years and is an amazing look back at the golden era of Hollywood. In a small museum next to the movie lobby, you can find vintage movie posters, projection memorabilia, signed photos of Hollywood stars who appeared here (anyone remember Fred MacMurray?), and early theatre memorabilia. One of the most curious artifacts is an original Schine usher uniform. It dates from the earliest days of the movie house and is complete with a double-breasted coat, fancy felt sleeves and collars, epaulets on the shoulders, and a red fez-like cap!

Essentials

What: Fulton County Courthouse

Where: 223 West Main Street, Johnstown; Fulton County

Contact

Fulton County History: www.fultoncountymuseum.com

Johnstown history and events: www.johnstownnyhistory.com

Old Fort Johnson: www.oldfortjohnson.org

Glove Theatre: www.glovetheatre.org

48

Vroman's Nose

Middleburgh
Schoharie County

The land of Tim Murphy. Photograph courtesy of the Schoharie County Chamber of Commerce.

New York is a hiker's dream. A hiker can actually explore mountains, gorges, caves, and forests in virtually every corner of the state. From the Shawangunk Range, which travels throughout the lower Hudson Valley near New Paltz to the steep chasms of Taughannock Park near Ithaca, the hiker will delight in one adventure after another. The Adirondacks have literally hundreds of walking paths, and the Finger Lakes also have many hiking trails; they are a lot less strenuous than those in the Adirondacks, and they offer some of the state's most stunning vistas.

I felt compelled to include a hiking trail in *Upstate Uncovered*, but which one? Some people suggested I include the trail that goes up and over the historic Kaaterskill Falls near Palenville. These falls have been painted since long before Thomas Cole's time and offer one of the great hiking thrills in the state. Others thought the nod should go to the hiking trail that takes you past the astonishing Elephant Head Vista at Ausable Chasm along the New York–Vermont border in northern New York. Still others said I should pick the hiking trails that lead to many of the old Adirondack fire towers still in existence throughout the state park.

Certainly, there was no shortage of "nominations" for a landmark hiking trail for this book.

I chose Vroman's Nose.

I have actually hiked this geological anomaly found in Schoharie County. It is the perfect marriage of moderate hiking and a sense of being in a place where important history occurred that really appealed to me. Vroman's Nose rises 480 feet from the floor of the Schoharie Valley near Middleburgh. It obviously got its comical name because it does in fact look like a giant nose sticking up from the flat valley bottomland. (The peak is named for the Vroman family, one of the region's earliest founding pioneers).

The hike up "the nose" is moderate to easy. The view from the top is nothing short of breathtaking. The total loop of the hike is about two miles. The path is wide at the bottom and fairly even. Nearer the top, the path becomes a little more obscured by nature and a little more difficult as you continue on over rock outcrops and small yet dramatic jumps in elevation. At the top, you will be rewarded with a fifty-mile view of the valley below, with the Catskill Mountains rimming the whole panorama. It can be intoxicating on a bright summer afternoon or with a bite in the autumnal air as you stand on a cliff and look at the farms below and the turkey vultures above. A large, level rock floor allows you to sit and enjoy the view at your leisure. This rock outcrop is called "the dance floor" and offers a totally unobstructed view of your surroundings. Benches have been placed along the way to relax on during your trek. It is a popular hiking trail and you will no doubt be welcomed along your journey by young couples, whole families with their dogs, and children scampering ahead of you in a "race to the dance floor."

Timothy Murphy is the great legend in Schoharie County. Murphy was a sniper drafted into the select Dan Morgan's Rifles. He fought at the Battle of Saratoga, where he is reputed to have shot and killed two British officers with a single shot. With their leaders gone, the British became deflated, and in due course lost the battle, which came to be called "The Turning Point of the American Revolution." Murphy settled into the Schoharie Valley after the war, satisfied that he had proudly served his cause, and he was constantly sought out for honors and awards as the "Hero of the Revolution."

The legend of Tim Murphy is filled with great tales, tall and otherwise. One of the most repeated stories has Tim Murphy being chased by a war party of Mohawks along the ridge of Vroman's Nose. With a pail of milk under each arm, he found himself backed up to the cliff side of the mountain. With no other choice, he made a jump for it over the side. In true heroic fashion, it is said that he landed safely some six hundred feet below the "dance floor" and never lost a single drop of milk! This story has been told for two centuries and those who live here believe it to be true, including the many residents in this region who still carry the last name Vroman.

One of the best views of Vroman's Nose can be seen from Tim Murphy's gravesite at the top of Middleburgh Cemetery. Photographers, painters, and tourists all make their way to Murphy's grave monument to read the story found on a large bronze plaque and to take in the awesome view of "the nose" directly across the fertile area that what once called "The Breadbasket of the Revolution."

Other Nearby Attractions or Sites

Just six miles from Vroman's Nose is the historic Old Stone Fort. Truly a historic fort from the days of the American Revolution, it has many Tim

Murphy artifacts and other items from the early settlers of the region. A curious object here is Old Deluge #1, a fire truck reputed to be the oldest in the United States.

The exterior of the fort still shows a cannon ball hole in the roof where the British and their allies laid siege to the fort in 1780.

Essentials

What: Vroman's Nose

Where: Middleburgh; Schoharie County

Contact

Vroman's Nose: http://cnyhiking.com/VromansNose.htm. This is a central New York hiking website with information, directions, and some nice color photographs of the hiking trails and the view from the "dance floor" on top of the mountain.

Vroman's Nose Preservation Corporation: This is a Facebook page managed by a group that cares for the hiking property at Vroman's Nose. It includes photographs and the remarks of those who made the hike to the top; https://www.facebook.com/VromansNosePreservationCorp

Old Stone Fort Museum: www.theoldstonefort.org

49

Cross Island Chapel

Oneida
Oneida County

The world's smallest church.

Okay. But how do you get to it?

The Cross Island Chapel sits in the middle of a pond at the end of a dead-end road just a dice-throw away from the giant Turning Stone Casino. It is odd looking, but very cute. And, yes, you get to it by rowboat.

The Cross Island Chapel is out of the way and not visible to anyone who is not looking for it. It is a small white chapel in the middle of the thick, gooey algae-covered pond on a tiny island made of wooden pilings. A tall white steeple immediately identifies it as a house of God. Next to it, occupying its own tiny island, is a large wooden cross.

The chapel is not really a church. It does not host a denomination, parish, or congregation. But it is used for worship, fellowship, and even weddings. Brides, a word to the wise: don't have a long veil if you are planning on getting hitched here. Veil room is very limited.

An informational sign on the waterfront explains that the dimensions of the Cross Island Chapel are 51 by 81 inches. Yes, you read that right. Inches. The total is less than thirty square feet.

The chapel is not attended unless you have made an appointment with a preacher to host an event for you. Another word of advice to the bride: keep your wedding party small. Let me rephrase that. Keep your wedding party nonexistent. The chapel has enough room for just three people. The bride, the groom, and the preacher.

A rowboat is usually laid up on the grassy edge of the pond for those who are seized by the moment and just have to go out and see the interior of this record-holding church with its two stained-glass windows.

The pond is in the middle of a populated neighborhood, so there is no public parking.

Upstate New York is filled with unique and unusual churches—perhaps a whole separate book's worth. I have included five remarkable ones in this book. The Church in the Middle of the Street in Medina, The Church of Seventy-Two Doors in Auriesville, The Oneida Castle Church in Danube, Our Lady of Victory Basilica in Lackawanna, and this little white church in the middle of a pond in the shadow of Upstate's largest gambling casino.

Yes, all of these churches are amazing. Our Lady of Victory Basilica, near Buffalo, is one of the largest churches in New York State. Her massive copper dome is second in size only to the dome atop the U.S. Capitol in Washington, D.C. Over a thousand can be seated in the church at one time.

You could fit fifty Cross Island Chapels on the basilica's altar alone.

Other Nearby Attractions or Sites

The Turning Stone Casino, a mile north of the Cross Island Chapel, is the largest casino in Upstate New York. Nearly five million guests come to this rural central New York location annually to enjoy the casino. The largest employer in Oneida County, it has a full range of Las Vegas–style gaming opportunities, PGA golf, A-list entertainment, and four-star dining and accommodations. The complex hosts many different buildings over its sprawling thirty-four-hundred-acre site. As a major conference center, Turning Stone offers more than a hundred thousand square feet of meeting space. The twenty-one-story hotel tower is the tallest building between Albany and Syracuse.

The casino and resort are operated by the Oneida Indian Nation. It is now one of the top five tourist destinations in the state.

Essentials

What: The world's smallest church

Where: Sconondoa Road, Oneida; Oneida County

Contact

Cross Island Chapel: There is no website. It is located at the end of a dead-end road, Sconondoa Road, a half mile off Route 385.

Turning Stone Casino and Entertainment complex: www.turningstone.com

50

Brooks' House of Bar-B-Q

Oneonta
Otsego County

The largest indoor barbecue pit in the east.

You actually see it before you smell it.

As you drive east from Binghamton to Albany (or reverse) along I-88, it looks like there's a pretty hefty fire cranking away a couple of miles ahead of you. Or, depending on which way the wind is blowing, you may first see a misty, smoky haze that then forms a large wave of white smoke, first going up and then floating down and across the interstate.

Then your nose starts to ring the alarm. You smell a sweet barbecue aroma just about the time you see it up ahead at the exit—Brooks' House of Bar-B-Q, a family chicken barbecue business more than a half-century old, and perhaps the most famous barbecue joint in Upstate New York.

Brooks had its humble beginnings just down the road at the site of the now gone Del-Sego Drive-In. Here, Griff Brooks and his wife Frances began selling their popular barbecue chicken dinners in 1958 under the giant screen of one of Upstate's many outdoor theaters. On June 10, 1961, they opened a brick-and-mortar restaurant, which has expanded over the years as future generations of Brookses took over the family business. Today, in the hands of grandson Ryan Brooks and his wife Beth, the family chicken dynasty has become one of Upstate's most familiar landmarks. In between Griff and Ryan, Ryan's parents, John Brooks and his wife Joan, crowned the family business with their signature jewel, the largest indoor charcoal barbecue pit east of the Mississippi. It is nearly forty feet long!

Today the business employs dozens of cooks, wait staff, retail clerks, and facility managers. The restaurant can and often does hold more than three hundred, and the family has added its own sauce-bottling plant, an ice cream parlor, a banquet room, and a retail gift shop. The Brooks family remains an honored and beloved part of life in lower Otsego County, and their vision for the future is robust and creative as they continue to spread the word about the best chicken barbecue in Upstate. They do this in several ways, not least through their catering services. Brooks' trucks can be seen as far as two hundred miles away, setting up for parties, weddings, and fundraisers throughout Upstate. Got a family reunion for fifty people at a lake you want catered by Brooks'? Not a problem. Got a corporate function for five thousand you want to treat with a full range of Brooks' specialty chicken dinners? Also not a problem.

Oneonta is a college town. Nearly seven thousand students attend either the State University of New York at Oneonta or the private university, Hartwick College. Those students, from far-flung areas throughout the Northeast, have been the restaurant's own personal review service over the decades. As they have graduated and moved away, they have spread the word about "this great chicken barbecue spot up in the mountains" around the United States and the world. The sight, smell, and taste of a barbecued chicken half from Brooks' always remains one of their great, lingering memories of their time in Oneonta.

And as proof of this, try to get a table at the restaurant during any of the college alumni weekends. You can't. Or Mother's Day either. Or any other holiday; you will find the parking lot packed and traffic so jammed on the highway out front that often you can't even find a blade of grass to park your car on. On any regular weekday the restaurant can grill, turn, and serve more than five hundred chicken halves. On a weekend that number can more than double.

To paraphrase Yogi Berra, "Nobody goes to Brooks' anymore. It is too crowded."

Other Nearby Attractions or Sites

Many famous people have chomped on chicken at Brooks' over the years, including entertainers, writers, visiting luminaries to the colleges, and more. Even First Lady Hillary Clinton began her famous "listening tour" of Upstate in the early days of her senatorial candidacy by ordering a chicken half at Brooks'. Probably the biggest segment of notables, however, is the baseball stars who have traveled to Cooperstown (twenty miles north of Oneonta) over the years for the induction ceremony at the National Baseball Hall of Fame. So, while you are seated in the spacious, sunlit knotty-pine dining room having your half-chicken with a side of slaw, keep your eyes open. You never know who will be sitting right next to you!

Several of the major food and travel shows on cable television have filmed segments at Brooks. And in 2009, barbecue expert and chef Paul Kirk, in the book *America's Best BBQ: 100 Recipes from America's Best Smokehouses, Pits, Shacks, Rib Joints, Roadhouses and Restaurants*, called Brooks' the tastiest chicken wings in Upstate. That's something I'm sure nobody ever dared tell Ryan Brooks's neighbors to the west in Buffalo!

After your meal, wander out behind the main dining room and get a photograph of yourself next to the most famous pickup truck in Oneonta, a 1936 beauty originally owned by Frank Sinatra. In fact, the Brooks family are only the second owners of Frank's green Chevy pickup truck, and they still ride it in parades around the area. John Brooks bought the truck when it first came up for sale in an auction of items from Sinatra's estate. The truck is the same make and model as the one his parents, Griff and Frances, used when they first started their small chicken farm.

Essentials

What: The largest indoor charcoal barbecue pit in the East

Where: Brooks' House of Bar-B-Q, NYS Rt. 7, Oneonta; Otsego County

Contact

Brooks' House of Bar-B-Q: www.brooksbbq.com

Otsego County history, events, and tourism: www.thisiscooperstown.com

51

The Little Red Caboose

Oneonta
Otsego County

A railroad icon.

Oneonta is a small city in central New York that has successfully transitioned from a grimy past as a smokestack community to a lean and green city of clear skies and humming state-of-the art manufacturing plants. Today glassmaker Corning's high-tech manufacturing center replaces the old cigar makers. Ioxus, a futuristic developer of ultra-capacitors and modules, has replaced the many dress-making workshops that dotted the city a century ago. Two colleges support thousands of students within the city limits, and medical centers, retail hubs, and tourism all play major parts in keeping the "City of the Hills" green and productive.

Perhaps the grimiest and most famous of Oneonta's backstories relates to the empty rail yards along the "Lower Deck," an area of town where Italians and other immigrants gathered to raise their families and work on the railroad that rolled right through their backyards.

Oneonta was once the home of the world's largest railroad roundhouse. Hundreds of locals worked there, tending to train repairs and refitting the incoming locomotives, which rotated on a massive seventy-five-foot steel table. The train cars would then be directed into one of the fifty-two stalls. It was a sight to see, for sure.

We know this only from archival photographs and old pictures, for the historic Oneonta roundhouse fell victim to the wrecking ball beginning in 1954 and ending with the disappearance of the last stall in 1993.

But one piece of Oneonta's glorious railroad past survives, now sheltered from the elements and time itself, in a little pagoda in the city's main park.

"The Little Red Caboose," a Delaware and Hudson four-wheel caboose, was the scene of a historic gathering in Oneonta on September 23, 1883. On that day, eight Oneonta trainmen organized the Brotherhood of Railroad Trainmen, becoming the first national union for railway workers. Over time, they strove to improve safety for workers, to establish pensions for retirees and survivors, and to initiate a structure for pay equity. The caboose is often said to be "the most historical railroad car in America."

It is a whimsical sight, sitting in its little pagoda in the middle of the green space of Neahwa Park. Children run around the bright red caboose, perhaps unaware of its historic significance. Picnickers and fans attending the nearby minor-league baseball park pass by with nary a glance. But there it is, still regal despite its diminutive stature, a testament to this city's legendary railroad past. Glass now encases the caboose to prevent vandalism from taking away that what time could not erase. Plaques on the caboose describe its past glory and give the names of the original union organizers from 1883.

Today "The Little Red Caboose" is lovingly cared for by the Leatherstocking Railway Historical Society. At one point, though, Oneonta was in danger of losing its little treasure.

"Several years ago the Smithsonian Institution in Washington, D.C., expressed an interest in having the caboose as an object of significant historical value," Oneonta city historian Mark Simonson told me. "They found that it was still intact here, although slowly deteriorating by being exposed to the elements. They sent representatives to Oneonta to look at it and make a case for enshrining the caboose in a safe locale in our nation's capital for all to see. Our mayor at the time, Jim Lettis, was incensed at this potential robbery and he marshaled the forces, both in and out of local government, to save our caboose.

"Four local men, all with keen interest in our area's railroad history, got together to form the Leatherstocking Railway Historical Society with the goal of keeping, and preserving, the Little Red Caboose in Oneonta. Russ Hawkins, Jim Louden, Dave Jones, and Bruce Hodges pooled their creative talents to form the society in 1982 and quickly raised more than ten thousand dollars to secure an enclosed pavilion in one of our city's parks."

The caboose is without a doubt a national shrine.

"It really is a symbol of Oneonta's past. An important one, too. There is almost nothing left to remind people of the glory days when the railroad was king in our city. The roundhouse is gone, the stalls are gone, there is almost no trace of the importance of the Albany and Susquehanna or the Delaware and Hudson railways and how they changed our city for the good and helped her prosper. Sure, to most people, it is just a little red caboose. But it represents our identity. Imagine Binghamton without its remaining carousels. Or even Syracuse without her famous twenty-four-second clock, which changed the sport of basketball. These are vital symbols, and we really must keep an eye on them and make sure they do not disappear. And besides that, let's face it. It is pretty cool," Simonson told me.

Spoken like a true city historian.

Other Nearby Attractions or Sites

One can do a lot more than just eye an old caboose when visiting this former railroad center. Just up the road, again under the auspices of the Leatherstocking Railway Historical Society, you can actually take a ride on a historic train. Built in 1869, the Cooperstown and Charlotte Valley railroad runs from a train station in Milford, N.Y. (less than ten miles from Oneonta) along a leafy, bucolic main line to the village of Cooperstown. Regularly scheduled train rides are very popular in the summer and the leaf-peeping season. The Susquehanna River Valley never disappoints, and the train actually crosses the river twice over steel-trussed bridges. Theme trains are extremely popular, including train robberies, Easter Bunny trains, Oktoberfest rides, a Jurassic Express, barbecue trains, and a Santa Express resplendent in hundreds of holiday lights. A rocking and wailing Blues Train, complete with live music, adult beverages, and wide-open cars for dancing while rolling along, is one of the hardest tickets to get in the summer.

Author's note: Mr. Simonson's reflections on important icons in some small Upstate cities mention the famed carousels of the Triple Cities in the Southern Tier as well as the historic twenty-four-second clock in Syracuse. Both of these icons are covered in chapters in this book.

Essentials

What: The historic Little Red Caboose

Where: Neahwa Park, Oneonta; Otsego County

Contact

Leatherstocking Railway Historical Society (including train ride information): www.lrhs.com

Oneonta history: www.oneonta.ny.us

Otsego County tourism: www.otesegocounty.com

52

Senator Daniel P. Moynihan's Office

Pindars Corners
Delaware County

The senator's schoolhouse.

His image was unmistakable, loping across the floor of the U.S. Senate. Well over six feet tall, with a shock of white hair illuminating his way; half-glasses lazing somewhere across the lower part of the bridge of his nose; lips pursed in thought; bow tie cocked jauntily at an angle; arms buried under color-tagged reports and copious briefing papers and binders bearing the embossed seal of the Senate on the front.

Daniel Patrick Moynihan was first elected to the U.S. Senate from New York State in 1976 and then re-elected in 1982, 1988, and 1994. To become the candidate in his first Senate election he defeated some of the most famous New York liberals of his time, including Bella Abzug, Ramsey Clark, and Paul O'Dwyer. In his many successive elections he was so overwhelmingly popular that his only election opponents were a sad litany of unknown Republican sacrificial lambs; ever hear of Robert McMillan or Florence Sullivan? In 1988, Moynihan won with nearly 70 percent of the vote.

For a man whose name was recognizable in the halls of power around the world (he was an ambassador to both the United Nations and India), Pat Moynihan was most at home at his secluded farm in rural Delaware County, New York. Proudly calling himself "The Man from Pindars Corners," he bought the farm just weeks after President Kennedy's assassination. He and his wife, Liz, raised their family there, spent as many weeks a year there as their busy schedules would allow, and relished the mundane tasks of farm life, such as building a fence or painting a barn. He was also a frequent guest at the local chicken barbecue dinners held at the Pindars Corners Volunteer Fire Department.

The Moynihan farm (known as "Derrymore," Gaelic for "ancient oak") is no ordinary one-tractor, two-chicken-coop setup like in a Ma and Pa Kettle movie. For sure, Pat and Liz Moynihan were not the Kettles. The farm consisted of two large residences, two barns, several outbuildings, an in-ground swimming pool, and more than six hundred acres of pristine Upstate heaven.

The senator decided it was time to sell the farm in 2000 after living there for thirty-six years. But not before one last hurrah.

On July 8, 1999, Hillary Clinton came calling on the senator, who was retiring. Clinton was the First Lady of the United States and was about to throw her hat in the ring and run for Moynihan's Senate seat. Her courtesy call on the Senate legend brought with it all the hoopla and pageantry of the arrival of royalty. More than a thousand people, supporters and otherwise, lined the country road leading to the Moynihan farm, and dozens of supernatural-looking network satellite trucks were scanning the skies looking for that perfect digital connection to capture this rural kissing of the ring.

Moynihan, ever the ham and loving his final role, graciously met Mrs. Clinton as her entourage emerged from a cloud of dust up the dirt road. They waved and smiled and hugged and laughed for the cameras and then went into the schoolhouse for a lesson in real, pure politics.

Later, they left the most famous little schoolhouse in the country (for one day only) and strolled leisurely down the country lane to the main house, where Moynihan endorsed Mrs. Clinton for his old Senate seat. As the senator, wearing loafers and an open-collar shirt, smiled and tipped his white baseball cap to the press and the onlookers, Mrs. Clinton, dressed in a fish-out-of-water dark pant suit among the hay bales, beamed and smiled from ear to ear. The only thing missing was the whistled theme song from the old Andy Griffith television show.

"Yes, people still talk about that day up here on the hill," Steven Wade told me. He is the current owner of the Moynihan property.

The schoolhouse sits on the far edge of the farm (now dubbed "Sterling Farm" in tribute to Wade's late father). It was built around 1850, and with its red paint, white shutters, and American flag flying overhead, it looks as if it had been lifted from a Grandma Moses painting.

Inside is a large potbellied stove, a small anteroom, and a wide-open space (formerly the classroom) where the senator did his writing while at his summer retreat. He added the shutters and a stone floor in the tiny building soon after he purchased the property. The only personal touches in the schoolhouse were his personal electric typewriter, an easy chair, and an ancient wall map of the surrounding area. He also installed a patch of comfortable carpet, which he had taken from the U.S. Senate Chamber.

"He wrote all but one of his eighteen books right here in this schoolhouse," Wade told me.

Old papers discovered when restoring the schoolhouse revealed that in the late 1800s it had employed three teachers, and as many as twenty-five schoolchildren were enrolled. The advent of school buses in 1945 ended the century-long history of reading, writing and arithmetic here.

The senator died on March 26, 2003, just three years after selling his beloved farm. He is buried in Arlington National Cemetery.

And then there is the grave. Not the senator's. The little boy's.

Near the front of the schoolhouse is a small white gravestone surrounded by a picket fence. There is quite a story to be told about this sad little corner of Derrymore.

"Years ago when they widened the road in front of the schoolhouse, the workers uncovered a worn gravestone. They placed it in the schoolhouse which, pre-Moynihan, was used for storage," Steve Wade said. "It just lay around and got moved from one place to another over the years, and I found it when I purchased the place after the senator left. It intrigued me."

I asked the new owner how the stone got into such remarkable condition and who moved it to its present place?

"I always thought the story was kind of sad. The inscriptions on the front of it reads: 'Filial affection erects this to the memory of John S. M., adopted son of A. H. and P. Durham of Athens, N.Y., who died while on a visit to the town of Dedenport [a misspelling of the actual town of Davenport]. On the 10th of February, 1825, age 3 years, 10 months, 7 days.'"

"The story in the valley here is that the child was riding with his family on a stagecoach along what was then the Susquehanna Turnpike. He died in transit, probably of scarlet fever and probably right in front of where the old schoolhouse is now. He was buried where he died because the stage company felt obliged to do so."

"So what was the biggest mystery that touched you?" I asked.

"Well, several actually. How could the child be buried here in February when the ground is frozen solid? If the family came back to give their child a gravestone, why didn't they just move his remains down to Athens, about an hour from here? Why does it mention that he was adopted? The stone is quite elaborate for that of a small child, so did the family have money?

"I just found the story to be so poignant, so touching that I kind of took it upon myself to care for this little boy's memory. He never saw his mother and father again, and is buried in a place far from home. I took the weathered stone up to a local expert stone-repair company, Cherry Valley Memorials. They cleaned it, straightened it, and made it look like new. They put it on a new pedestal and brought it down here to the schoolhouse. I planted flowers around it and put up a little white picket fence. I invited friends and neighbors from up and down the valley to come for a celebration of this little boy's life. We all stood around little Johnny's grave, said some prayers and sang 'Amazing Grace.' I feel like we gave that child the sendoff that he never had back in 1825. It made me feel good about what we did."

Other Nearby Attractions or Sites

There are two remarkable country landmarks within five miles of Senator Moynihan's former farm. Hanford Mills Museum in East Meredith is one of America's finest working water and steam mills and is a major attraction in this northern corner of sprawling Delaware County. The West Kortright Centre is a cultural and arts center located in a stunning rural Presbyterian church built at almost the exact time as the Moynihan schoolhouse (1850s). Many of the school children who attended school at the old schoolhouse also worshipped at this church. "Art in the Sticks" brings national entertainers to this beautiful, acoustically pristine church for lively nights of music in the summer.

Essentials

What: Senator Daniel P. Moynihan's schoolhouse office

Where: Pindars Corners, half a mile south of Rt. 23, at the corner of Rathbun Hill Road and MacDougall Road; Delaware County. Note: This is private property, but the schoolhouse and the child's grave can easily be viewed.

Contact

Delaware County history: www.dcha-ny.org

Biographical information on U.S. senators: Bioguide.congress.gov

Hanford Mills Museum: www.hanfordmills.org

West Kortright Centre: www.westkc.org

53

H. P. Sears Restored 1930 Service Station

Rome
Oneida County

Fill 'er up!

Here in the heart of Rome stands one of Upstate's most beloved nostalgic treasures. The H. P. Sears Service Station rises up from the landscape of government buildings, parking garages, and old churches to beckon you to stop and spend a couple of moments in the past.

Howard P. Sears (1896–1984) was a bit of an overachiever. At fourteen, he quit school and started a bicycle repair and sales business, and at fifteen, with automobiles far outpacing bicycles, he "switched gears" and hand-printed an automobile-parts-and-accessories catalog he called the Sears Auto Supply Company. Remember, he was all of fifteen at the time.

By 1919, Howard was in the oil business, purchasing his first delivery truck and establishing himself as one of Rome's most successful young entrepreneurs. His son, Howard Jr., began in the business at his father's knee at age ten. He would later head the company.

In the days rolling into the baby boom post–World War II era, the red-white-and-blue oval Sears Service Station sign was a ubiquitous sight along the city highways and back roads of central New York. A series of gas stations were erected, and at one time more than a hundred tanker trucks carrying Sears gasoline traversed the Upstate roads.

Today, there is one service station from the chain left. And it is remarkable.

Now turned into a little museum, the Sears Service Station is just a block from Rome's city hall. It is unlike anything this writer has ever seen in traveling and researching Upstate New York. Tucked nice and neatly into a little corner parcel, this original 1930 Sears gas station is complete with everything, except gas. The first thing you will notice is the color white. Everywhere. The pump islands, the little attendant's building, the art-deco lampposts, the old-fashioned fencing, everything is painted white. The brilliant dashes of color are provided by the bright red found on the illuminated glass globes on top of the pumps (reading "Sears Premium") and the blue stripes circling the pump stations. Red-white-and-blue. Just like Howard Sears, Sr., planned it. For a little bit of the exotic, the roof is covered with bright orange tiles. It would be hard to miss this Sears station when driving by in 1930.

Oh, and take a look inside one of the gas pumps and get ready for some good old sticker shock. Gasoline: thirteen cents a gallon!

There is just so much to see here on the outside. One thing that I found to be especially memorable was the Toledo Air pump station. Perhaps the only one of its kind in existence, this big red tire air pump displays a balancing arm behind a glass window that showed you that the pump was actually weighing the air going into your tires. When your tire was filled to capacity, a whistle would blow. Weighing air? Neat.

However, the real eye-catcher here is the drive-over oil change pit. It is hard to imagine that there was a time when you pulled into your local corner gas station for an oil change, slowly drove over a deep pit, and then just sat in your car as an attendant walked down a small set of stairs and did the oil change from underneath. The used oil was emptied through an attached funnel on the wall, which took it to an underground storage tank. No muss, no fuss. And it is all still right here, all original and, frankly, all still hard to imagine.

The restoration of this historic 1930 service station has been recognized by many preservation groups for its amazing attention to detail. In fact, a comparison between the Sears Service Station of today and a black-and-white photograph of it open for business in the 1930s reveals almost no changes whatsoever.

Inside the little attendant's building is a museum dedicated to the H. P. Sears Company and its beginnings and history. Items range from old oil cans carrying the Sears logo, to advertisements, archival photographs, and vintage gas-station equipment. I particularly like the old brown cap worn by the Sears "fill-'er-up guys" in the 1930s and 1940s.

This is a perfectly wonderful little place to spend a few moments in the past, viewing it all through your well-worn rose-colored glasses As you drive away and give a wistful glance in your rearview window, you half-expect to see the 1930 Sears Service Station vanish into thin air, like a warm and nostalgic Brigadoon located right there on a busy corner in downtown Rome, N.Y.

Other Nearby Attractions or Sites

Rome is one of Upstate's most historic cities, known as the birthplace of the "Pledge of Allegiance" as well as the home of what was once one of the U.S. Air Force's most important northeastern bases, Griffiss Air Force Base.

Of course, the reason most visitors come to Rome is to explore historic Fort Stanwix. Now a National Monument administered by the National Park Service, Fort Stanwix has been called one of the most accurate examples of an eighteenth-century American fort in the country. The fort, known at the time as Fort Schuyler, was the scene of many important events during the American Revolution. In August of 1777, the fort withstood a twenty-day siege from British forces, and on the second day of the siege, August 2, 1777, the Colonial troops raised the first American flag to fly in battle. When British general Barry St. Leger demanded surrender, the fort's defenders, lacking a proper flag of their own, stitched together red, white, and blue stripes from shirts and cloaks and flew the banner high over the fort as their defiant answer.

Fort Stanwix, located in downtown Rome, attracts thousands every year and hosts many events, including reenactments. A large, modern visitor's center and gift shop have been added in recent years, where you can begin your visit by viewing a short video of the history of the fort.

Essentials

What: H. P. Sears Service Station Museum

Where: 201 North George Street, Rome; Oneida County
Fort Stanwix National Monument: www.nps.gov/fost

Contact

H. P. Sears Station Museum: www.hpsearsoil.com

Fort Stanwix National Monument: www.nps.gov/fost

Griffiss Air Force Base (now closed), 1726 Black River Road. The base is now used for public and private purposes and is inactive as an Air Force base. However, it is still worth a visit to see the giant B-52 bomber on display at the entrance. This behemoth, dubbed *The Mohawk Valley*, is a popular photo op for visitors. Griffiss Air Base was named for Townsend E. Griffiss of Buffalo, the first U.S. Air Force casualty in World War II.

Francis Bellamy is buried in Rome Cemetery, 1500 Jervis Avenue. The words to his "Pledge of Allegiance" are chiseled on his grave marker.

54

New York's Number-One Mineral Bath Destination in the Nineteenth Century

Sharon Springs
Schoharie County

Spring Village of Schoharie County.

On a low, humid summer day the odor is unmistakable. That "rotten egg" smell that we all wrinkled our noses at when we were kids. It is still here, faintly, in Sharon Springs.

The mineral fountains, wells, and baths of Sharon Springs made this tiny community a major Upstate tourist destination from about the 1830s to the 1930s. Some of the richest natural waters in the nation flowed down from the hills surrounding the community. Great "temples" were built surrounding these springs, and people came from near and far to imbibe and luxuriate in their magical waters.

Today, no water flows through these temples. Several of the famous springs and baths still exist, but all but one are in private hands. It is hoped that these iconic structures will one day again be a drawing card to this beautiful hamlet of around six hundred people.

"Oh, yes, people know about Sharon Springs," Maureen Lodes told me. She is the proprietor of one of the several cute-as-a-bug shops along the community's tiny Main Street. "In the nineteenth century and into the early part of the twentieth century, we had tens of thousands of visitors each summer. They came for the 'water treatment' and to soak in the wonder baths of our community. Many of them were European Jews who came here and established huge hotels and resorts. Years later, a large segment of them moved north to Saratoga. You can still see the empty hotels throughout Sharon Springs."

These hulking ghosts of the past are well worth a visit by themselves to this lively little burg off of US 20. Several are beyond repair, others are on a waiting list to be given new life, and some others are actually undergoing restoration as this book is written. The largest property is the former Hotel Adler, its nearly two hundred rooms still empty after more than a half century.

"We understand that a Korean group has bought the Adler and the surrounding mineral springs and plans on developing them for use in the future," Lodes told me. She is a past president of the Sharon Springs Chamber of Commerce. "The massive Roseboro Hotel right on Main Street has just recently been purchased and is undergoing a facelift too. The community does own one of the mineral springs, the Chalybeate Temple."

I took a walk down to the Chalybeate along Main Street and had no problem conjuring up the images of Sharon Springs's halcyon days. Long lines of men in bowler hats and women in bustles holding parasols emerging from their horse-drawn carriages along the street and strolling down to the "temple" for a glass of the cure. The Chalybeate is in good shape, has an ornate roof, and is in a parklike setting that makes it a welcoming place. Informational signs display archival photographs, and the text highlights the glory days of the mineral springs and the community itself.

"Many said that Sharon Springs had the most pure, natural water in the state rolling right off the hill behind our village. Water that was pure, natural sulfur, magnesium, and chalybeate—meaning anything having to do with iron," Lodes told me. In fact one of the informational signs at Chalybeate says that the water from this particular spring, while valuable for those with certain ailments, contained so much iron that it would turn one's teeth brown after just a small amount.

Sharon Springs is experiencing a sort of resurgence right now, one of many it has gone through over the last couple of hundred years. Today the focus is on retail, rather than history. Several unique shops bustle during the weekends, and all of a sudden the village finds itself a destination again. TV stars "the Beekman Boys" have opened a popular high-end mercantile store on Main Street, and the stunning American Hotel, co-owned by the village's mayor, has a statewide reputation for fine food and overnight accommodations. Marilyn Lodes's store, Cobbler and Company, is a cute little gift shop that carries fanciful gifts, cards, jewelry, candy, soaps, home and garden accessories, and more, all stocked floor-to-ceiling in a twelve-room former shoe repair shop on Main Street.

Maureen Lodes is an active longtime member of the Sharon Springs Historical Society. "We get lots of new visitors now to Sharon Springs all the time. And that is great and we are thankful. But it is our mission to make sure we relate our history to these visitors. Our community is much more than just our little shops and festivals. It is a history unlike any other in the Upstate region."

I asked her for an example.

"Well, most people have no idea of the history of our community following World War II. After the war, Germany was forced into making reparations to the victims of its aggression. Because of this, many Jewish survivors of the Holocaust, actual concentration camp survivors, were flown at Germany's own expense here to Sharon Springs. Once here, they were put up in our grand hotels and fed and cared for. They were entitled to bath treatments at our healing mineral springs.

"Many of these survivors endured unspeakable horrors during the war. Depending on the severity of their treatment in the camps, they were allowed time to soak in our baths to alleviate their pain, ailments, and stress. It was amazing. Some told of survivors arriving in wheel chairs and walking out. They were allowed twenty minutes in the bath and then forty minutes out. Some of the most desperate, those that actually had to deal with corpses at the camps and such, were allowed to come here one month every year after the war. All expenses were paid by Germany. These are the unknown stories of Sharon Springs," she told me.

Today, several of the baths are visible to the general public. The Chalybeate Temple is in a small park along Main Street and is completely accessible. The Imperial Bath building, just a shadow of its former grandeur, is in private hands and is also located along Main Street. At the end of the street, also privately held but clearly visible from the sidewalk, is the magnificent Magnesia Temple.

The Magnesia Temple was perhaps the most famous of them all. During its long lineage, it was purchased by Max Schaefer, the beer baron. Schaefer moved his family to Sharon Springs, where he became a major hop investor.

"Yes, the Magnesia Temple is magnificent," Maureen Lodes told me. "The domed structure itself, which is still standing, is remarkable. It is the oldest iron mineral bath in the country, and the temple covering it is the largest metal structure of its kind anywhere."

Of course there is no water flowing in any of these springs today. And most of the buildings are off limits to the general public.

"That is true but we hope people will come and see for themselves the rich history of what our little community once was. It really is unlike any other place. And we are hopeful that in the days ahead the public will have access to all of these wonderful icons from our past. We keep changing. For a century our area was known as the 'Breadbasket of the Nation.' Then we were a hops-growing mecca. Later we were one of the most famous resort communities in the East, with more than forty thousand visitors coming each summer. We have some farms that are in the seventh generation of the same family. Now we are known for our retail diversity and our festivals. Sharon Springs is like the proverbial Phoenix rising from the ashes. We just keep going and going. We are very excited about our future here."

Maureen Lodes is a charming and effervescent advocate for Sharon Springs. She would be delighted if you came for a visit to a festival or for dinner or for a shopping day. But if you do, take my advice and stop by Cobbler and Company and ask her about the mineral spas of old.

Maureen has a fascinating story to tell you.

Other Nearby Attractions or Sites

The recent rebirth of Sharon Springs is in no small part due to the arrival several years back of Josh Kilmer-Purcell and his partner Brent Ridge. Known as "The Fabulous Beekman Boys," the pair star in their own reality television show and have authored several bestselling books. Their 1802 Mercantile on Main Street is a high-end retailer with a national following. The Beekman Boys won the reality challenge show The Amazing Race in 2012, and with it the million-dollar prize. The pair are the catalysts for several high-profile seasonal festivals in Sharon Springs, including a harvest festival, a spring garden party, and a Victorian Christmas festival. Each routinely brings thousands to this tiny village.

Essentials

What: The famous mineral spas and water cure baths of the nineteenth and early twentieth centuries

Where: Sharon Springs, Schoharie County; all are along Main Street.

Contact

Website: www.sharonsprings.com

Beekman 1802 Mercantile: www.beekman1802.com

Cobbler and Company Antiques and Gifts: http://www.cobblerandcompany. com

55

Oneida Community Mansion

Sherrill
Oneida County

Free love.

The Oneida Community Mansion takes a back seat to none of them.

John Humphrey Noyes built this massive abode in 1848. It was meant to be the center of his utopian society. Noyes founded his "community" in Vermont but relocated to Upstate New York when he was chased out of the Green Mountain State one step ahead of the sheriff (adultery charges). Noyes's community was based on the tenets of hard work, free will, and free love. It is the free love part that got him in trouble. He believed that men and women should live freely among each other in his community, sharing the duties, responsibilities, and concepts of his view of "Perfectionalism." This also meant sharing each other.

It was Noyes who coined the phrase "free love," a mantel carried on by the hippie culture of the 1960s, a century later. The inhabitants of the Oneida Community Mansion frequently had sex with each other, regardless of marriage status, with the men practicing a policy of self-control taught by Noyes himself. This meant there were few unwanted children in the sect. Each sexual encounter was logged in a journal, and if by chance a child was born, the residents raised it communally as their own. Despite the rigorous adherence to male continence during the sex act, over a dozen unplanned births took place inside the mansion.

The commune in Sherrill was very industrious. They worked together, men and women alike, establishing many different businesses, which enriched the group and provided them with a sustainable lifestyle. Of course, the most famous of these businesses would be their Oneida cutlery empire. By the twentieth century, Oneida Limited was recognized as the leading cutlery maker in the world, turning out millions of pieces of exquisite flatware, stemware, and specialty products.

The company is no longer located in Sherrill. And Noyes's dream of a perfect world at his commune died out in a short time. His sect never had more than about three hundred followers living in the mansion, and without a chance to self-propagate a new generation of followers due to his strict sexual discipline, the group was disbanded in around 1880. The last surviving member of the Oneida Community, Ella Underwood, died in 1950 at the age of one hundred.

Now, to the house.

Reportedly constructed with a million red bricks, this house does not disappoint. Located on 160 acres, the mansion sprawls over ninety-five-thousand square feet. It consists of a large main building with two wings at each end. I have been in this mansion several times. It is labyrinthine, historic, and not a little bit creepy.

The halls are dark, the ceilings are tall, and it is very quiet. Almost too quiet. The last time I visited (it is open to the public, although many of the rooms inside are rented out to tenants), there was no one to greet me at the front door. I entered and padded along the carpeted floors poking my head into each room I came to. A large library, lit by long slanting skylights, housed thousands of books, old and new. The furnishings of the library are straight out of the *Mad Men* television show. Wicker chairs and tables, tall 1950s-era lamps, a giant world globe, wicker window blinds. In fact, there are several libraries here, and they are all fascinating.

A central lounge makes for a generous meeting place for the residents and the public. Fireplaces, couches, and easy chairs dotted the expanse of carpeted floor. A long wall of windows overlooks the patio and landscaped grounds. Upstairs is a cavernous meeting hall. This is where Noyes would gather his followers each night for lectures and orders of the day. Large photos of Noyes and his extended family gaze down on the rows of empty pews.

The front of the hall is graced by a performance stage. Here, even to this day, speakers, singers, theatre groups, and dancers frequently entertain large crowds. The public is often invited to the Oneida Mansion to participate in events and social engagements.

In the rear of the mansion are a well-stocked cocktail area and a large, well-appointed dining room. The public has embraced this venue for dining and live entertainment. This is also a popular spot for weddings and celebrations. The setting is really quite beautiful. Again, a little creepy, but quite beautiful.

There are several dozen private rooms lining the long hallways. These were the apartments of the original members of Noyes's sect in the 1800s. Today almost all of them are rented out to locals on a permanent and long-term basis. You never know what you are going to find when you explore the seemingly endless halls and passageways of the mansion. Here is a giant grandfather clock from the original owners, still stoically chiming away in a hidden sitting room. Over there is a glass case with an odd collection of antique souvenirs from around the world. On that wall is a large, unusual decoration that demands inspection; it turns out to be an ornate wreath made out of human hair!

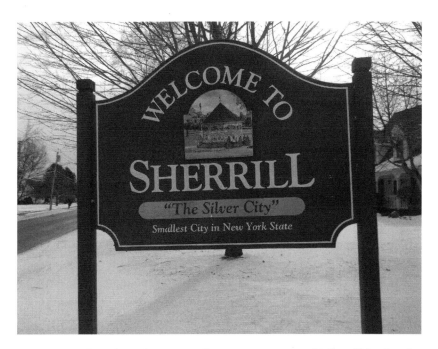

Known as "The Silver City," according to census records Sherrill is also the smallest city in New York State.

Like I said, for the curious road warrior this house does not disappoint.

Other Nearby Attractions or Sites

Located directly behind the mansion is the Oneida Community Golf Club, founded in 1900 by Oneida Limited for its employees and administrators to use. If you choose to play a round on this beautiful public course, you can make arrangements to stay at one of the rooms owned by the golf club inside the mansion itself. A breakfast and free tour will come with your overnight accommodation.

In an odd juxtaposition of extremes, just five miles up the road from the mansion is the mammoth Turning Stone Casino. This is the largest casino in Upstate New York. At the other extreme is, well, Sherrill itself. As the sign coming into town reads, "Welcome to Sherrill. The Smallest City in New York State." Yes, its 3,147 residents just barely push Sherrill onto the list of New York cities. It is in last position, but it is a city nonetheless.

Essentials

What: The Oneida Community Mansion

Where: Sherrill; Oneida County

Contact

Oneida Community Mansion: www.oneidacommunity.org; they do give tours

Turning Stone Casino: www.turningstone.com

Oneida Golf Course: www.oneidagolf.com

56

Grace Brown's Grave

South Otselic
Chenango County

An American tragedy.

Pretty Grace Brown was barely twenty years old when she became the focus of the "Murder of the Century." Brown was born in South Otselic, a rural hamlet of less than a thousand residents, and never strayed too far from home her entire two decades on this earth. In 1904, the eighteen-year-old moved to nearby Cortland and took up employment at the Gillette Skirt Company.

Once she began her job, it wasn't long before the slender, dark-haired beauty became the object of affection of Chester Gillette, the owner's nephew. He tried to keep his flirtations a secret from the plant managers, but he was at first completely smitten with the pretty young working girl. They soon began secretly dating, and the relationship blossomed into a sexual fling. In 1906, Brown became pregnant, a startling and unhappy circumstance for an unwed young woman early in the twentieth century. Scandalized by his predicament and getting nervous over its denouement, Gillette planned a trip to the Adirondacks with his girlfriend, perhaps under the guise of an elopement.

The two made their way north from their central New York home to Utica, where they spent the night. The next day they continued to the remote lakeside community of Big Moose Lake, deep in the Adirondack forests. On July 11, 1906, Gillette took his very pregnant girlfriend for a boat ride out to the middle of the lake, beat her with a tennis racquet, and then dumped her body overboard.

He hurried back to shore, tried to cover up his deeds, escaped briefly, and then was arrested at the nearby town of Inlet. By that time poor Grace's body had floated to the surface, revealing her dark secrets.

Gillette always steadfastly proclaimed his innocence. He said Grace was despondent over the fact that she was pregnant and unwed, and that she impulsively jumped over the side of the boat in an act of suicide.

The Chester Gillette trial was the most sensational trial ever held in Upstate New York at that time. The dashing young heir to a thriving business, the pretty, naïve girl who became the object of his love and lust, her unplanned pregnancy, his foiled plot to get away with her murder. At the trial, Grace's private, fawning love letters to Gillette were read aloud with relish by the district attorney. Courtroom drama was unchecked. At one point, a prosecutor brought to court a large cloth-covered glass jar. He never uncovered the jar, leading many to think it contained a fetus taken from the deceased's body. Each trial day, hundreds lined the streets in the rain trying to gain entrance to the few seats allotted for the public.

All the elements for a tragic and heart-pounding murder story were in place, and the reporters came running. The New York City newspapers sniffed out a subscription bonanza and covered the trial in faraway Herkimer County from day one. The New York *Morning Telegraph* sent its ace reporter, the famous Bat Masterson, north to cover the trial. Reporters and seaplanes descended on the remote Adirondack lakes, bringing hard-bitten crime writers looking for "the big story." Theodore Dreiser used the crime as the basis for his now-classic novel *An American Tragedy* (1925).

Gillette was found guilty and executed in the electric chair at 6:14 a.m. on March 30, 1908, at Auburn Prison.

Gillette is buried in an unmarked grave at Auburn's Soule Cemetery. Grace Brown rests eternally beneath a small stone in Valley View Cemetery

Visitors and history seekers still are fascinated by the story surrounding the then "crime of the century."

in her hometown of South Otselic. Her gravestone reads "Grace Brown 1886–1906. At Rest."

So famous was the murder case that several entertainment vehicles spun out of the real life story, including a Broadway play. Two major Hollywood films depicted the case, loosely. *An American Tragedy* (1931) starred actress Sylvia Sidney in the Grace Brown role. *A Place in the Sun* (1951) starred Shelley Winters in the role of the doomed twenty-year-old.

Other Nearby Attractions or Sites

For those seriously interested in this famous Upstate murder case, the region is replete with benchmark locations. One of the best is the Herkimer County Court House where the trial took place. Across the street is the Old Herkimer County Jail; Gillette's cell is on the third floor. In the basement is a museum with many period artifacts, including a complete two-thousand-page trial manuscript.

Farther north, at Big Moose Lake, you can actually visit the site where Gillette and Brown entered their rowboat on that fateful July afternoon more than a century ago. A New York State historical marker denotes the place where Gillette docked his rowboat. The original Glenmore Hotel, which was on site and operating at the site of Gillette's boat launch, burned down in 1950. A newer hotel overlooks the lake today, keeping the story alive with readings, events, and a display of historical artifacts. In 2006, followers of the Grace Brown saga gathered at the Glenmore for a memorial service and then entered a small boat, just like she had done a century before, and rowed to her assumed death spot. There they floated a memorial wreath in her memory.

Young Grace Brown was buried without fanfare in the Brown family plot in her hometown. When you enter the main driveway of the cemetery, proceed halfway down and stop. Grace's grave is located on your right near the roadway.

Essentials

What: Grace Brown's grave

Where: Valley View Cemetery, South Otselic; Chenango County

Contact

The Glenmore Bar and Grill, Eagle Bay, located at the site of the Grace Brown murder The original Glenmore burned in 1950 and this structure replaced it. It is still a popular bar, restaurant, and overnight hostel; glenmorebarandgrill.com

Herkimer County history, events, and tourism: www.herkimercounty chamber.com/historical

57

The Twenty-Four-Second Shot-Clock Monument

Syracuse
Onondaga County

The shot (clock) heard around the world.

In 2013, six teams in the National Basketball Association pulled in over 800,000 fans each. The Chicago Bulls sold almost a whopping 900,000 tickets to lead the league in seats filled. Much of the credit for this sports success can be attributed to Danny Biasone.

Ever hear of him? Not many outside of Syracuse have.

Biasone (1909–1992) was an Italian immigrant bowling-alley operator on Syracuse's East Side in the 1940s; he also had an interest in the then little-played sport of basketball. He spent less than five thousand dollars of his own money to create the Syracuse Nationals. The teams in the basketball league were typically from the Midwest at the time, and the Nats became the easternmost team in the league. With their fellow Upstate team, the Rochester Royals, they were the catalysts in bringing this upstart sport to two of Upstate New York's small cities.

The game was cumbersome from the start. Loose rules, poorly maintained venues, and lackluster stars hindered the sport's growth; the country was still very much in love with the rough and tumble of professional football, and the glory-draped pageantry of major-league baseball.

One of the biggest drawbacks to pro basketball was that it was, well, a yawner. Initially, there was no time limit on how long a team, or a player, could retain the ball. The "stall of the ball" was the dominant ingredient in any game-winning strategy but it produced a money-losing result at the box office. Players would literally stand around and pass the ball between two of their tallest players while their shorter opponents flailed helplessly away, for minutes at a time. Scores were routinely no higher than twenty points per game.

Like I said, a yawner.

With revenues drying up and professional basketball about to get its ultimate time out, Syracuse owner Biasone came up with an idea to speed the game up and make it more appealing to the fans. After reviewing one particular disaster of a game, he made his move. On November 22, 1960, the Fort Wayne Pistons put on a glacial display of nonchalance by defeating the Minnesota Lakers, 19–18. The game was maddeningly slow (only four points were scored in the fourth quarter as the Pistons tried to shut down Lakers' six-foot-ten superstar George Mikan), signaling the oncoming death of the sport.

Biasone and others, including Coach Howard Hobson of Oregon and Yale, came up with the idea of a twenty-four-second clock, forcing players to move the ball around every twenty-four seconds, as a tool to keep the ball in motion, keep the game moving, and keep the fans in their seats. They divided 2,880 (the number of seconds in a game) by 120 (the average number of shots taken in each game) and came up with the magic number of twenty-four.

The owner employed his new timer clock for the first time in a scrimmage game at Syracuse's Blodgett Vocational High School on August 10, 1954, in front of NBA executives. The shot clock made its NBA debut in the 1954–55 season, and it was a hit. Jittery players were getting rid of the ball in fifteen and twenty seconds, afraid that the new buzzer would call them for stalling at the twenty-four-second mark. The results were immediate. Scores soared (by an average of fourteen points a game), fans loved the new court excitement, and a rebirth of professional basketball was underway.

Oh, and Biasone's Syracuse Nationals won the NBA championship in the first year of the owner's new creation.

Today, Biasone is recognized as one of the sport's great innovators and is hailed as a savior of professional basketball. In downtown Syracuse, amid the trendy stores and vibrant sports bars of Armory Square, stands perhaps the most unique and unusual landmark in Upstate New York: a slightly larger replica of Danny Biasone's shot clock, with flashing numbers forever counting down from twenty-four seconds, towers above the sidewalk. A plaque affixed to its base tells the story of how this clock, and the little Italian immigrant bowling-alley operator from Syracuse's Eastwood neighborhood, saved the National Basketball Association.

The fifty-thousand-dollar cost of the monument was paid by an anonymous basketball fan. It was dedicated with great fanfare on March 26, 2005, with several of the surviving members of the Syracuse Nationals' 1955 NBA Championship team in attendance.

Danny Biasone's original twenty-four-second shot clock is on public display at LeMoyne College in Syracuse.

"We could not be more honored to have Mr. Biasone's twenty-four-second clock on our campus," Joe Della Posta said. He is the director of communications at LeMoyne College. "For years the original shot clock was displayed at his old bowling alley in Syracuse. After he died, his family presented it to us. Danny Biasone was close friends with Tom Niland, who was LeMoyne's first athletic director and first basketball coach. We originally installed it in the Danny Biasone Lounge but later brought it up and placed it in a large exhibit case in the front of our athletic center.

Kids, especially those interested in athletics, stop and look at the story of the shot clock and are amazed.

"It is a neat thing to have here, and we are proud to be the custodians of such an historic piece of basketball history. And yes, we always make it part of our campus tour," he said with a smile.

If the LeMoyne Athletic Center is open, the large Daniel Biasone Memorial is right inside the front door. The display cases hold trophies, awards, archival photographs, and more. One interesting item is the original score sheet from the March 10, 1955, winning championship final game against Fort Wayne. It lists the starting lineup of beloved Nats players for that decisive game: Dolph Schayes, Red Rocha, Earl Lloyd, Red Kerr, George King, and others. If the building is closed you can still clearly see everything from the large glass entranceway.

The original twenty-four-second clock is obviously the pride and joy of the memorial. It is mounted in the middle of the display cases. It is 25 percent smaller than the one in Armory Square. The original is weathered and beaten and has obviously seen its share of play. The inscription on it reads: "The original 24-second clock. 1st used in the 1954–1955 N.B.A. season. The 24-second rule was originated and developed by Danny Biasone, President of the Syracuse Nationals. The rule revolutionized basketball."

Other Attractions or Sites

Syracuse makes for a great weekend destination. Be sure and stop at Clinton Square in downtown for a full panoramic glimpse of the city's history. The Erie Canal ran through here until it was filled in in 1925. Many early-twentieth-century buildings provide a dramatic backdrop to one of Syracuse's great gathering spots for festivals, street fairs, and celebrations.

Essentials

What: Original NBA twenty-four-second shot clock

Where: Armory Square (replica), LeMoyne College (original); Syracuse; Onondaga County

Contact

LeMoyne College (athletics): www.lemoynedolphins.com

58

Tipperary Hill

Syracuse
Onondaga County

Green over red.

You know from the first time you see it coming up Tompkins Street that something looks, well, a little strange. As you turn off W. Fayette Street at the massive St. John the Baptist Ukrainian Church you can see a number of hanging traffic lights strung out over the ascending intersections before you. But the one at the top. The last one. Yes, it is different.

The green light is at the top of that signal and the red light is on the bottom.

The "green-over-red" light has been a Tipperary Hill neighborhood landmark since the early twentieth century. The original immigrants to the blue-collar area of Syracuse were English. As was the custom with the founding population of a new neighborhood, they named their streets to honor their native English writers, poets, and personalities. Many of the streets on "Tipp Hill" still bear witness to such legendary English writers as Lord Alfred Tennyson and Samuel Taylor Coleridge. When the Irish laborers of the Erie Canal moved into the neighborhood in the 1830s, they too wanted to celebrate their homeland. By the late 1800s, the neighborhood was well known as Tipperary Hill, with many of the "newer" families here originating from County Tipperary in Ireland.

When Syracuse began installing electric traffic lights at intersections throughout the city in 1925, one was placed at the intersection of Tompkins Road and Milton Avenue. Milton Avenue had long been named to honor the English poet John Milton. Neighborhood lads quickly objected to the "British red" over the "Irish green" on the traffic light and soon began pelting it with rocks to knock the red light out.

This happened so frequently that the city was bombarded with requests from the neighborhood residents to leave the permanent "green-over-red" signal in place. The neighbors were concerned that the constantly broken and out-of-order light would lead to increased accidents at that intersection, and the city, frankly, was tired of sending work crews out to Tipp Hill to replace the red bulbs that were knocked out.

On St. Patrick's Day, 1928, a neighborhood organization called the Tipperary Hill Protective Association met with Syracuse officials and said that if the colors were not switched on the traffic light, they could not guarantee that the vandalism against it would not continue. The Irish residents of the neighborhood were steadfast in their nationalistic claim of wanting the green to rule over the red. The city went to New York State transportation officials to plead for the waiver on the order of the light colors. The Tipp Hill neighbors won their case.

The legend of the teenage stone throwers is one that is held close to the heart in this section of a city, which claims that 15 percent of its population as Irish. The gang of ruffians was known by their individual Irish handles: Packy, Stubby, Jacko, Duke, and others. The owner of the corner grocery store, a one-legged Irishman named Dinty, acted as the protector of the stone throwers and would cover for them if police came to investigate. These were some of Tipp Hill's most colorful characters. They were considered heroes in their day.

Coleman's Irish Pub has been a Tipp Hill mainstay since the actual days of the stone throwers. It opened its doors in 1933 and has been the heartbeat of the Irish neighborhood ever since. Stories of the "green-over-red" traffic light flow like Guinness on St. Patrick's Day here, when many

Statues in tribute to the stone throwers are located in a small park at the street intersection guarded by the "green-over-red" light.

254

a glass is raised to honor the young lads who forced the city to change its ways.

Today a memorial to the stone throwers stands at the intersection of Milton and Tompkins. Set in a plaza officially dubbed the Tipperary Hill Heritage Memorial (but referred by all as simply "the stone-throwers statue"), it is a life-sized bronze tableau of a typical Irish family of the day. The father is pointing to the light over the street. The mother and daughter look skyward. The young lad, dressed in an Irish woolen sweater, knickers, and knee socks, stands with his arms on his hips ready for action. A closer inspection of the statue reveals a slingshot in the boys back pocket. He clearly knows what he has to do. The rest of the plaza is adorned with Irish flags, paving bricks, park benches, and a green wrought-iron fence with a shamrock motif.

As if to add an official imprimatur to the whole "green-over-red" legend, Irish prime minister Bertie Ahern made Tipp Hill a stop on his American visit in 2005. On St. Patrick's Day weekend, the Irish leader's motorcade wound its way up through the blue-collar homes of Tompkins Street and stopped at the intersection with Milton Avenue. A large crowd applauded and waved their Irish flags as the prime minister exited his black limousine, walked into the middle of the intersection right under the famous traffic signal, and raised his hands in victory. As they say in the sports world, the crowd went wild.

The Tipp Hill upsidedown traffic light is the only one if its kind in the United States.

Other Nearby Attractions or Sites

While a visit to Tipperary Hill should include the requisite "pint at Coleman's," another suggested side visit would be to the grand St. John the Baptist Ukrainian Catholic Church. It is one of the largest houses of worship in Syracuse and is topped by several significant copper onion-shaped domes. Its distinctive three-story red-brick facing acts as the official starting point for any visit to Tipp Hill. It is located at the bottom of Tompkins Street; Coleman's Pub is in the middle and the stone-throwers memorial is at the top.

The interior of the church is resplendent with Byzantine artwork, gold-leaf adornments and incredibly intricate wood carvings. A statue of

Ukrainian poet and freedom fighter Taras Shevchenko stands in front of the church. It was donated to the church by pub owner Peter Coleman.

Essentials

What: Green-over-ed traffic light

Where: Tipperary Hill, Tompkins Street at Milton Avenue, Syracuse; Onondaga County

Contact

Irish History of Syracuse: Ancient Order of Hibernians; www.syraoh.com

Coleman's Authentic Irish Pub: www.colemansirishpub.com

St. John the Baptist Ukrainian Church at Tipp Hill: www.stjohnbaptistucc.com

59

The Home of Boy Scout Troop #1

Unadilla

Otsego County

The pride of the Village Beautiful.

I truly believe that every little town and village across Upstate New York has a story to tell. I have been to hundreds of communities over the years while researching and writing my several books about the region. Sometimes you have to look for the story, sometimes you have to ask what the story is, and sometimes the story is right there, out in the open for all who pass through to see. Unadilla falls in the last category.

This town of forty-five hundred hugs the Susquehanna River in the lower southwestern corner of Otsego County. Its wide Main Street is lined with large, elegant homes with wide porches. In fact, on a recent drive through the village, only a half-dozen of the one hundred homes along the road lacked a wrap-around or awning-covered porch. These homes, some of them minimansions, speak of a time when Unadilla flourished with manufacturing, banking, and farming. Today it is a sleepy bedroom community to the larger nearby cities, but it retains its beauty and a patina of charm in the face of the hectic pace of today's life. It cherishes its long-time sobriquet: "The Village Beautiful."

When visitors drive through Unadilla on N.Y. S. Rt. 7 (Main Street), I am quite confident they say to themselves, "What a lovely town. I'll bet nothing ever happened here." Well, this is where the storytelling comes in to play. The village does have a tale to tell, and years ago they decided to put it out in the open for everyone passing through to see. Hanging off the light poles along Main Street are long ornamental banners proclaiming "Welcome to Unadilla. Home of Boy Scout Troop #1!"

Now that is how you tell a story!

Unadilla was by no means the first Boy Scout troop in the United States. It's confusing. In 1910, when the Boy Scouts of America started registering troops across the country, Unadilla got in line and was the 166th troop so registered, on April 9, 1910. More than four thousand charters were issued that year. Even though it is registered as Troop #166 in line, the other 165 troops have long since disbanded, and Unadilla is now literally the earliest recorded troop in the U.S. They are called "America's Centennial Troop" because the local troop is in fact as old as the Boy Scouts of America organization as a whole.

Rev. Yale Lyon, a local minister, was the troop's first scoutmaster. He had five boys signed up for BSA 1 by the end of the first year. The following year, 1911, the first New York State Encampment of the Boy Scouts of America was held in Cooperstown. Rev. Lyon walked his little troop the forty miles to join the gathering. Rev. Lyon stayed on as scoutmaster for almost three decades. He was considered a great leader of boys and men and served as the rector of the Saint Matthews Episcopal Church in Unadilla from 1910 to 1942. He is buried in the church cemetery.

To celebrate the hundredth anniversary of Unadilla's scout troop in 2010, nobody had to walk anywhere to go to the state encampment. It was held in Unadilla!

A scouting museum is located in the Unadilla Community Center. Among the many artifacts are scout uniforms, manuals, photographs, awards, insignia, books, pamphlets, and other items associated with scouting history.

The Unadilla organization readily admits that it is not the first Boy Scout troop in the country. The way troops were registered in the beginning led to confusion within the association. In fact, even today many other communities boast about having Boy Scout Troop #1. Despite these claims, the official proclamation on the small group in Unadilla is that since they have weathered two world wars, a Great Depression, and the changing tides in family structures and technology, and they have successfully maintained a charter consistently month after month for over a century, yes, Unadilla is in fact the home of the longest continuously chartered Boy Scout troop in the United States.

Other Nearby Attractions or Sites

Unadilla is home to one of the Northeast's most prestigious horsebreeding farms. In fact, Milfer Farms has been called one of country's top stud farms several times by racing's Thoroughbred Times.

The six-hundred-acre farm is located just outside of Unadilla at the site of the D. M. Ferry mansion. Ferry was a businessman and millionaire seed entrepreneur. He is credited as the first person to sell seeds to individuals in small packets. Ferry's mansion was designed by the famous architect Albert Kahn. Included on the estate was Honeymoon Cottage, one of the first pre-fabricated residences in America.

The mansion was once owned by Chester Davis, Howard Hughes's personal attorney. Mr. Davis died here at his horse farm on May 8, 1983. Milfer Farms is now owned by Davis's son, Jon, an internationally recognized veterinarian.

Among the long list of illustrious thoroughbreds who have resided at Milfer Farms for stud, none was more famous than 1979 Kentucky Derby winner Spectacular Bid. This champion racehorse spent the last twelve years of his life at Milfer Farms and was popular with fans of all ages. The horse sired 250 winners, and because his stud syndication set a record at twenty-two million dollars, he is considered by many to have been one of the most successful stud horses ever.

Spectacular Bid died of a heart attack on June 9, 2003. He is buried at Milfer Farms in Unadilla.

One other thing. Unadilla is home to one of New York State's dwindling number of drive-in movie theatres. The Unadilla Drive-In has been in operation since 1956. There are currently fewer than 30 drive-ins left in the state. At the peak of drive-in popularity (1963) there were more than 160.

Essentials

What: Boy Scout Troop #1

Where: Unadilla; Otsego County

Contact

Unadilla Boy Scout Troop #1: This website includes history, museum information, and photographs; http://trp1bsaunadillanyhist.blogspot.com.

Milfer Farms: www.milferfarms.com

Unadilla Drive-In: www.drive-in.ws

60

Owen D. Young Central School

Van Hornesville
Herkimer County

A truly remarkable rural school.

Owen D. Young is one of those names now lost in the dusty pages of our history books. Although he rose from humble beginnings in remote, rural Upstate New York, he became one of the true American giants of the first half of the twentieth century.

Young's credits could fill an entire chapter. It hardly does his reputation justice to offer a flash-card review of his many accomplishments. He founded RCA; he was a diplomat who worked for five U.S. presidents; he oversaw German reparations following World War I; he was *TIME* magazine's last "Man of the Year" before the Great Depression struck; he was president of General Electric; he became one of the leading international financial statesmen of his era; and much more.

But it is this little stone schoolhouse in tiny Van Hornesville that remains one of his most precious and lasting gifts to Upstate New York.

Young attended one-room schools in Herkimer County and went on to attend St. Lawrence University in Canton, N.Y. Young always dreamed of building a new, modern school facility in his hometown, and did so in 1930 with great zeal.

Van Hornesville School, located near the farm where he was born and grew up, is a model of country perfection. It is unlike any other small school in New York. With Young's unlimited checkbook behind it, the school did not go begging for any amenity available at the time. Classrooms were modern, well-lit, and spacious. The grounds were meticulously kept, the staff was top notch. The building is constructed of large stones and has a slate tile roof. The school library furniture replicates the furniture found in Philadelphia's Independence Hall. The school science lab is dedicated to Nobel Prize winner Marie Curie, a friend of Mr. Young. The guest of honor at the school's first commencement ceremony in 1931 was Owen D. Young himself. The commencement speaker was Franklin D. Roosevelt.

The first graduating class at Van Hornesville School (now known as Owen D. Young Central School) numbered eight students—seven girls and one boy. The boy was named Owen Smith, Mr. Young's namesake. By the way, the graduating class of 2014? Ten students.

For a community that doesn't even reach hamlet size, Van Hornesville has seen a lot of history over the years. Owen D. Young lived here his whole life and is buried in the small cemetery at the edge of town. The aforementioned Madame Curie was a friend of Young's who visited his home here in 1929. Another famous friend was the writer and Pulitzer

Prize winner Marjorie Kinnan Rawlings, author of the classic children's tale *The Yearling*. At Mr. Young's suggestion, Ms. Rawlings bought a farm in Van Hornesville to immerse herself in the ways of country life while writing her final novel, *The Sojourner*. She remained a frequent visitor here until her death in 1953.

The road to and from Van Hornesville is a classic Upstate New York twisting, winding country road. When you enter the community (from the south on NYS Rt. 80), you see a picture-postcard view of a village green. At one corner, an ancient stone gargoyle spits out fresh, cold water. Around the green you can see a half-dozen beautiful, large Victorian homes with wide awning-covered verandas and well-tended front lawns. The Methodist church (which Young helped finance) shows off its large stained-glass windows, bright red doors, and high, open-sided bell tower. And that is about it. On my last visit to the community no businesses could be seen.

Van Hornesville looks like a place just begging for a winter's heavy snowfall. It has a Currier and Ives feel to it, one that is perfectly suited for a Christmas setting. Owen D. Young must have thought so, too. No matter where in the world this legendary globetrotter found himself in December, he always headed home to spend the holidays with his family at his farm.

Other Nearby Attractions or Sites

Located right behind the Owen D. Young School is one of Upstate's greatest secrets. The Robert P. Woodruff Outdoor Learning Center is one of those wondrous little places that you almost hate to tell anybody about. It is just so special. The Center is actually a fifty-acre wilderness with a path that literally takes you down through the pages of local history. As you enter the deep, dark woods (the paths are well kept and clearly marked) you find yourself on an old byway that used to travel from Fort Plain to Cooperstown in the seventeenth and eighteenth centuries. George Washington was said to have actually traveled this trail on his way to Cherry Valley, the site of one of the American Revolution's most infamous massacres.

The path leads you deeper and deeper into the forest until there is almost no sunlight. You come on the remnants of an old mill, some man-made dams, a cheese factory, and other relics of the past two centuries. As you enter the heart of the forest you can hear (but not yet see) the Otsquago Creek roaring below. Eventually you come on a set of wooden stairs that descend several stories into a grotto. This is where the real magic of this nature park lies.

The grotto is surrounded by huge hollowed-out caves, some more than eight feet high. Far above you the Otsquago Creek comes pouring over a cliff, creating one of Upstate's most refreshing hidden waterfalls. The pond below it is cool and clear, a perfect place for wading or swimming. The solitude is inviting, and the presence of Mother Nature in the form of caves, cliffs, waterfalls, forest, fauna, stony creek beds, and more, is totally invigorating.

Informational signs, picnic tables, and restroom facilities are all accessible.

Essentials

What: Owen D. Young Central School building

Where: 2316 State Highway 80, Van Hornesville; Herkimer County

Contact

Owen D. Young Central School and the Robert Woodruff Outdoor Living Center: www.odyoungcsd.org. (For an interesting glimpse of the school's history and the man who made all of this possible, log onto the school's website. Along the top you will find several tabs on the home page. Click on to the page that says "Community." This leads you to a remarkable and historic black-and-white video of the actual first graduation ceremony of the school in 1931. The clip is stunning in its clarity. You can see and hear Governor Franklin D. Roosevelt give his commencement address, and you can see Owen D. Young himself. It is humorous to watch at the close of Roosevelt's address as a man jumps up and leans into the microphone and starts talking. He is the announcer broadcasting the events for WGY radio in Schenectady, owned by GE, a company that Owen D. Young was once the president of!)

REGION FOUR

Catskills, Hudson Valley, Capital District

*Including parts of Albany, Delaware, Dutchess, Orange,
Rensselaer, Rockland, Saratoga, Schenectady,
Sullivan, Ulster, Washington, Westchester,
and Rockland Counties*

61

Hook and Ladder No. 4

Albany
Albany County

Upstate's most beautiful firehouse.

Hook and Ladder Company No. 4 is not the oldest firehouse in Albany. That title goes to Engine House No. 7 (1874). It's not even the second oldest. That is Engine House No. 1 (1892). But, coming in at number three, this one, dubbed "The Big House," has been called one of the most beautiful fire stations in Upstate New York.

Maybe beauty is just in the eye of the beholder. Maybe not.

Architect Marcus T. Reynolds (1869–1937) was one of Albany's most dominant designers. Many of his grand edifices still exist, noted for their sweeping flourishes and touches of the Dutch traditions of old Albany. The Marcus building that is *not* listed on the National Register of Historic Places is rare.

He designed banks, schools, private residences, industrial buildings, libraries, carriage houses, and hospitals. His magnum opus was the massive Delaware and Hudson Railroad Company building (1912–1918) at the foot of State Street on the banks of the Hudson River. This hulking yet graceful structure is so imposing that many mistake it for the New York State Capitol. The sprawling stone complex, now home to the State University of New York administration offices, comprises nearly a quarter of a million square feet of office space. The centerpiece is a thirteen-story tower that reflects the form of the famous medieval Cloth Hall in Ypres, Belgium. It is topped with a unique item from the architect: an eight-foot iron weather vane depicting Henry Hudson's ship the *Half Moon*, designed by Marcus personally.

On a smaller scale, but no less magnificent, is this tiny firehouse that Marcus designed for Delaware Avenue. The building, built in 1912 and squeezed in between houses and businesses in one of Albany's busiest neighborhoods, is adorned in Dutch finery. The brick and stone work is done in the old Flemish Bond style, with one stretcher brick between the header bricks, which in turn are aligned over the stretchers in the row below. This intricate pattern gives the structure a beautiful quilt-like appearance, especially when the sun casts shadows over the exterior walls. The hipped roof is copper, and the many peaks and multistep gables are adorned with whimsical terra cotta shields and beaver gargoyles displaying Albany's coat of arms. Old-style iron crosses are embedded in the outside walls at various places.

In the rear one can still see the stable doors where the fire horses were brought in. High above these doors you can still see the iron hooks that were used to grapple the large hay bales and lower them down to the hungry animals. Inside the firehouse, you can still see on the old wainscoted ceiling signs of the big leather harness contraptions that dropped onto the backs of the horses when the fire bell rang. Two shiny brass fireman's poles extend from the ceiling to the floor. These are original to the structure, and today's firemen still make the twenty-foot slide from the living quarters above to the trucks below.

Obviously, this architectural gem is one of Albany's great treasures, and attempts to change it in any way are met with fierce resistance from the local preservationist community. When century-old, ill-fitting window jambs began allowing drafts into the building, the firehouse requested that sets of storm windows be placed over the original, single panes of glass. It evolved into a battle between the old and the new. The preservationists prevailed, and storm windows were allowed—but only on the inside of the building!

Tony Opalka, the Albany city historian, says the firehouse's beauty comes directly from the architect's love for Albany. "Marcus T. Reynolds was brought up by descendants of the Van Rensselaer family. Their roots go back to the original Dutch patroons of the city. Reynolds felt a strong attachment to this family and its Dutch heritage, and it is manifested in the design of Hook and Ladder No. 4. The design of the firehouse is Reynolds's bold statement of his enthusiasm for Dutch design.

"He clearly wanted this structure to stand out. It is very different from anything else along the Delaware Avenue neighborhood. It was an emerging area when Reynolds got the commission to build the firehouse, and he felt that this might be his last chance to put a 'Dutch stamp' on the neighborhood before things changed dramatically."

I asked Opalka what the relationship is between Albanians and this little structure.

"For sure, everybody knows about this building," he told me. "It's funny, because the interest never really wanes, even after more than a century. We recently had a members-only open house for people with the Historic Albany Foundation. It sold out quickly, and in fact we had more people jammed in here than we really should have. They just can't get enough of it. We went upstairs in the hayloft and studied the wonderful architectural flourishes of the structure, things like the horse's bays and the turreted staircase. It was amazing and in fact the hayloft looked and smelled as if the horses were still employed to take the firemen on their calls—the station began using firetrucks in 1916. The open house was a tremendous success."

Delaware Avenue is called "Albany's New Main Street." It has undergone a major facelift over the last decade. Now, trendy coffee shops and wine bars dot the street, there is a wonderful old movie house, the Spectrum, that is very popular, and some Italian markets and ethnic restaurants have opened up more recently. The neighborhood is popular with young professionals who work at the nearby Empire Plaza, and with families.

"The beautiful old firehouse is really an anchor to this neighborhood," Opalka told me. "I have to tell you, the day we had our open house, two actual fire calls came in during our event. We all stood by, here in this century old landmark, and watched as the firemen sprang into action, opened the huge front doors, and delicately maneuvered the big hook-and-ladder trucks out into the busy street. It made me feel good that Marcus Reynolds's masterpiece of old was still a vibrant and vital part of this neighborhood."

Other Nearby Attractions or Sites

After a visit to the Hook and Ladder No. 4 fire house, you are within a ten-minute walk of one of Albany's most interesting neighborhoods. Lark Street (an extension of Delaware Avenue) is alive with eclectic shops, bars, live entertainment venues, and restaurants. This area, known as Central Square, backs up to Washington Park, which is one of Upstate's greatest urban green spaces. Built in the 1870s, it includes eighty-five acres, including a five-acre pond, an entertainment amphitheater, miles of walking paths, and many sculptures and statues by renowned artists. Lark Street and the park are separated by a single block.

Two of Upstate's most popular festivals are held here. LarkFest, a street fair with live music and food vendors, is the largest single-day street fair in Upstate, attracting nearly a hundred thousand people annually. Lark Street is closed to traffic for the daylong party. Albany's famous Tulip Festival, on Mother's Day in Washington Park, celebrates the city's Dutch heritage and the arrival of spring against a backdrop of 125,000 colorful tulips.

Essentials

What: Upstate's most beautiful firehouse

Where: Hook and Ladder No. 4, Delaware Avenue at Marshall Street, Albany; Albany County

Contact

Albany Fire Stations (info on all stations, including Hook and Ladder No. 4): www.albanyny.org/government/departments/publicsafety

Marcus T. Reynolds (this book has much information about Reynolds and other key Albany architects): *Architects in Albany*, by Diana Waite (Mt. Ida Press, 2009)

Tony Opalka (a biography of the city historian and contact information regarding research and tours): www.nysm.nysed.gov/albany/bios/stafftopalka

Tulip Festival: https://www.facebook.com/pages/Tulip-Fest-Albany-New-York

LarkFest: www.larkstreet.org/events

62

Nipper the Dog (RCA Statue)

Albany
Albany County

His master's voice.

Nipper, the longtime canine mascot of the RCA Victor Company, actually was a real dog.

The terrier belonged to Mark Henry Barraud. They lived over a theatre in England. When Mark died his two brothers, Francis and Philip, took custody of Nipper (named so because he was always nipping at the trousers of strangers passing by). The dog died in 1895. In 1898 Francis, who was a painter, memorialized the dog in a portrait. Having once seen Nipper looking curiously down the bell of an old-fashioned recording machine, Barraud came up with an idea. The result is a realistic painting titled *Dog Looking at and Listening to a Phonograph*. The painting was well received by the artist's friends and colleagues, and he was encouraged to try and sell it to a music company.

The Gramophone Company, a forerunner of RCA, bought the painting for a hundred pounds, and an advertising legend was born. Over the years, the musical apparatus that we see Nipper listening to changed from the original gramophone to successive recording devices, but the pup's endearing, quizzical expression has remained the same: eyes focused, head tilted, ears at the ready. Magazine and print advertisements used the simple slogan "Look for the dog" to encourage people to buy the new music machine. With an eye for immediate recognition, the company decided to change the stodgy, cumbersome title, *Dog Looking at and Listening to a Phonograph*, and held a competition inviting the public to christen the new logo. An Englishman named Ralph Mountain came up with the now iconic title, *His Master's Voice*.

Over the years, Nipper has been painted by some of the greatest illustrators in America and featured in countless print advertisements. His image has been a marketing bonanza. Any antique shop or collectible store worth their salt should be able to come up with at least one of the logos on many product handouts or artifacts. Nipper has appeared on infant clothing, coffee mugs, plush toys, water glasses, refrigerator magnets, doorstops, Christmas ornaments, coin banks, children's toys, lapel pins, T-shirts, key chains, and much more.

Emile Berliner, co-inventor of the gramophone, applied for a trademark for the logo and the catchphrase "His Master's Voice." He was granted trademark number 34,690 on July 10, 1900, and promptly ordered twenty-four copies of the painting to be made by Barraud.

Nipper can still be found in various configurations all over the world. At one time every RCA distributor's warehouse had one on their roof. In Moorestown, New Jersey, for example, more than thirty fiberglass Nippers dot the downtown landscape, each painted by a different local artist. At the end of a certain time period, these little Nippers are auctioned off for charity. Moorestown was the home of Eldridge Johnson, who bought the American rights to the painting in 1900 and used it to advertise his Consolidated Talking Machine Company. In London, a large plaque marks the dog's actual final resting place. It was placed there in 1984 on the hundredth anniversary of the dog's birth by a member of the Johnson family. It is located along Nipper Alley. The street sign bears the logo of the dog peering into a phonograph.

Perhaps the most world-renowned incarnation of the iconic dog is in Albany, New York. Here, along the warehouse area of Broadway near the Hudson River, a massive dog still sits, striving mightily to catch the faint whisper of his master's voice.

Nipper, all four tons of him, sits atop the Arnoff Moving and Storage Building, 7 Tivoli Street. He was erected in 1954 and has been one of the most recognizable (and beloved) hallmarks of the downtown landscape. The twenty-four-foot-tall steel terrier is bathed in light in the evening. Sometimes these lights reflect holidays or community events. Every February the dog is bathed in a red glow in recognition of the American Heart Association's "Nipper Goes Red" promotion. A long boom sticks out from the dog's left ear holding the light fixture. Its original purpose was to alert low flying aircraft to the statue, which at one time was the tallest object in the city.

Of all the many RCA warehouse Nippers over the years, only two are left. One is in Baltimore. That dog can actually be seen listening to a phonograph and is painted in several colors. The other is in Albany. The Albany pooch is black and white only and has never had a phonograph on the roof to listen too.

Albany's Nipper is acknowledged to be the largest man-made dog in the world.

Other Nearby Attractions or Sites

New York State's capital city has much to look at and enjoy. A visit to the Empire State Plaza will showcase the city's modernistic answer to its Old

World, Dutch, and Romanesque architecture of the past (Albany is the oldest chartered city in the nation). One of the most visually stunning aspects of the Plaza is a performing arts center known to all as the Egg. Its design was approved by then-governor Nelson Rockefeller, a well-known lover of modern art. It evokes a spaceship taking off from a tiny launching pad. Inside the Egg are two state-of-the art theatres holding a total of fifteen hundred patrons. The Corning Tower is the most recognizable attribute of the plaza. It soars 660 feet above the city and features an observation deck on its forty-fourth floor. The building is named in honor of Erastus Corning II, who was mayor of Albany for more than forty years. It is the tallest building in New York State outside of Manhattan.

Essentials

What: Nipper the dog (RCA statue)

Where: Arnoff Building, Broadway at Tivoli Street, downtown Albany; Albany County

Contact

The Arnoff Storage and Moving Company building is not a public building. You will not be alone, however, as you position yourself on the sidewalk out front to get a photograph of Nipper. Rarely does a tourist leave Albany without trying to squeeze in a selfie with Nipper from the sidewalk below.

Empire State Plaza: For information about the various buildings at the plaza, including the New York State capitol building, visit www.ogs.ny.gov/esp/. The Corning Tower Observatory is open daily and is free to the general public.

63

The Anti-Rent War

Andes
Delaware County

Lead can't penetrate Steele.

You would be hard pressed to find a more peaceful, bucolic part of Upstate New York than Andes, in western Delaware County. The village of fifteen hundred residents sits high on the northern rim of the Catskill Mountains surrounded by fertile farmlands, lush forests, and sparkling streams and creeks. Its elevation affords the visitor spectacular vistas of the purple mountains of the Catskill range undulating to the south of the village. Mount Pisgah, in the town, rises over thirty-five hundred feet. Andes. As in Andes Mountains of South America. Yes, that is actually the reason it was named so.

In the first half of the nineteenth century, Andes was a far different community. Smaller, more remote from the outside world, more agrarian, more, well, tucked away if you will. Still, in the 1840s, Andes was the focal point of one of the least-known insurrections to take place in Upstate New York. It was the Anti-Rent War, and in 1845 Andes was at the epicenter of the final, violent death throes of this farmer's revolt.

For many years a patroon system of land ownership was in place throughout the Upstate. Patroons were the fabled landowners of massive tracts, mainly in the Hudson Valley. Led by the great Dutch founding family of Killian van Rensselaer, these landowners amassed huge swaths of Upstate New York and had a system in which the tenants, acting as serfs, tilled the land, gave parts of their bounty to the patroon owner, lived under his rules, and paid rents and taxes to their "master." Ownership of the land was never possible for these farmers.

A revolt against these chafing rules started bubbling up in the late 1830s as farmers began meeting in secret, plotting ways to resist paying land taxes and to unite for the right to own land. Meetings were held at night in secret places to discuss ways to rebel. The last fading remnants of the patroon system fought back against this challenge to their supremacy. Dissident farmers were arrested, meetings were busted up, and threats of fines and imprisonment were posted throughout the rural counties to thwart further resistance. This emboldened the anti-renters even more.

The insurgents started showing up at farm foreclosure auctions. They would dress in sheepskin masks and calico robes to hide their identities. They intimidated bidders, supported farmers who were forced to give up their farms because of overdue taxes to the absent owners, and even resorted to clearly illegal means. There are reports that if a bidder bought a farmer's livestock despite the threats from the Calico "Indians" at the auction, the Indians would simply step forward, kill the animals, and then pay the farmer out of their own funds. The word of the Calico Indian insurgents spread across the Delaware County area. Some of their meetings would attract more than a thousand attendees and potential recruits. They were heady days for the anti-renters. But it would all come to an end, right here on Dingle Hill Road in Andes, on August 7, 1845.

Word had gone out that day that a local farmer, facing an impossible payment of sixty-four dollars in back rent due to his landowner, was to lose his farm at an auction. The Calico Indians prepared to attend the auction of sixty-four-year-old Moses Earle's farm in full force, and in full Indian regalia. Osman Steele was the undersheriff of the town and the constable in Andes. By all accounts, he was an ill-tempered, hot-headed, overzealous lawman who was determined to confront the anti-rent rebels at the Earle farm. He and his deputy, Erastus Edgerton, stopped at a local watering hole in Andes on the way out to Dingle Hill. Here the sheriff downed several shots of whiskey. The Hunting Tavern, still located on Andes's Main Street, was a place of boastful swagger and alcohol-infused courage for Steele, Edgerton, and others in his posse. Legend has it that when a customer asked the lawman if he was afraid of what would happen out on Dingle Hill if the Indians created trouble, Steele swallowed a shot of whiskey (which he had reportedly laced with a dusting of gun powder), slammed the glass down on the bar, and declared, "Lead cannot penetrate Steele." It would be the last words ever spoken by the sheriff at the Andes Hunting Tavern.

What happened a short time later at the Earle farm is well documented in this Delaware County village. Steele and Edgerton did ride up to the farm, to be met by a large contingent of disguised Calico Indians. Others arrived from neighboring towns, swelling the anti-renters' numbers to over two hundred. It wasn't long before ego, alcohol, bragging rights, and personal vanity all conjoined to make a witches' brew. Shots were fired—nobody knows who fired first—and Steele fell to the ground mortally wounded. The Calicos quickly dispersed. Farmer Earle came out and knelt over the dying law officer and cradled his head. Steele whispered to the farmer, "Earle, if you had just paid your rent this wouldn't have happened." The farmer replied, "If you had minded your own business none of this would've happened." Undersheriff Osman N. Steele, shot three times, died later that day.

The Anti-Rent War is well known today in Andes and this corner of Delaware County, but is still a largely forgotten page in the story of Upstate New York. The signs welcoming travelers into Andes declare their footnote in history: "The Epicenter of the Anti-Rent War."

Other Nearby Attractions or Sites

The Hunting Tavern, where Steele boasted about being impenetrable, is still here, now acting as a museum. Many anti-rent items are on display here, including posters, paintings, and examples of Calico Indian costumes used by the insurgents. There is a marker and an informational kiosk on Dingle Hill Road just outside the village limits, showing the location of Moses Earle's farm and the site of that fateful encounter in 1845. The ghostly image of Calico Indian masks is still seen in stores, murals, and artwork throughout the village. Many books a have also been written about the subject.

Essentials

What: The Anti-Rent War
Where: Andes; Delaware County

Contact

Andes Society for History and Culture: www.andessociety.org

64

Buddhist Peace Pagoda

Grafton

Rensselaer County

Na-Mu-Myo-Ho-Ren-Ge-Kyo.

While the exterior of this exotic pagoda is visually striking, the inside is empty.

The Grafton Peace Pagoda took eight years to build (1985–1993). It is located about halfway between Troy and the Vermont state line.

The exterior of the pagoda offers a striking departure from the rolling farmlands that are the signature of this area of the state. It is stark white, topped with gold adornments, architectural flourishes, stone walls, and a large staircase. A large statue of Buddha sits prominently at the entrance. Depictions of his life are carved into the exterior walls. The inside is empty, as are all other peace pagodas.

The pagoda was built by Jun Yasuda, a Buddhist nun famous for her long walks for peace. She is a member of the Nipponzan Myohogi order. This diminutive Japanese woman has walked literally thousands of miles around (and across) the United States. Her first was the "Longest Walk," which took her from San Francisco to Washington, D.C., in 1978. She has done several of these marathon walks, all the while beating on a small drum and chanting "Na-Mu-Myo-Ho-Ren-Ge-Kyo," a Buddhist prayer for peace whose literal translation means "I devote myself to the Lotus Sutra of the Wonderful Way."

Usually a lonely figure at the beginning of her marches, like a rolling stone the nun gathers followers and believers all along her journey. On the anniversary of the September 11, 2001, terrorist attacks on America, Yasuda commences a Peace Walk that takes her from Grafton to New York City. To date the nun has walked across the United States four times.

A remarkable bit of information about this pagoda is that it was built by an army of volunteers using donated funds and (mostly) recycled materials. There are approximately eighty of these peace pagodas around the world. The only other one in the United States is located in Leverett, Massachusetts, about fifty miles east of Grafton. A third location for a future peace pagoda has been secured for eastern Tennessee.

Getting to the Grafton Peace Pagoda takes an intrepid spirit. You divert off a main road, onto a secondary road, and then turn up a seasonal dirt road. Next, you have to park and walk into the site. The grounds have plantings, ponds, footbridges, and Japanese memorial icons. Two Asian animal figurines "guard" the main steps up to the Buddha situated at the top of the pagoda stairs. Jun Yasuda's rustic residence is off to one side, and a log temple is also located on the grounds. The temple welcomes visitors to enter and worship (shoes must be taken off). It is resplendent with tapestries, plush prayer pillows, magnificent statuary, and other Buddhist hallmarks.

Despite the remoteness of the Peace Pagoda, you almost always find visitors wandering the grounds. On my most recent visit, I encountered a large group of middle-school students from western Massachusetts exploring the site. Several popular events bring small crowds here, for the remembrance services recalling the bombing of Hiroshima that helped end World War II and for a spring flower festival.

Other Nearby Attractions or Sites

Grafton sits near the border of New York State and Vermont. Two of New England's great small cities are within a twenty-minute drive of the Peace Pagoda.

Bennington, Vermont, just northeast of Grafton, is home to many historic sites, including the Bennington Battle Monument. This 306-foot stone obelisk commemorates General John Stark's victory over a larger British army on August 17, 1777. The stone tower has an observation portal at the top that allows the visitor to see Vermont, New York, and Massachusetts. President Benjamin Harrison attended the dedication ceremony of the monument in 1891.

The Bennington Museum, opened in 1928, is the repository of the largest private collection of paintings by famed folk artist (and native of nearby Eagle Ridge, N.Y.) Grandma Moses.

Williamstown, Massachusetts, is just southeast of Grafton. This small yet vibrant college community (Williams College) has several cultural amenities that are among the best in New England. The Williamstown Theatre Festival has featured works by acclaimed writers as well as performances by Tony-award-winning performers since its inaugural opening in 1954. Many shows started here have ended up on Broadway.

The Sterling and Francine Clark Art Institute is one of the finest private art museums in the East. Mr. Clark, an heir to the Singer Sewing Machine fortune, began collection art in the 1920s. The entire museum, from its inception, construction, staffing, and collection, was overseen by the Clarks. They are buried on the grounds.

Today, this world-class museum exhibits works by Homer, Degas, Sargent, Renoir, Gilbert Stuart, Frederic Remington, and many others.

Essentials

What: The Grafton Peace Pagoda

Where: 87 Crandall Road, Grafton, Town of Petersburgh; Rensselaer County

Contact

Grafton Peace Pagoda: www.graftonpeacepagoda.org

Bennington Museum: www.benningtonmuseum.org

Williamstown Theatre Festival: www.wtfestival.org

Clark Art Institute: www.clarkart.edu

65

Honest Eddie's Tap Room

Hancock
Delaware County

Eddie Murphy: the last honest man.

Bass' Hancock House Hotel is the most imposing structure in this historic community located on the Delaware River just a stone's skip across from Pennsylvania. The hotel has three floors, the top two sporting elegant verandas running the full length of the building. Its location in the heart of this hamlet of fewer than a thousand residents makes it a perfect location for relaxing and people watching on the sidewalk below.

This old landmark hotel has had some serious renovations over the years, and today it remains one of the nicer places to stay and dine along this neck of the river. The taproom on the first floor is comfortable and welcoming. I was particularly interested in the name and some of the items prominently displayed on the walls of the pub.

"Honest Eddie's Tap Room" said the blinking neon sign. I knew there had to be a story here. And I was right.

Eddie Murphy was born in the Hancock House Hotel on October 2, 1891. His parents owned the place. Eddie was a natural athlete and dreamed of becoming a big-league baseball player. After high school, he graduated from local teams to the Eastern League and was such a good hitter and fielder that his progression to the majors was assured. He signed with the Philadelphia Athletics in 1912. The following year he played in the 1913 World Series with the team. Murphy's contract was bought out by the Chicago White Sox in 1915 and he stayed with that team for six more seasons. The timing of his playing for the White Sox could not have been worse. Murphy would play in one of the most notorious World Series spectacles in baseball history.

The Chicago White Sox were accused of throwing the 1919 World Series and subsequently cashing in on bets they had made. The scandal rocked baseball and almost ended the professional sport. Front pages across the country blared out the unseemly details involving "Shoeless Joe" Jackson and seven other teammates. Although they were eventually acquitted of the fraud, the indelible stain would follow them forever. All eight players accused of throwing the series were banned from baseball for life.

But what about the "ninth man?"

Eddie Murphy, beloved native son of Hancock, N.Y., and a valued member of the Chicago White Sox championship team, escaped all hint of scandal and emerged as "the last honest man." Murphy and any other teammate who refused to go along with Shoeless Joe and his cohorts were rewarded with a check from the team's owner for $1,500 for their integrity. As Murphy would later tell the press, "Well, I guess it is true. Honesty does pay."

Murphy went on to rack up impressive numbers in baseball before retiring in 1926. In fact he played in three World Series. He died in Dunmore, Pennsylvania on February 21, 1969, at the age of seventy-seven.

Today, Honest Eddie Murphy's Tap Room pays tribute to this legendary baseball player. The barroom is an homage, a shrine if you will, to the man and his career, all right here in the building he was born in. The walls feature several artifacts from his playing days, and, in fact, family members and distant relatives still stop by for a visit to their namesake's living memorial. The tavern is a convivial gathering place popular with those in town, and the restaurant attached, the Maple Room, has been renovated to mirror the style it was built in more than a century ago.

The connection between Eddie Murphy and Babe Ruth has been well talked about over the years. Both Ruth and Murphy were children of owners of barrooms or saloons. On the day that Babe Ruth first took the mound as a pitcher for Boston in 1914, the first batter he ever faced was Eddie Murphy. In 1918, Murphy and Ruth were almost dead even in the batting-average race (Ruth with .300; Murphy with .297). One other eerie six-degrees-of-separation connection between the two has to do with a baseball bat.

At the time that Babe Ruth began slugging home runs at a historic pace, he was using a Louisville Slugger. Despite their name, the famous bats were made for nearly a century in Eddie Murphy's hometown. Murphy once said that the first bat Ruth ever homered with was probably carved from a Hancock tree.

Other Nearby Attractions or Sites

Fishing fanatics and outdoorsmen come to Hancock from all over the world to troll the trout-laden bottom waters of the Delaware. The West Branch Angler's Resort in Hancock is one of the most popular destinations for these anglers. The resort has modern riverside cabins and a complete outdoorsman's supply store; it can provide you with some of the best fishing and river experts in the region. The resort's River Run Restaurant is one of the best along the river; they host private parties, corporate gatherings, and even weddings.

One of the most prominent natural features in Hancock is Point Mountain. This large hill, which appears to come to a point, has a story to it. Two rivers, the east and west branches of the Delaware River, come together here and surround the mountain. Years ago, a prominent local doctor, Dr. Lester Woolsey (1872–1962) decided he wanted to be buried on top of the mountain. He bought the property and constructed an elaborate, medieval-looking castle-like building, on top which was to be his mausoleum. Eventually he and nearly thirty members of his family were buried there. Over time, weather (and vandals) took a toll, and all of the bodies were removed to a Pennsylvania cemetery. The mausoleum's ruins are still an eerie attraction for adventurers with a little spunk and derring-do.

Essentials

What: Honest Eddie's Tap Room

Where: Hancock House Hotel, Main Street, Hancock; Delaware County

Contact

Bass' Hancock House Hotel and Honest Eddie Murphy's Tap Room. The hotel also owns a series of cabins located a few miles away for use as weekend getaways; http://hancockhousehotel.com

Hancock travel, history, and tourism: www.hancockny.org

West Branch Angler's Resort: www.westbranchresort.com

66

Grandma Moses's Grave

Hoosick Falls
Rensselaer County

Anyone can paint.

If you had asked central casting to send you "a kindly, grandmotherly type" for a movie, they could have done no better than to send Anna Mary Robertson Moses.

With her wire-rimmed glasses, high starched collars, and the tightly bound white bun piled on top of her head, this elfin figure captured the imagination of the art world from the late 1940s through the early 1960s. She was a talented farm woman raising her chickens and her kids on a small farm in Hoosick Falls, N.Y. Here in the remote confines of Upstate's Rensselaer County, "Mother Moses" enjoyed the country life and honed her creative talents. Her art was in the form of embroidery in those days. Her fancy stitch work became highly praised and highly prized by her farm friends and neighbors.

A nasty attack of arthritis in her seventies forced her to turn to painting as an outlet for her creative energy, and even though she never picked up a paintbrush before the age of seventy-six, she showed an early knack for painting, what she called, "old timey things." She was a tireless one-woman painting machine, churning out over two thousand paintings in less than thirty years. She sold her paintings to her friends and family, and sometimes to strangers who asked for them, for as little as five dollars each.

Soon dubbed "Grandma Moses" by the press, her fame began to spread from her home in Eagle Bridge (in the town of Hoosick Falls) near the Vermont–New York border. Her subjects were a balm to a public weary of war and the Depression. She painted barn raisings and butter churnings, swimming holes and horse wagons, children's Christmas pageants and checkered tablecloths flapping on a farm wife's clothesline.

When she was seventy-eight years old, and still a relative unknown, she was convinced to display some of her works in the front window of the little drugstore on Hoosick Falls's Main Street. Not long after, Louis Calder, a New York City art collector, happened by and bought them all for less than twenty dollars. He asked about the painter and was directed to her home in Eagle Bridge. He went there to visit the artist and found that she had ten more paintings similar to those in the drugstore window. He bought them all. The story goes that Grandma Moses had been alerted that the man was on his way to buy the rest of her paintings and that she took a particularly large one and split it in half to make two smaller, individually priced paintings. Calder's purchases of the earliest of Grandma

Moses's works cost him less than fifty dollars. Today, of course, they would be worth a small fortune.

The lid came off the next year for the spry little artist. Three of her folk-art paintings were shown in an exhibit titled *Contemporary Unknown American Painters* at the prestigious Museum of Modern Art in New York City, but to lackluster response. In 1940, she was the focus of a one-woman show at the Galerie St. Etienne in New York. The show was titled *What a Farm Wife Painted* and was a great success. She was the star of the show and her notoriety as an American original was assured.

Grandma Moses created countless of works of art, and many of them ended up being reprinted on calendars, mugs, cards, posters, china plates and other merchandise. Hallmark signed her to a commercial contract, and sales of her Christmas cards number in the millions. Even today, her paintings turn up on every imaginable kind of item, easily recognizable and universally loved.

Grandma Moses continued painting until a few months before her death at the age of 101.

Once she became famous, the image of the tiny, birdlike woman, in flowered hat, cameo pin, dainty gloves, and lace cuffs, was ubiquitous. She was invited to the White House by President Truman and was given honors by museums around the world. In 1950, a documentary on the farm wife artist, narrated by Archibald MacLeish, was nominated for an Academy Award. The same year she published her autobiography, *My Life's History*. Actress Lillian Gish portrayed her in a television show. In 1953 she was on the cover of *LIFE* magazine, and her iconic celebrity status was affirmed for all time. She was a media darling at the age of ninety-three.

In 1955, Edward R. Murrow hosted a special edition of his hit television show *See It Now* featuring Grandma Moses. Murrow, the crusty investigative reporter known for his gruff, direct style was effortlessly charmed by his guest. When Murrow asked her what uniquely qualified her to be an artist, she pooh-poohed and tisked-tisked her answer to him. She pushed a piece of paper toward the host and said, directly, "Here. Draw a tree. Anyone can draw."

You can see this legendary exchange between two of the 1950s' most recognizable celebrities at the Bennington Museum in Bennington, Vermont. The museum, just over the state border from New York, has the largest collection of original Grandma Moses paintings in the country. They also have many items of memorabilia from the artist's life and home, including the unique tilting desk on which she painted. A looped tape of her appearance on *See It Now* plays for museum visitors.

Grandma Moses exhibits are still held at major museums around the country. Her output was incredible (more than 250 of her paintings were finished after her hundredth birthday), and fans are eager to see as many in her collection as can be displayed. One of her most famous paintings, *Sugaring Off* (1943), sold for over a million dollars. A far cry from the two- and three-dollar paintings she used to display in Thomas's Drug Store.

When Anna Mary Robertson Moses passed away on December 13, 1961, President John F. Kennedy praised her as "our national treasure." She was 101 years old.

Author's note: Perhaps the most famous and beloved American artist is Norman Rockwell. He was a fan of Grandma Moses and he several times drove an hour from his own studio in Stockbridge, Massachusetts, to Eagle Bridge to visit her.

Other Nearby Attractions or Sites

The long border area between New York and Vermont is one of the prettiest regions in the state. This area is not very wide (thirty miles at most) yet it is home to art galleries, small-town festivals, covered bridges, old-time general stores, and classic village greens. Washington County, just five miles north of Hoosick Falls, is home to four historic covered bridges. The county is also known for its cheese. A popular "cheese tour" allows the visitor to go to several cheese makers to sample their wares. All of this is just minutes from Hoosick Falls.

Essentials

What: Grave of Grandma Moses

Where: Maple Grove Cemetery, Hoosick Falls; Rensselaer County

Contact

Maple Grove Cemetery is located on Main Street just south of the business district of Hoosick Falls. Signs point the way to Grandma Moses's grave in the new section. The inscription on her gravestone reads: "Anna Mary Robertson Moses. Grandma Moses. Her primitive paintings captured the spirit and preserved the scene of the vanishing countryside." A blue-and-yellow New York State historical marker is located on the roadside in front of the cemetery identifying this as her final resting place.

Bennington Museum: www.bennington museum.org

Galerie St. Etienne: Grandma Moses had her first success at this gallery in 1940. It is the oldest gallery in the United States specializing in expressionism and self-taught art. They have several of Grandma's original paintings in their permanent collection. www.gseart.com

Rensselaer County Tourism: www.renscotourism.com

Washington County Cheese Tour: www.washingtoncountycheese.com

Washington County Tourism: www.washingtonnycounty.com

67

Col. Elmer Ellsworth's Grave

Mechanicville
Saratoga County

First Union casualty of the Civil War.

In 1861, just four weeks after the start of the Civil War, the Confederates were in Alexandria, Virginia, and they wanted to make sure the Union forces, and the president, knew it. They commandeered a prominent hotel in town and raised a Rebel flag large enough to be seen on a clear day even by the president in the Oval Office directly across the river.

Col. Elmer Ellsworth was well known as a leader of men and was one of the Union Army's most prominent drillmasters. He was a lawyer and had worked with Abraham Lincoln in his law office in Illinois and later worked toward electing his friend president. When the president went to Washington, so did Ellsworth.

Lincoln looked on Ellsworth more as a son than a military man. In fact, one local New York State historical marker, in Malta, N.Y., says, "Ellsworth was mourned by Lincoln as a son. He once called the diminutive Ellsworth, 'the greatest little man I ever met.'" Before long the mocking Confederate flag became too much for the citizens of our nation's capital to bear, and Col. Ellsworth took a group of soldiers across the Potomac to take it down.

On the morning of May 24, 1861, Ellsworth and his troops entered Alexandria and went to the Marshall House Inn. The Confederate flag flying above the hotel, Ellsworth and his men entered and went up the stairs to the roof. After cutting down the flag, Ellsworth came back down the stairs, where he was confronted by an angry James Jackson, the proprietor of the inn. Words were exchanged, and Jackson shot Ellsworth, killing him instantly on the staircase of the Marshall House Inn. A soldier accompanying Ellsworth lunged his bayonet at the hotel owner before he could reload, killing him. That soldier, Corp. Francis Brownell of Troy, N.Y., was awarded the Medal of Honor for killing Jackson.

Ellsworth became the first conspicuous Union casualty of the Civil War.

When President Abraham Lincoln first heard the news of the death of his friend, he collapsed. He wept, wracked with self-blame for allowing Ellsworth to undertake his fateful mission. Lincoln ordered an enormous ceremonial funeral for the twenty-four-year-old Upstate New York native. Ellsworth's body first reposed in state in the East Room of the White House, where President Lincoln sat grief stricken throughout the mourning period. Later, Ellsworth's body was taken to New York City by train. Along the route, thousands came out to pay tribute to the young Union martyr. Flags flew at half-staff throughout the North. From New York City, the soldier's body was taken to the Hudson, where a naval cortege took it up the river to his final resting place in Mechanicville, N.Y. It is estimated that as many as a million people observed the sad last journey of Col. Ellsworth from Washington to Upstate New York.

Much like the battle cries "Remember the Maine" and "Remember Pearl Harbor" would rally Americans to the cause of future wars, the rally cry "Remember Ellsworth" echoed throughout the North, and enlistment rolls were quickly filled with those who called themselves "Ellsworth's Avengers." Some 200,000 new enlistees were signed up within three months of his death. In the months following, people even started naming their babies after Ellsworth, and the site of the Virginia hotel became a pilgrimage destination for hundreds of Union soldiers, who visited merely to touch the same railing that Ellsworth had touched in his dying moments.

Col. Ellsworth had just turned twenty-four years old when he was shot and killed, becoming the first officer killed in the Civil War.

Ellsworth is buried in Hudson View Cemetery. His final resting place is unmistakable. A forty-foot obelisk marks his grave. On top is a large eagle about to take flight. A large bronze image of the soldier decorates the base, surrounded by laurel wreaths. The inscription at the back of this most impressive monument recalls the young soldier's dying words: "I am confident that he who knoweth even the fall of the sparrow will have purpose even in the fate of one like me."

Another inscription can be found on the reverse side of the monument:

"Col. Elmer E. Ellsworth. Commander of the 1st Regiment of the New York Fire Zoaves. Killed taking the first Rebel flag in the war for the Union."

So, was Col. Elmer Ellsworth of Mechanicville the first casualty of the Civil War, as many reference books call him?

That question seems unanswerable. Surely another soldier died in the six weeks between the start of the war and May 24, 1861. But if so, who? Many references hedge their bets by calling Ellsworth "the first conspicuous casualty" of the Civil War. Others say he was the first officer. Others say he was simply the first Union officer killed. And on it goes. But one thing is for certain. Ellsworth was the first hero of the Civil War, and he died trying to defend his country's honor on a crowded wooden staircase in Alexandria, Virginia, in the opening days of the engagement.

Another controversy pertains to whether Ellsworth was the first successfully embalmed prominent figure. The practice of embalming was still new in the 1850s, and was used mainly to keep cadavers intact for medical students. Ellsworth's embalmed remains stayed remarkably intact throughout the protracted funeral ceremonies and procession that took his body from Washington to his hometown some 350 miles away. It took many days for his body to travel from Washington, D.C., to New York City, and then up the Hudson River to the New York State Capitol, where his body again lay in state, and then on up to Mechanicville. Ellsworth's family was still able to view their son one last time as he was presented to them in an open casket before he was buried.

Other Nearby Attractions or Sites

After visiting the astonishing monument to Ellsworth in the Hudson View Cemetery, travel the fifteen miles northwest to Saratoga Springs. Here you will find the New York State Military Museum. It is one of the best in the state.

Among the precious artifacts held by this museum is an entire display case filled with Elmer Ellsworth memorabilia. The informational narratives here tell this local man's story in both pictures and text. Perhaps the most amazing piece in the museum's collection, however, is the actual uniform that Col. Ellsworth was wearing on the day he was killed. There is a jagged hole in the jacket where the fatal blast was fired near his heart

Essentials

What: Grave of Col. Elmer Ellsworth

Where: Hudson View Cemetery, Mechanicville; Saratoga County

Contact

New York State Military Museum: http://dmna.ny.gov/historic/mil-hist.htm

68

Home of the Annual Bagel Festival

Monticello
Sullivan County

The bagel capital of New York.

The 1940s and 1950s were the booming days of Upstate's famed Borscht Belt. A series of massive hotels and resorts once dotted the countryside here, beckoning millions of tourists over the years to come up from the steamy summer confines of metropolitan New York and enjoy the fresh air and relaxation provided at places such as Grossinger's (Liberty), Brown's (Loch Sheldrake), the Concord (Kiamesha Lake), and the Nevele (near Ellenville).

As the era of the show palaces, Jewish resorts, and convention centers began to wane in the late 1950s, the area tried to resuscitate its reputation as an entertainment mecca by opening the sprawling Monticello Raceway, one of the state's largest horse-racing facilities. The track opened on June 27, 1958, and is still in operation.

Today, when Monticello is mentioned, it's usually in the context of "what will happen in the future." All of the resorts eventually closed in the face of easy access to a number of entertainment venues, such as Atlantic City and several large resorts and casinos in Connecticut. The advent of universal air-conditioning in the 1960s also meant that the trek to the cool forests and lakes of the Catskills in the summer was not quite as imperative. The hotels, many with hundreds of rooms, slowly closed, one by one, becoming ghosts in the woods; many were eventually leveled. Some are trying to make a comeback today, and there is always hope that new liberal casino regulations might breathe life back into this beautiful area, which faces inordinate economic pressures; Sullivan County has several times been the county with the highest unemployment in the state.

For Monticello, the hope for the future, in a small way, may come from the lowly bagel.

The bagel, as we all know, has been around for centuries. It got its name from the Yiddish word "beygal," which means bracelet or ring. Bagels have long been associated with the huge inner-city Jewish enclaves in the cities of the Northeast, primarily New York City. As the Catskills began to grow in the 1920s, led mostly by the establishment of Jewish resorts and bungalow colonies, the bagel made its way into the mountains as well.

Today, Monticello is considered the "Bagel Capital of New York State," and in a region that is hard put to brag about receiving any new, exciting accolades, this city of seven thousand plans to milk their title for all it's worth.

Bagel shops are everywhere in Sullivan County, and they are all uniformly excellent. The bloodline of the bagel runs right through Sullivan County. An area man, Louis Wichinsky, invented the first bagel-making machine, which could initially turn out six hundred bagels an hour. The Monticello Bagel Bakery, an institution on Broadway (Monticello's main thoroughfare), was opened in 1967 by the Fleischman family, and a Fleischman still runs it today. Their bagel shop was one of the first-ever bagel bakeries to be located outside of New York City. The Bagel Bakery is ground zero for bagels in Monticello.

On the day I stopped in, a long line of customers was queued up ordering their bagels and schmears. The menu board above the counter listed a series of types of bagels, from the traditional plain to those with poppy seeds, sesame seeds, cinnamon and raisins, and even more exotic combinations. The accompanying toppings ran the gamut from plain butter to lox, salmon, olive oil, cream cheese, and a walnut spread.

I commented to the harried counterman about an unusual piece of art in the front of the store. It is a six-by-five-foot American flag made entirely of red, white, and blue bagels. Talk soon revolved around the

You will find an American flag made out of bagels inside the Monticello Bagel Bakery on Broadway.

annual Bagel Festival. Each year thousands descend on Monticello for a weekend celebration of the "roll with a hole" all along Main Street. There are many family-oriented events, live music, a parade, the crowning of the King and Queen of Bagels, vendors' tents lined up on both sides of "Bagel Broadway," and more. Louis Wichinsky's original bagel-making machine is on display in the history tent, attesting (somewhat) to Monticello's claim to be the birthplace of the bagel.

I chatted up a customer at the Bagel Company who volunteered that he had been coming ever since the festival began.

Mort Tambur, seventy-seven, a Long Island resident who summers in the Monticello area, told me about the weekend events. "I bring my kids and grandchildren and we have a ball," he began. "It really is quite exciting to see so many people out in the street, laughing and enjoying themselves along Broadway. More communities need something like this. And when it is time for the bagel chain, everybody really gets worked up."

The bagel chain?

"Yes, it is wonderful. They line up everybody along Broadway, and they all hold a rope or something and they start stringing bagels along it all up and down the street. The kids love it. All ages, all colors, men, women, everybody having fun. It is wonderful. They say the Guinness Book of Records people came to see if it was the world's longest bagel chain. I don't know if it made it or not, but it was a lot of fun," he laughed.

The Bagel Festival was a hit and looks like it will be an annual event that will draw thousands to Monticello every August. The first year saw five thousand visitors, and there are projections for crowds of fifteen thousand or more in the coming years.

I had to look up the official New York State legislative resolution declaring Monticello the "bagel capital of New York." And there it was, dated February 5, 2013, entered by state senator John Bonacic. Among all the "whereases" on the citation is one that reads "Monticello, with its rich and diverse past, has sealed its place in history as a unique innovator and as a world symbol of fine baked goods. . . . We commend the Village of Monticello upon the occasion of being named 'The Bagel Capital of New York.'"

Other Nearby Attractions or Sites

The 1969 Woodstock music festival was held just ten miles west of Monticello in Bethel. Visitors today can observe the famous "muddy field" that held nearly a half-million concert goers, and also visit the new, modern Bethel Woods Arts Center at the site, which includes a Woodstock Museum dedicated to the most famous rock concert in history.

Essentials

What: The Bagel Capital of New York
Where: Monticello (Sullivan County)

Contact

Bagel Festival: www.thebagelfestival.org
Monticello and Sullivan County travel, tourism, and events: www.scva.com
Bethel Woods Arts Center: www.bethelwoodscenter.org

69

The World's Largest Kaleidoscope

Mt. Tremper
Ulster County

Jewels in a Catskill silo.

There is a world of difference between the foothills of the Catskill Mountains and the region's northern section. The foothills gained notoriety in the early twentieth century as the famed Borscht Belt. It became known for Jewish enclaves, bungalow communities, dazzling nightclubs, Elizabeth Taylor, Eddie Fisher, Debbie Reynolds, Jennie Grossinger, and cool, fresh air. It included cities and towns such as Liberty, Monticello, and Ellenville.

The other part of the Catskills is much different. Far more rural and remote, this region is known as the High Peak area and became known for its cool, fresh air, trout fishing, recreation, and ski mountains named Windham, Hunter, and Plattekill.

"Either way you looked at it, the Catskills were a major escape destination from the close confines of New York City," Tony Lanza told me. He is the chief operating officer of the Emerson Resort and Spa. The Emerson is one of the most spectacular resorts in the Catskills, offering world-class accommodations, four-star fine dining, and a famous spa and wellness center, all wrapped up in the bosomy embrace of Mother Nature.

"Our facilities are without peer," Lanza told me. "And to think here we are right in the middle of the most beautiful part of the state. In fact the Esopus Creek, which runs right behind our property, goes all the way to New York City, where it joins other Catskill tributaries to provide the metropolitan area with more than 90 percent of their drinking water.

"We think the Emerson is such a special place. We are just two hours from the George Washington Bridge, yet our guests enter a whole new world when they come to the Emerson. Even the climate is different. Sometimes when it is eighty-five degrees in Manhattan, it can be seventy here in the Catskills. Folks just love it. We are in the shadow of Mt. Tremper and Mt. Pleasant, and we are situated in one of only two of America's constitutionally protected parks, the Adirondacks being the other one."

"Our natural setting makes this a perfect place for a weekend getaway," Kayleen Scali offered. She is an administrative assistant at the resort. "We have weddings here every week. Our restaurants are the finest in the Catskills, and we offer a large retail component at the Emerson, which really sets us apart from other resorts. For sure, most of our guests come up from the metropolitan New York area, but we also have guests who visit us from all over the world."

Okay. So what about the kaleidoscope? For that story we go to Linda Prinzivalli. She is the Emerson's kaleidoscope curator.

"I came to Emerson looking for a job," she began. "I ended up here in the kaleidoscope store."

This is certainly no ordinary store. The "kaleidostore" store sells over five hundred varieties of kaleidoscopes, of all sizes and all prices. "I really had no great attachment to the kaleidoscope when I began, but over time I have grown so fond of them. They are magical instruments. I am an artist so I really appreciate the wonder of the interactive relationship between the instrument and the human. You actually participate in the joy of a kaleidoscope when using it. I just love them now."

People travel from all over the world to visit the collection at the Emerson. There is a kaleidoscope organization called the Brewster Kaleidoscope Society, named after Sir David Brewster, who coined the term "kaleidoscope" in 1817. It has about three hundred members, and the Emerson belongs to the group.

"We have kaleidoscopes for sale here ranging from below ten dollars to over four thousand dollars. Our collection is among the finest in the world. In fact, we recently had a guest at the Emerson who came here from Texas A&M University. He spent two whole days just looking at and admiring our kaleidoscopes. He had seen virtually every collection in the world and deemed ours the best."

One of the most fun attractions at the Emerson is "The World's Largest Kaleidoscope." It is about the most unusual experience you can have in the Catskills.

"Our giant kaleidoscope started out as a fifty-six-foot-tall cow grain silo. Obviously, to us, it looked just like a giant kaleidoscope so that is what it became. We opened it to visitors in 1996 and the Guinness Book of World Records came and certified it as the world's largest kaleidoscope."

I have experienced the giant kaleidoscope several times, both with my children when they were little and as an adult by myself. You enter a small door at the base and find yourself on the "floor" of the silo. The walls are black; there are leaning back rests along the curved walls and a large carpeted space in the middle. People position themselves leaning back on the wall rests, looking up to the ceiling to see the show. What happens when the lights go out is hard to describe. But it was great fun.

"I tell people to just go in and lay on the floor," Prinzivalli said. "That way you get the whole experience. You are looking way up to the top and you can let experience envelope you. We have three thirty-seven-foot tapered mirrors at the top and they reflect the myriad of colorful images produced by our special artists for a total multimedia sensory experience. Each mirror weighs over two tons. Charles Karadinos, a kaleidoscope artist, came up with the original idea. Isaac Abrams and his son, Raphael, created the 'Kaatskill Kaleidoscope' program. The whole cost was over $250,000. Abrams is a world-renowned artist who has exhibited at the Whitney Museum of American Art in New York City and is considered the 'Father of Psychedelic Art.' Our first program opened on July 4, 1996, and was titled *America, the House I Live In*. It had a patriotic theme, and the twelve-minute show is accompanied by some original orchestration created just for us and piped throughout the silo. It was amazing. Since then we have added other kaleidoscope shows, including *Metamorphosis*, which features images of the Catskills' landscapes, and a popular holiday show. We now have young parents bringing their children to share the experience they themselves had as children. The shows are very popular."

The Emerson is a remarkable place. Situated in a stunning setting, it features fine dining, world-class amenities, top-notch accommodations, and a reputation for exemplary service. Add to that a touch of childhood fancy, in the form of the world's largest kaleidoscope, and you have yourself a truly unique Upstate landmark.

"People come here for a true mix of the old and new," Tony Lanza said. "They come to ski, to hike, to kayak, or to enjoy a fine meal and a comfortable room. Or, with a tip of the hat to yesteryear, they come for a quiet weekend just to sit on our porch and listen to the creek, or curl up in front of a fire and read a good book. And, yes, they come for our kaleidoscopes too. It's perfect."

Other Nearby Attractions or Sites

This part of the Catskills is rife with great restaurants and quirky overnight accommodations. Just a CD's throw down the road from the Emerson is Kate's Lazy Meadow Motel. The rooms here are funky and far out, and the Lazy Meadow has become a popular motel for those seeking an out-of-this-world overnight baby-boomer-era experience. Think plastic furniture, geometric bedding designs, lava lamps, and a retro 1950s kitchenette. The owners are Kate Pierson and Monica Coleman. Pierson is the lead singer of the B-52's rock band. Their 1989 signature hit, "Love Shack," was named by Rolling Stone magazine as one of the top five hundred rock-and-roll songs of all time.

Essentials

What: The world's largest kaleidoscope

Where: Emerson Resort, Mt. Tremper; (Ulster County)

Contact

Emerson Resort: www.emersonresort.com

Kaleidoscope Society: www.brewstersociety.org

Kate's Lazy Meadow Motel: www.lazymeadow.com

Catskill-area information: www.visitthecatskills.com

70

Historic Huguenot Street

New Paltz

Ulster County

The oldest authentic street in New York State.

Huguenot Street is unlike any other street you will find. It is the oldest street, located in one of the oldest neighborhoods, in America. The Huguenot Historic District in New Paltz consists of a pretty ten-acre campus-like neighborhood of seven homes plus a 1717 restored church and a graveyard dating back to the days of the first settlers in the Hudson Valley.

To walk among these historic homes, all built of stone and timbers, is to walk along the footpaths of history. Literally.

Over the years, this ancient neighborhood has had Indian, French, Dutch, African, and English residents, among others. Each home retains the rich historical patina of its original owners. The homes are open on special-event days, and it is well worth putting a visit on your must-see list. First settled in 1678, the area has been designated as a National Historic Landmark District. There is a visitor's center and guided tours are provided.

The houses are all sturdy, graceful, and odd looking. There are Dutch styles as well as English styles common in the 1700s. They are massive, not so much for the area they take up, but rather for their sheer heft. It is easy to imagine this as a busy little neighborhood with children, families, businesses, and churches.

The Pierre Deyo house looks the biggest, having been added on to several times over the centuries. Christian Deyo and his son, Pierre, were two of the original twelve Huguenot patentees in New Paltz (the dozen were known to the French as "The Dusine"). He built the first stone house in the district in 1692. It was built in the style of a Flemish manor but was transformed into a Victorian-style residence two centuries later. In 1971, the Deyo family donated it to be used as a public meeting house and museum.

The Jean Hasbrouck house was built in 1712 by another of the original patentees. For many years, the building was used as both a residence and a general store for the small community. It is the largest home in the historical district. Since 1899, it has been the home of the Huguenot Patriotic Historical and Monumental Society. Like many of the original Huguenot Historic District buildings, it has a historical marker in the front which gives a glimpse of the background of the building. The one here tells us that cockfights once took place in the kitchen!

The Bevier-Elting house, built by patentee Louis Bevier in 1698, has an unusual subcellar. The LaFevre house interior features over two hundred years of the family's portraits. Built in 1799, this residence's design

New Paltz's historic district is dotted with fascinating historical markers like this one.

marked the first shift from the classic, original French concept to the more prevalent Dutch architecture of the lower Hudson Valley. Daniel Dubois built his home, Fort Dubois, in 1706. The historical marker here reminds us that "as a fort this was the first redoubt in the village, and that port holes can still be seen in the east end."

Each house is different. And yet, remarkably, all are the same in some respects. Large stones make up the walls, tall sweeping roofs hide storage attics and haylofts, substantial timbers provide support, and old oaken barrels still anchor the corners waiting to collect rainwater.

One fun thing about a visit to the Huguenot Historic District is that it is located just a couple of blocks off the main business area of New Paltz. The village is a hip enclave of high-end specialty shops, pubs, cafés, art galleries, bookstores, vinyl record shops, and eateries. The trend is "easy breezy" here, like a younger version of their neighbor to the north, Woodstock. The thousands of students at the State University of New York add mightily to the youthful ambiance of the village. Surrounding it all are the impressive Catskills in the far distance and the much nearer Shawangunk Mountains (known as the "Gunks").

If you are planning a visit to New Paltz, we strongly suggest visiting around Halloween. The entire village, including the 330-year-old houses in the Huguenot Historic District, gets involved with the spooky festivities. Halloween revelers have numbered in the thousands over past years' events.

Other Nearby Attractions or Sites

The Mohonk Mountain House is one of America's most storied and beautiful inns and resorts. The massive inn, with nearly three hundred rooms, towers over the privately owned Lake Mohonk. It was started by twin brothers, Alfred and Albert Smiley, and it is still owned by the Smiley family. Since the original brothers, both Quakers, began the family inn in 1879, it has been expanded greatly over the years. Today the mountaintop has nearly a hundred miles of hiking trails and carriage paths. Located just west of New Paltz you have to drive up a narrow one-mile driveway to enter the grounds. The view from the top is among the best in the Hudson Valley. Presidents from Abraham Lincoln to Bill Clinton have stayed here.

The Mohonk is also famous for one of the finest Sunday brunches in New York. Served in their high-ceilinged dining room, the brunch is a bountiful harvest of carving stations, seafood specialties, chef-prepared entrees, and copious homemade desserts. It costs more than sixty dollars a person, but don't let the sticker shock scare you away from this unforgettable dining experience.

Essentials

What: The oldest street in America

Where: Huguenot Street Historic District, New Paltz; Ulster County

Contact

Huguenot Street Historic District: www.huguenotstreet.org

Mohonk Mountain House Resort: www.mohonk.com

Ulster County Tourism and Events: www.ulstertourism.info

71

The National Purple Heart Hall of Honor

New Windsor

Orange County

The first Purple Heart. Photograph courtesy of Peter Bedrossian, Program Director at the National Purple Heart Hall of Honor.

On May 3 and June 10, 1783, Gen. George Washington ordered a special military commendation and awarded it to three soldiers. The award was known as the Badge of Military Merit. The first three recipients were Sgt. Elijah Churchill, Sgt. William Brown, and Sgt. Daniel Bissell. All three of them served in the Continental Army out of Connecticut. Washington had ordered a badge of this type to be created a year earlier, and he designed the badge himself. A small, purple heart with the word "merit" in white letters across the face of it lay on a small patch of white silk. Washington determined that this special badge would be given based on "a singularly meritorious military action," and when worn by the recipient it would allow him to pass unimpeded through sentry lines without showing papers. After the Revolutionary War, the Badge of Military Merit was never issued again. It returned to favor at the anniversary of the creation of the award and on the bicentennial of George Washington's birth. The medal "resurfaced" with a new design and a new name: the Purple Heart.

Of the three original awards given out more than 225 years ago, the only one remaining of the original design can be seen at the National Purple Heart Hall of Honor. It was awarded to Sgt. Elijah Churchill. William Brown's badge, found discarded in an old barn in the 1920s, is now reported to be in the possession of the Society of the Cincinnati (New Hampshire). This badge does not have the word "merit" on the front. The medal that belonged to Sgt. Bissell was lost in a house fire in 1813.

The original Badge of Merit gets its own special place here at this museum. As you walk down a long corridor detailing the timeline of the badge and of military involvement in general, you come to a small glass cubicle in the wall. In it is Churchill's small, unremarkable-looking award. Of course the history of the medal is very remarkable indeed. Over time the rules for receiving it have changed, and we all know that today a military person must be wounded to be awarded the Purple Heart.

This museum is very interesting and really should appeal to all ages. It begins with a gripping fifteen-minute video on the history of the medal. You may then enter any number of tall bunker-like semiprivate kiosks situated in a large room. There you may sit and listen to stories recorded by actual Purple Heart recipients while a video montage plays just for you. The booths are evocative of a bunker, a ship, and an airplane.

While not a traditional museum, the Hall of Honor does have a museum feel to it. There are many exhibits, dioramas, displays, and video presentations, some of them graphic, about the horrors of war and the inspiring stories of those who fought on our behalf. The Hall of Honor hosts events and activities throughout the year, many with an educational focus for young people; others are for veterans and Purple Heart recipients.

The organization that runs this venue is actively seeking information about as many Purple Heart recipients as possible. It's a daunting task—nearly two million of the awards have been given—but the effort encourages a connection between those who come here and the award itself. Visitors are welcome to peruse the vast database compiled by the military and to submit names on their own for inclusion in the Purple Heart Hall of Honor. To date, over two hundred thousand have done so.

The facility is designed to conjure up the image of a farm or wilderness fort, and the building's subtle lines blend in perfectly with the bucolic countryside. The National Purple Heart Hall of Honor sits adjacent to the New Windsor Cantonment.

Other Nearby Attractions or Sites

The Continental Army spent the winter and spring of 1782 here. The New Windsor Cantonment was the last place that General Washington ever mustered his army. A veritable city grew up in the Hudson Valley pastureland as Washington marshaled nearly eight thousand soldiers, along with five hundred family members, to the forest adjacent to the Purple Heart Hall of Honor. Washington built a camp of six hundred buildings here, and it was from these grounds that he issued the cease fire order ending military hostilities in the Revolutionary War. When the word went out throughout the camp that the end of the war had been ordered, it is said that Washington's troops drained the immediate area of all of its rum supplies to toast the good news.

This last cantonment of the Colonial Army is now a New York State Historic Site. Among the existing buildings at the camp are a chapel and several log buildings resembling those constructed by Washington's army. It is believed that some of the stone walls that lace the forest were made of stones from the fireplaces of Continental Army residences.

The National Purple Heart Hall of Honor and the New Windsor Cantonment Historic Site share the property and can be explored during a single visit here.

An interesting side note to this chapter is that one of the first three original recipients of the award is buried in Upstate New York. Daniel Bissell is buried in Allen's Hill Cemetery in Richmond (Ontario County). On his tombstone are the words: "He had the confidence of Washington from whom he received the badge of Merit."

Essentials

What: The first Purple Heart

Where: National Purple Heart Hall of Honor, 374 Temple Hill Road, New Windsor; Orange County

Contact

National Purple Heart Hall of Honor: www.thepurpleheart.com; the Hall of Honor also hosts an active Facebook page. On this page they regularly feature stories submitted by readers about how they received their own Purple Hearts or they retell stories of those who have passed away. https://www.facebook.com/NationalPurpleHeartHallofHonor

New Windsor Cantonment State Historic Site: http://nysparks.com/historic-sites/22

Orange County history, travel, and events: www.orangetourism.org

72

Sing Sing Prison Museum

Ossining
Westchester County

Up the river to the Big House.

Sing Sing Prison was the third prison built in New York State. It followed an early New York City prison (Newgate) in Greenwich Village, in 1797, and Auburn Prison in 1816. By 1828, Newgate was closed. Auburn still operates at maximum capacity. Sing Sing also is still operational.

The oft-heard phrase "going up the river to the Big House" is a direct reference to New York City prisoners (in the post-Newgate era) being shipped the forty miles up the Hudson River to the stone-walled confines of Sing Sing. The maximum-security prison still holds anywhere between seventeen hundred and two thousand prisoners. Among the most famous jailbirds ever held behind the gun-turreted walls were the Cold War–era husband-and-wife spies Ethel and Julius Rosenberg, child rapist and professed cannibal Albert Fish, serial killer David Berkowitz (known as "The Son of Sam"), and notorious bank robber Willie Sutton.

Sing Sing was infamous for being the home of "Old Sparky," a well-used electric chair. On June 4, 1888, New York governor David Hill, faced with a growing public revulsion regarding death by hanging, ordered the construction of an electric chair to be used in carrying out death sentences. A quick, body-frying jolt of electricity was somehow deemed more politically correct than the many gruesome, botched hangings that had taken place previously. Old Sparky was first employed at Auburn State Prison on August 6, 1890, on convicted murderer William Kemmler. After this execution, the electric chair was moved to Sing Sing, where it was employed with great regularity.

Between 1890 and 1965 (when New York abolished the death penalty), Sing Sing electrocuted 614 prisoners. The oldest was a sixty-five-year-old man; the youngest was a twenty-seven-year-old woman. The last person to die in Old Sparky was murderer Eddie Lee Mays, thirty-four, who was put to death on August 15, 1963.

Several films make reference to this infamous prison, and one, *20,000 Years at Sing Sing*, starring Spencer Tracy and Bette Davis, had several scenes filmed here (1932).

There has been a call to establish a Sing Sing Prison Museum for many years. Plans have been started and aborted for using existing unused parts of the actual prison to host the museum. While these plans were being discussed, an organization was formed to create a "temporary" museum in Ossining to tell the story, albeit it a grim one, of the city's most famous institution. From the outside, the Joseph G. Caputo Community Center looks like a hundred other anonymous, low-slung, windowless brick public venues. All sorts of Ossining groups avail themselves of this multi-use public building, from seniors to government agencies.

Inside, however, is a real find for museums hunters.

The Sing Sing Museum sits in its own little wing. It is small and well lit, and it has an interesting array of original prison artifacts and provides many informative stories about Sing Sing. Among the most surprising are two prison cells. The steel-and-cement iron-barred "suites" give you an immediate sense of the dreariness and monotony of life in "the Big House." Each cell is only three feet wide and seven feet deep. There is a commode, a sink, a tiny table, and a bed, which is really nothing more than a cot. One cell is left open so you can enter and feel its claustrophobic nature (and also take that special goofy selfie of you posing in a prison bed!).

Other parts of this minimuseum display various other means of punishment meted out at the prison. These included the "cat-o-nine tails," a barbed whip that was used to lash prisoners across the back. The heyday of the "cat" was 1843, when Sing Sing prisoners received a whopping three thousand lashes in less than one year. The "Iron Cage" was a cumbersome, heavy iron cage that was fitted and then locked around the prisoner's head, to be worn day and night for three days at a time. The ball and chain was a common punishment in which an inmate had to drag around a solid iron cannonball attached to his leg. And the ghastliest of all was the "shower bath." In this early form of waterboarding, the prisoner was placed in a chair, gagged, and then doused with water to the point of near drowning. Again, the heyday for this torture was in 1860, when 161 shower baths were given to the unruliest prisoners.

Of course the pièce de résistance in this museum is Old Sparky. Well, not the original electric chair, but an exact replica fashioned by prison inmates many years ago. The inmates created this electric chair by following the engineering specs of the actual first chair ever built back in 1888. In fact, the designers patented blueprints are framed on the wall over the chair.

This chair is made of solid oak. It has a metal cap that was screwed down onto the prisoner's skull and heavy leather straps to hold him in place. Foot holes anchored the inmate's feet. It is an eerie sight that will make even the unqueasy, um, well . . . queasy.

The museum, which has no admission charge, is unattended, so your questions, and there are sure to be many, will go unanswered. However, the Sing Sing Museum provides a rare glimpse inside the walls of one of America's most infamous prisons, and it is a stop that you should put on your itinerary the next time you are visiting the lower Hudson Valley.

Other Nearby Attractions or Sites

The prison itself is located just a mile from the museum. It sits along a beautiful Hudson River shoreline near the Ossining train station. There is not a lot to see (unless you are there to visit an inmate, of course), but you will again have a tremendous sense of foreboding just being close to the armed guards along the wall, the turreted security towers at each corner, the miles of shiny razor wire encircling the prison like a demonic Slinky gone wild, and the security checkpoints at the entrance.

The most jarring sight of all? A children's playground outside the prison walls with an armed guard tower right in the middle of the play area.

Essentials

What: The Sing Sing Prison Museum

Where: 95 Broadway, Ossining; Westchester County

Contact

Sing Sing Prison Museum: www.facebook.com/singsingmuseum

Ossining history, tourism, and events: www.villageofossining.org

73

The Shandaken Eagle

Phoenicia
Ulster County

On the wings of eagles.

The original Grand Central Station was a magnificent, massive Beaux Arts structure built by William Vanderbilt to usher in the era of mass rail transportation to the city of New York. The structure, taking up an entire city block, was torn down in 1910 to make room for an even larger, newer Grand Central Station. Among the most exquisite of the building's architectural signatures were large, iconic cast-iron eagles.

These dozen eagles were situated at each of the four corners of the railroad terminal "guarding" the comings and goings of the thousands of passengers on the street below. Three eagles were stationed around each clock tower, twelve in all. When the demolition of the original building began, there was quite a conundrum about the future of the famous eagles. Who would want these monstrosities? Each weighed in at more than two tons, and the eagles' wingspans of thirteen feet made them a particular tricky item to sell or give away.

Eventually William Vanderbilt took one out to his mansion at Centerport, Long Island, where it still is today. Over the years there has been a curious scavenger hunt to find the other eagles. Nine of the original twelve can be located. Most are situated along the Hudson River Valley, and most are in private hands.

"A guy named David McLane, who was a photographer for the *New York Daily News*, bought one of the eagles for a hundred bucks," said Rick Ricciardella. He is the longtime water commissioner and has been a local realtor in Phoenicia for more than a half-century. "This guy kept that big old eagle in his backyard for years. Finally he donated it to our community when he moved here. Best hundred dollars he ever spent. We held a big parade and all kinds of hoopla when the eagle arrived," he told me.

Dubbed the Shandaken Eagle (Phoenicia is in the town of Shandaken), the magnificent bird was refurbished and given a brand new shiny bronze covering by Dakin Morehouse, owner of the Phoenicia Forge Arts Center. Townsfolk donated items and memorabilia to be put in a time capsule that was buried at the base of the eagle when it was dedicated (the time capsule is to be opened in 2076). Not everybody was happy to see this gigantic bronze eagle as the new welcome sign for Phoenicia.

"Myself, I thought we don't need something from New York City to tell people about our little Catskill Mountain village. I just thought it didn't fit. But I have mellowed and like everybody else now, I have a soft spot in my heart for 'our bird,'" Ricciardella told me.

New York State Rt. 28, which goes from the Adirondacks through the Catskills, has more than its share of oddities along the way. You will see everything from a life-sized dollhouse to a seven-foot Indian along the way, but the Shandaken Eagle is no tourist-trap attraction. It sits proudly on a large boulder with beautiful landscaping surrounding its base. Red, white, and blue bunting drapes the base of the eagle. A tall American flag waves from a pole next to it. It is impossible to pass it without a second look. A historical plaque tells of the bird's flight from Grand Central Station to the Catskills. It reads "The Shandaken Eagle, dedicated on August 23rd, 1986. This sculpture originally stood high atop one of the towers of Grand Central Station in New York City at the turn of the century. Initially coated with white cement this cast iron eagle was restored with a bronze surface at the Phoenicia Forge. The eagle was donated to the people of the Town of Shandaken by David and Gilbert McLane."

"I get people all the time stopping in to my real estate office asking about the eagle. Our town is now more than 60 percent second-home owners. Lots of people from the city come here. There are more movie stars and television stars in Phoenicia at any given time than you can shake a stick at. And they all make the turn off the main highway at our big eagle. It's kind of neat," he said.

I asked him if celebrity sightings are kind of a game with all the tourists and locals in the area.

"No sir, not a game. They just come. They can't help it. Why just two days ago Vice President Joe Biden was down the road a mile attending his nephew's wedding. There were Secret Service agents everywhere. And yesterday he attended mass at our little Catholic church. My wife sat right next to him," he laughed.

Phoenicia has no more than five hundred permanent residents at any one time. Of course, the number swells in the summer when the vacationers arrive. The main street is lined with interesting shops and restaurants (several are owned by Ricciardella's family). On the day I was there, the town was full of out-of-state license plates, families, aging hippies, and stroller-pushing soccer moms. You'd never know that just two years ago this town was almost wiped out.

"Hurricane Irene and Tropical Storm Lee. Two thousand eleven, boy, that was a bad year. We almost lost it all. The Esopus Creek came pouring down Main Street, wiping out everything. We were without power for days. We lost forty-four homes and eight bridges. Yessir, that was a bad one," he sighed.

I asked him if the Shandaken Eagle was damaged. "Nope, she stood tall through it all," he smiled.

Other Nearby Attractions or Sites

Phoenicia would make an excellent day trip if you are a resident of New York City (ninety miles to the south) or central New York. Outdoor activities are plentiful here. One favorite pastime seems to be river tubing. A bus labeled the "Tube Taxi" can be seen roaming the hamlet's streets picking up happy vacationers heading down to the bubbling Esopus Creek.

I had a delicious meal at a tastefully decorated restaurant on Main Street, and there were shops selling everything from fine art to old books and vinyl records. A must-see is the Mystery Spot. This too is a Main Street landmark. You can't miss it. A ten-foot tall statue of Davy Crockett stands out front.

The shop has everything from hundreds of old *TV Guide* magazines, to vintage mink coats, Catskill souvenir bric-a-brac, folk art, retro furniture, and other odds and ends. The full name of the shop is Homer and Langley's Mystery Spot. The name conjures up the images of the infamous brothers Homer and Langley Collyer, America's best-known hoarders, who died in their New York City home surrounded by tons of junk in 1947.

If you visit the Mystery Spot (and you should), be on the lookout for the ashes of 1940s screen siren Veronica Lake. Rumor has it that owner Laura Levine has the actress's ashes and they are enshrined here in a display with a Veronica Lake "peek-a-boo" cookie in it!

Essentials

What: The Shandaken Eagle

Where: Phoenicia, town of Shandaken, Rt. 28 at County Rt. 214; Ulster County

Contact

Town of Shandaken history: www.shandakan.us

Rick Ricciardella (water commissioner and local realtor): www.ricciardellarealty.com

The Mystery Spot: www.lauralevine.com

Book about the eagle sculptures: *The Cast Iron Eagles of Grand Central Station*, by David Morrison (self-published, yet it is the definitive work on the statues and the hunt to find their current whereabouts)

Water tubing: The largest company to provide whitewater tubing on the Esopus in Phoenicia is Tinker Town Tube Rental, and they are the ones with the ubiquitous Tube Taxi; www.towntinker.com.

74

The Orchards of Concklin

Pomona
Rockland County

America's oldest family fruit farm.

Pomona is named after the Goddess of Fruit. They have been worshipping that goddess here at the orchards of Concklin for more than three hundred years. Eleven generations. Of the same family.

Nicholas Concklin first came to this area in 1711. He docked his boat in the Hudson River and walked inland until he found a suitable place to start a farm. He bought about four hundred acres of land here from the Kakiat patent, which covered the land in this area all the way to New Jersey. Concklin purchased lot number one, and his family has been farming on the property ever since.

The Orchards of Concklin is a full-service fruit farm. Outside are acres of orchards and u-pick fields, which swarm with visitors during the harvest season. Inside the large store are displays of hundreds of the finest fruits of the Concklin family's labors. Rows of shiny red apples, fruits of all sorts, homemade pies, and jellies and jams all line the walls mirrored in shiny produce cases. Candy is sold by the pound, and a bakery produces some of sweetest-tasting pies and cookies in the Hudson Valley. During the fall, cars are parked all along the highway as throngs come to pick from the thousands of pumpkins available and to taste some homemade cider donuts and cider pressed on the orchard grounds. A harvest festival featuring orchard fruit, pies, family fun, live music, and local barbecue is a highly anticipated event in the Pomona area.

To fully grasp of the age and lineage of the Orchards of Concklin one must make a brief stop just inside the front door. Here you will see many framed items and historical documents attesting to the eleven generations of the same family who have farmed this area since 1711. Old photographs, maps, legal papers, newspaper articles, and even some ancient indenture and survey documents confirm that this is the oldest continuously operating fruit farm in America . . . and all run by the same family!

Eleven generations and still going strong. You do the math. This is an awesome place.

Other Nearby Attractions or Sites

Haverstraw is a village of about eleven thousand residents. It is just five miles east of Pomona and has played a significant role in local and national history. One of the most infamous acts of treason in American history took place here during the American Revolution when Gen. Benedict Arnold and British Maj. John André concocted a plot to surrender West Point to the British in Haverstraw, in a house that still stands today known as the Treason House.

"Haverstraw" is Dutch for "oat straw," the long, grassy straw-like vegetation that grows along the village's Hudson River waterfront. The riverbed also produced rich yellow, blue, and red clay suitable for making bricks.

For many years Haverstraw was known as "The Brick-Making Capital of the United States." In 1910, there were more than thirty brick manufacturing factories in Haverstraw, making that industry by far the village's biggest employer. The bricks were taken by river to New York City to be used in the building boom of the early twentieth century. At its peak, the Haverstraw brick companies were making more than three hundred million bricks a year.

Today, many fine brick homes and public buildings can still be seen in the historic district of Haverstraw. A Brick Museum tells the story of the village's glory days as the brick center of the nation. A wall of bricks doesn't sound like the sexiest exhibit in the world, but when you see row after row after row of handmade bricks, each stamped with the name of a different brick manufacturer, you come to understand the importance of this niche industry to Haverstraw.

Just north of Haverstraw is Stony Point Battlefield Park. It was here on July 16, 1779, that American general Anthony Wayne carried out a daring attack on an entrenched British position. His actions in leading his men to victory led to the general's nickname, "Mad Anthony" Wayne.

Essentials

What: The oldest family fruit farm in America

Where: 2 South Mountain Road, Pomona; Rockland County

Contact

Orchards of Concklin: www.orchardsofconcklin.com

Haverstraw Brick Museum: www.haverstrawbrickmuseum.org

Stony Point Battlefield State Historic Site: http://nysparks.com/historic-sites/8

75

Walkway Over the Hudson

Highland and Poughkeepsie
Ulster and Dutchess Counties

A walk in the clouds.

There is simply nothing quite like it in the world.

It is called the "Walkway over the Hudson," but it might be more aptly named the "Miracle over the Hudson." Until 1924, you could only get across the Hudson River (other than by boat) at one place, the railroad trestle between Highland and Poughkeepsie. It was the only river crossing between New York City and Albany until the Bear Mountain Bridge was built in 1924.

The railroad ceased running in the area in May, 1978, and the bridge lay dormant and rusting for decades until the idea to turn it into a foot-bridge surfaced in 1998. After a massive campaign to raise millions of dollars, construction on the Walkway began on September 5, 2000. Nine years later, on October 3, 2009, hundreds marched from one side of the Hudson to the other, some 212 feet above the water.

Crossing this skyway in the clouds is an unforgettable experience. On any given day, including those freezing, windswept days of winter, any number of strollers, runners, and bikers can be found absorbing the mind-bending effects of being so safe so high above the ground. The Walkway is very easy and level to walk, restrooms are provided at either end, and places to sit dot the entire 1.2-mile length of the walk. The views are spectacular. I have strolled the Walkway in the fall when the rolling hills on either side of the Hudson look as if someone gently laid a colorful crazy quilt over the landscape. The colors are that vibrant. In winter, with the ice narrowing the flow of the Hudson and with the puffs of smoke coming from a hundred smokestacks in Poughkeepsie, it is easy to think you are in a Currier and Ives painting. In the summer, both sides of the river are lined with lush green forests.

An amazing show takes place far below. Small pleasure craft dart up and down, sending up flumes of white spray. Massive, slow-churning freighters slowly creep from the docks of New York City to the Port of Albany, carrying everything from oil to cars to giant spider-leg windmill blades for the wind farms of the North Country. Amtrak zips along the east bank of the river. In October, thousands line the bridge to enjoy the fall foliage vistas.

As you stroll with your family on a bright summer day across the Walkway, it is hard to remember that you are actually traversing a mon-umental engineering achievement. The statistics on the creation of the pedestrian bridge are incredible: forty million dollars; twenty thousand tons of steel; a million iron rivets; forty thousand tons of stone, timber and concrete; and 973 prefabricated steel plates, each weighing fifteen tons, hold the whole project up. On select nights you can walk over the bridge in darkness aided by eighty thousand LED illuminators.

With so much time, energy and fortune wrapped up in this one-of-a-kind project, there was some consternation as to whether it would be a success. The Walkway welcomed its one millionth visitor on July 4, 2011, and it is expected to generate over twenty million dollars annually for the local economic base.

Because of the nature of its flat open surface, the Walkway is a natural place for gatherings and events of all kinds. Among the celebrations on the bridge are fireworks on July Fourth, a visit with Santa on the bridge, nighttime moonwalks, road races, and more. One of the most popular revolving events is the flag-changing ceremony. Frequently, the flag in the center of the bridge, which marks the boundary between Ulster and Dutchess Counties, is changed, with specific flags being flown in honor of a veteran or organization. Events (which must be scheduled far in advance) can range from a gala fundraiser attended by thousands to an intimate wedding ceremony held on the bridge itself.

The year 2000 saw the inaugural running of the Walkway Marathon, which attracted over fifteen hundred runners.

Guided tours of the bridge are very popular and need to be scheduled at least two months in advance. "Walkway ambassadors" narrate the history of the pedestrian pathway, its construction, and the dynamics of producing this historic venue.

The Walkway over the Hudson pedestrian bridge runs parallel to the Poughkeepsie Mid-Hudson Bridge. This bridge is now officially called the Franklin D. Roosevelt Mid-Hudson Bridge, as both the then-governor and Mrs. Roosevelt attended the bridge's ribbon-cutting ceremony on August 25, 1930.

Now an official New York State park, the pedestrian bridge has been named to the National Registry of Historic Places and is considered an International Civil Engineering Landmark. From its humble beginnings as the very first bridge in the valley to go over the Hudson River in 1889, to its current position as the most beautiful skyway path in the world, the Walkway over the Hudson is nothing short of a miracle.

And, it is free!

Other Nearby Attractions or Sites

You can enter the Walkway from the west in Highland (Ulster County) or from Poughkeepsie in the east (Dutchess County). The Highland entranceway is still a work in progress, although it is complete as an entrance to the bridge. There just is not a lot else to do on the western side of the Walkway. At the entrance to the Poughkeepsie side, you will find refreshment kiosks, a large paved parking area, an elevator to the street below, and easy access via an attractive stone staircase to the business neighborhood below. There you are within walking distance of several nice cafés, pubs, and restaurants.

Essentials

What: The longest pedestrian bridge in the world

Where: Walkway over the Hudson State Park, Highland and Poughkeepsie; Ulster and Dutchess Counties

Contact

Walkway over the Hudson: www.walkway.org

76

Pratt Rock

Prattsville
Greene County

America's first Civil War monument.

When Zadock Pratt rededicated his famous sculpture monument to his son, Colonel George Watson Pratt (1830–1862), who was killed at the Battle of Bull Run, he probably did not realize that he had just created the first Civil War memorial in the United States.

And that is the least of the historical milestones associated with this amazing landmark in Greene County. Zadock Pratt (1790–1871) was one of the most influential men of his era in Upstate New York. He was financier, soldier, politician, builder, and the founder of the largest tannery in the world. He basically built Prattsville from the ground up. He was one of the early great entrepreneurs of the Empire State and created one of its most important new wilderness towns.

"Zadock Pratt was a brilliant, creative man," Carolyn Bennett, director of the Pratt Museum, told me. "He was always on the go, always looking forward, always expanding. After he created the most modern town in the wilderness, he wanted people to come and visit it. So he built hotels, businesses, parks, and, yes, even Pratt Rock."

As you enter the village of Prattsville from the south on Rt. 23 you see a large sign saying "Pratt Rock" on your right. Looks can be deceiving. It looks like just a simple, shady place to rest and picnic. A small parking pull-off allows you to stop and explore. But what you will find after taking a well-marked half-hour hike, is something you will not soon forget.

At the top of the hill you come upon a large clearing faced with towering walls of solid rock. At first, the curious carvings dotting this canyon wall seem unintelligible and confusing. But once you know the story of Zadock Pratt, it all becomes quite clear.

"Pratt and five other itinerant stone carvers spent years creating elaborate stone carvings on the rock face, basically depicting Zadock's life. You will see horses, which were important in his logging business, hemlock trees, which were the source of his famous tannery, an arm with a chisel, and many other carvings designed to entertain his guests. He even scrawled his name in giant letters for all to see: 'Zadock Pratt, Born October 10, 1790.'"

There is also a life-sized bust of his son, Col. Pratt, carved on the mountainside. He led the 20th New York State Militia during the Civil War; their motto was "This Hand for Our Country." Perhaps in a fog of sadness, Zadock carved this motto near his son's likeness, but he changed it to read, "This Hand for My Country."

It has recently been discovered that Pratt actually terraced the ground around his stone monument.

"We believe this to be one of the earliest examples of an Eastern-style terraced public garden in the state. Perhaps Mr. Pratt brought this concept back with him from one of his trips to Korea. He was an inveterate world traveler, and always brought something home with him from his trips, whether it be an item or an idea."

Robert Ripley, of Believe it or Not fame, came to Pratt Rock once and declared it "New York's Mount Rushmore."

"I find that a little humorous," Bennett told me. "Since Pratt Rock predates Mount Rushmore by nearly a century, I think it would be more appropriate to call Mount Rushmore 'America's Pratt Rock.'"

Thousands of visitors have climbed the sloping trail to wonder at this array of carvings and take in the amazing panorama of the valley alley below. But still, not many know the story of Zadock Pratt the man.

"Our mission at the Pratt Museum is to try and entice those visitors to come up to the museum after they have visited Pratt Rock. Here, we can really fill out the story of this truly remarkable American. Pratt built his rock monument to be a pleasure park. It was definitely innovative. His pleasure park even predated New York's Central Park by several years. He made it very accessible to all ages. It is safe and beautiful but definitely in the wilds. I think some people think they are going to see lions and tigers and bears along the trail. But that isn't the case. Pratt loved his park and actually planned on being buried among his carved walls when he died. He had finished his tomb but found that rain water crept in through the porous rocks and the idea of a soggy coffin really ended that decision for him. So he is instead buried in the lower cemetery along the Schoharie Creek. In the custom of the old days, the largest grave stone in a cemetery was usually saved for the most important person in town. You can be assured that Zadock's is by far the largest grave in that cemetery," Bennett said with a smile.

Prattsville is a spunky little community that has certainly dealt with its share of disasters. None was more horrific than Hurricane Irene, which just about capsized the town in August 2011. Governor Andrew Cuomo declared that no other community in New York State was as heavily damaged as Zadock Pratt's pride and joy. Virtually every structure in Prattsville was destroyed or severely damaged. Even the Pratt Museum, housed in the founder's original residence, was heavily damaged.

"Many of us in the community are trying to revert back to the pre-flood days as we think about the future of Prattsville. We continue to look forward, much like our founder did many years ago," she told me. "Prattsville is back and open for business. We hope everybody comes and hears the story of Pratt Rock and the incredible man who created it."

Other Nearby Attractions or Sites

A ten-mile side trip on Rt. 23 will bring you to the beautiful little Catskill community of Windham. This is a ski town and it is bustling in the winters and sleepy and relaxing in the summer. The main street is dotted with small markets, coffee shops, and pubs. Windham Mountain has fifty-two trails and includes slopes for all skill levels plus night skiing. It is one of the oldest ski resorts in New York State, opening in 1960. The picturesque village was also devastated by Hurricane Irene when over ten inches of rain fell on the small downtown area in less than six hours.

Essentials

What: Pratt Rock

Where: Prattsville, NYS Rt. 23; Greene County

Contact

Pratt Rock: www.greatnortherncatskills.com

Pratt Museum: https://www.facebook.com/pages/Zadock-Pratt-Museum/2610 92762203

Prattsville history: http://www.gchistory.org/prattsvillehistorichomes

Windham history: www.townofwindham.com

Ski Windham: www.windhammountain.com

77

Crailo State Historic Site

Rensselaer
Rensselaer County

The birthplace of "Yankee Doodle Dandy."

"Crailo" is one amazing, and very old, home.

It was originally owned by the Van Rensselaer patroon family. This was Hendrick Van Rensselaer's homestead, and it came with a nice brick house, some beautiful Hudson River waterfront, and just shy of sixty-two thousand acres. The old Dutch land barons didn't mess around when it came to owning property. Hendrick's grandfather, the legendary Kiliaen Van Rensselaer, owned more than a thousand *square miles* of early New York State.

The present day house dates back to 1707, but the foundation was actually laid in around 1640.

"The first impression I get from visitors here is about the age of the building," Geoff Benton told me. Geoff is the assistant site manager of the Crailo State Historic Site. "Not many people can get it into their heads when they come upon things that are more than two hundred years old around here. They say, 'I've lived here all my life and never even knew this place was here.' The Van Rensselaers actually lived in this house through the mid-1800s. After that came a period of neglect and deterioration, which continued until New York State bought it for preservation in 1928. They closed it immediately, spent several years repairing and renovating it, and then opened it up to the public again around 1935."

The interior of the home is a beautiful reimagining of life in a Dutch home back in the days when the area was still called New Netherlands, and Albany, almost directly across the river from the home, was still called Fort Orange.

"Yes, the renovation was pretty remarkable," Benton said. "The state worked with the D.A.R. and the S.A.R. and other historic organizations to locate and bring to the house rare and unique items reflecting the historic nature of the home. Although most of the items are not original to the Van Rensselaer family, they do tell a great story of the centuries over which they lived here. Our rarest item is a child's cradle made in the Hudson Valley in around 1700. It is hand carved, and still has the original paint on it. The headboard is painted with a tulip motif and the footboard is a biblical-themed painting of the Good Samaritan story. This one little item has been featured in many of the major antique and American furniture magazines."

The Yankee Doodle Dandy story is just one of the many historical anecdotes told within the ancient walls of Crailo House.

"Yes, it is a charming story," Benton began. "In 1758, during the French and Indian War, a British surgeon named Dr. Richard Shuckburgh crossed the river from Albany to have dinner with the Van Rensselaers at what was then called Fort Crailo. At the time, General James Abercrombie was preparing his troops for an assault on Fort Ticonderoga. While waiting for the Van Rensselaers to arrive, the surgeon sat on an old stone well, smoking his pipe, and watched with amusement as a large contingent of ragtag ruffian New England soldiers arrived at the training camp. Shuckburgh thought the sight of these bumpkin Colonial soldiers humorous and he scratched out a derisive ode that became 'Yankee Doodle Dandy.' It was later put to a melody, called 'Polly Lost Her Pocket,' and the song grew in popularity. Of course today every American knows the song by heart."

I told the site manager that it must be a great surprise to the visitors and tourists to find out that such a well-known and beloved patriotic ditty began right here.

"Around 1880, during the first attempt to save Crailo from destruction, the powers that be decided that using this patriotic hook was a good way to raise donations for the preservation of the home. That is when the site really started to highlight its association with the song. And it worked. People love the story and we love to tell it. When we conduct a guided tour of the home we never mention the 'Yankee Doodle Dandy' connection until the end. After a tour of the mansion we exit out the rear door to show our guests the beautiful gardens. It is here, at the very well where Dr. Shuckburgh sat smoking his pipe, that we retell the story of the song's beginning."

I told Benton that this must be quite a dramatic highlight of the tour.

"Oh, definitely," he laughed. "Especially the school groups. I usually ask the kids if they have ever heard of the song. Of course they say yes and then begin to sing it. After, I tell them that they are standing on the very spot where the song was written. They all gasp and get excited. It is fun to watch their reaction."

I asked Benton if there were any other places around the country that claim to be the birthplace of the song.

"There are a few. Nobody really knows for sure. But we have the most proof. We have papers and documents that a Dr. Richard Shuckburgh was actually at Crailo at the very time General Abercrombie was here training his troops, and the ditty became well known at that very time. So unless anybody else can prove otherwise, we feel quite confident that Crailo House is in fact the birthplace of 'Yankee Doodle Dandy.' "

Other Nearby Attractions or Sites

A wonderful side trip from Crailo awaits just over the bridge in downtown Albany. Here, the Dutch Apple cruise ship is docked along the waterfront. The ship provides entertaining and informative Hudson River cruises seasonally. A narrator describes the scenery, homes, and wildlife habitats along the Hudson.

The ship itself has three decks, two of them covered, and is modeled after the Hudson River dayliners that traveled the river in the nineteenth century. This cruise gives you a wonderful view of Crailo from the water. There is a lot of history in this area around Albany, Rensselaer, and the little towns and villages along the Hudson. It is a fun, relaxing, and fascinating way to spend a warm summer afternoon. And you may even see a bald eagle or two along the way!

You can't miss the *Dutch Apple* dock. It is located right next to the World War II destroyer escort, the *Slater*. This warship is the last of its kind still afloat in the United States.

Essentials

What: The birthplace of "Yankee Doodle Dandy"

Where: Crailo State Historic Site, 9 Riverside Avenue, Rensselaer; Rensselaer County

Contact

Crailo State Historic Site: http://parks.ny.gov/historic-sites/30/details.aspx

Dutch Apple Cruise: www.dutchapplecruises.com

USS *Slater*: www.ussslater.org

78

Revolutionary War Cemetery

Salem
Washington County

The old burying ground.

Salem is a small community of less than three thousand residents tucked away in the bucolic corner of Washington County. It lies twenty miles east of the Saratoga battlefield. The cemetery here, the Old Burying Ground, is known by all as simply the Revolutionary War cemetery. It is a solemn, beautiful, and eternally sad place. It has, perhaps, more Revolutionary War dead than any other cemetery in the state.

I have visited many cemeteries across Upstate New York, but none like this one. You enter on foot between two large columns. There is a wider entrance that was originally used by carriages and hearses bringing in the deceased. You are first struck by the sight of an unusual pattern of undulating, grass-covered mounds throughout the almost three acres. Not just "bumps" in the landscape, but actual mounds of earth. Pressed into these mounds are tombstones, many with their legends barely readable. These are mass graves containing the remains of entire early Salem families. It is also believed that many soldiers are buried in these mounds, the war dead from the Battle of Saratoga. As many as a hundred bodies were brought in through the carriage gate after the first day of battle alone and placed in one common grave or mound. No records were kept.

One historical reference says this possible mass burial was the work of the aptly named James Tomb. He was a teamster at the Battle of Saratoga, and he was responsible for removing the dead militiamen. He was from Salem and was familiar with the cemetery here, the only known burying ground within a day's drive of Saratoga.

What is known for sure is that of the 1,040 burial plots filled here since it opened in 1767, 101 are verifiably graves of Revolutionary War soldiers. With the assumption that at least a hundred others are buried in one of the common grave mounds, the total rises dramatically. Research has led to the placement of the Old Salem Burying Ground on the National Register of Historic Places (2003).

As you walk among the ancient stones, they seem to quietly call out to you. Intricate etchings, florid Biblical tributes, prose and poetry, and family histories can be made out on most of the still-readable stones. Many are carved in the unique rounded-angel head design of master carver Zerubbabel Collins (1733–1797). The Collins family of grave carvers was among the most famous in the Northeast, and examples of their work are prominent throughout Upstate New York, Connecticut, and Vermont.

341

The cemetery is surrounded by a slate stone wall. This is fitting, since this area of New York is rich with natural slate. In nearby Granville, in "Slate Valley," you can visit a museum that tells of the industriousness of the immigrant "slate farmers" who toiled in the back-breaking work of mining the slate, which may have been used for the very stones found here in Salem.

The earliest settlers of Salem came from the area around Ballybay, Ireland. Scotch-Irish soon populated the region, and it is believed that the tradition of burying descendants in "family mounds" may have been brought over with these settlers from the British Isles. There are many interesting examples of early cemetery traditions at this Revolutionary War cemetery. Soldiers were buried with their heads facing east as was the case in most cemeteries. Foot stones, a sure sign of an early New England cemetery, are plentiful. These tiny stones mark the length of the gravesite with the headstone at the top and the footstone at the bottom. Funerary art runs from carved angels to traditional signs of mourning such as trees and religious icons.

This hallowed resting place is worth a visit if for no other reason than the significant number of Revolutionary War burials. But the Old Burying Ground was operating before the war, and most of the graves are those of residents of Salem.

An interesting grave belongs to Joshua Conkey. His is a more modern, white stone (his original stone having been destroyed over the years). Conkey, a veteran of the French and Indian War, was captured and held by Indians during the Battle of the Snowshoes. In this battle Robert Rogers, the famous founder of Rogers's Rangers, engaged a much larger contingent of Indian fighters along the shores of Lake George. It was here that Rogers made his famous claim to have escaped capture by sliding nearly five hundred feet down a snow-and-ice-covered rock face to the safety of the frozen lake below. Conkey is buried here alongside his wife, Dinah, who accompanied him later in the Battle of Bennington. It is told that she baked bread for the soldiers as the battle raged around her.

Margaret Telford was known as "The Witch of Salem"—not to be confused with the other Salem, in Massachusetts, with their witch hysteria of a century earlier. Mrs. Telford was a curious citizen of Salem, N.Y. who became the center of a witch controversy that followed her to the end of her life. Although she was not strung up from a tree up on Gallows Road just outside of town, she bore the brunt of the town's scorn until she died in 1807. Her accusers, perhaps caught up in the tense environment of a war taking place just outside the village limits, challenged her in a public setting to answer the charges of witchcraft that had been leveled against her. She outlived many of her accusers and remained in Salem despite her public humiliation.

Her crime? A neighboring farmer accused her of casting a witch's spell on his cows causing them to produce cream that could not be churned into butter.

Like I said, this is a fascinating cemetery for many different reasons.

Other Nearby Attractions or Sites

At one time virtually every town in Upstate New York claimed a covered bridge of its own. There were hundreds of them. Today, only twenty-nine remain. Astonishingly, four of them are just minutes from Salem. The Buskirk, Eagleville, and Rexleigh covered bridges are all located within a fifteen-minute drive of Salem. An interesting side trip, however, would be to the Shusan Covered Bridge Museum. Here, just seven miles south of the Revolutionary cemetery in Salem, you will find a wonderful 1858 Town lattice-style plank truss bridge. It was closed to traffic in the 1960s and fell into disrepair. Eventually this majestic 161-foot span was saved by the Shusan Covered Bridge Association, which bought it, renovated it, and turned it into a museum dedicated to the "Bridges of Washington County."

Essentials

What: Revolutionary War cemetery (old burying ground)

Where: Salem, Rt. 22; Washington County

Contact

Salem Revolutionary War Cemetery: www.salem-ny.com/revcem

New York State Covered Bridges: This website has locations and descriptions of all four of the covered bridges in Washington County; www.coveredbridgesite.com/ny

79

Saratoga Race Course

Saratoga Springs
Saratoga County

The oldest sporting venue in America.

No name is as synonymous with a particular sport as Saratoga is with horse racing. The whole city of Saratoga Springs (population under thirty thousand) acts as a welcoming committee for the race track. They hold festivals, street parties, galas, and other significant events both at the track and on the busy streets of the city.

The race track is a hulking yet graceful ancient structure on the edge of downtown. Several of the original design flourishes still exist today, including the spikey spires that give it its famous profile, and the enormous wooden grandstand. The track can hold more than fifty thousand visitors at once and plays host to several key races in the annual schedule for American thoroughbreds. There are more than two hundred buildings on the vast campus of Saratoga Race Course, with several of them original to its founding in 1863.

Marylou Whitney, "The Queen of Saratoga," is the widow of Cornelius Vanderbilt "Sonny" Whitney. She has left her dainty imprint all over the Saratoga racing season. She inherited tens of millions of dollars on the death of Mr. Whitney, who was one of the most famous racing advocates of his era, and she is the dominant force for good, both as the leading socialite in the Saratoga region and as a benevolent philanthropist to various causes both local and national. She married John Hendrickson in 1997, and today they split their time among many residences, including their 130-acre Saratoga estate, Cady Hill. Yes, it is grand, and yes, it is opulent. But it is still one of the smallest of her residences She also owns one of the Adirondack's legendary "Great Camps," and that abode clocks in at more than 150,000 acres!

The Whitney Handicap, which is run every summer at Saratoga, is a lasting memorial to the Whitney family's long and illustrious love affair with thoroughbred racing. The race, along with the Travers, is the highlight of the season at Saratoga and always draw an SRO crowd. It is also the occasion for some of the wildest, most elaborate parties held in Upstate (Marylou, ever the daring, darling hostess, has been known to arrive at the parties in a hot air balloon, or in full costume regalia, accompanied by an equally costumed entourage). The Stakes offers a whopping purse of $1.5 million.

A day at this historic racetrack is always full of small, wonderful touches. Before each race, the horses are slowly walked directly through the immense crowd for a rare and thrilling up-close look at these beautiful behemoths. This is the only race course in the United States that allows this. Since Saratoga Springs was founded as a place for the rich and famous to visit and take a natural mineral water cure, it is no surprise that right in the middle of everything is the Big Red Spring. Fans are encouraged to enter the spring enclosure and sample some of Saratoga's "miracle" waters. The spring gets its name from two of racing's greatest champions, Secretariat and Man o' War. Both were magnificent chestnut thoroughbreds who were nicknamed "Big Red" by their legions of fans.

The spring is located in the sprawling picnic area, another unique feature of the race course. This area, known as the Backyard, is replete with more than a hundred picnic tables scattered underneath towering shade trees. Attached to these trees are numerous video screens to watch the races on. Outdoor parimutuel windows are everywhere for your convenience. This picnic area is a lively, popular place to set up camp on race day, and bringing in your own food and beverage (adult and otherwise) is a favorite tradition. A decades-old tradition of "covering the table" is all you need to do to hold or reserve your spot. So be sure and bring a tablecloth! Of course, there are formal and informal dining options available throughout the racetrack area, both inside and out.

Because the racing season is short at Saratoga, virtually every weekend is packed to the brim with spectators and race fans. On those special days when the track offers free handouts (hats, shirts, mugs, posters, blankets, etc.), the crowd can be a bit overwhelming. So get there early.

A day at the races in Saratoga is much more than just putting down a couple of bucks on a bet. It is about history, tradition, and long-lost elegance. You cannot help but be swept up in the grandeur and majesty of the place. Early in the day, you cover your table; later, you can reach out toward a massive thoroughbred loping through the crowd on the way to the race. A hand bell is rung precisely seventeen minutes before each race. After the thrilling end of the race, you can attend the photograph ceremony in the up-close-and-personal winner's circle. For the most part, they only race for one month here, so they mean it when they say, "Saratoga is the August place to be!"

And all of this for just five dollars admission!

Other Nearby Attractions or Sites

Saratoga Race Course is located on Union Street. This is a "street of millionaires," populated by some of the most magnificent Victorian homes in Upstate.

Across Union Avenue from the race track entrance is the National Museum of Racing and Hall of Fame. This is a great museum for all ages, especially for the racing fan. Videos, exhibits, statues, and racing memorabilia fill the floors and many rooms of the museum. Among the many familiar horses honored in the Hall of Fame are Man o' War, Seabiscuit, Seattle Slew, Whirlaway, Spectacular Bid, Kelso, and War Admiral.

The museum features dozens of priceless racing paintings as well as more than seventy sculptures.

Essentials

What: The oldest sporting venue in America

Where: Saratoga Race Course, 267 Union Avenue, Saratoga Springs; Saratoga County

Contact

Saratoga Race Course: www.saratogaracetrack.com

National Museum of Racing and Hall of Fame: www.racingmuseum.org

Saratoga Springs history, tourism, and events: www.saratoga.com

80

Wedgeway Barber Shop

Schenectady
Schenectady County

The oldest barber shop in New York State.

It is called the Wedgeway Barber Shop because the building started out as a wedge-shaped structure in downtown Schenectady along the Erie Canal.

"The Wedgeway was once the busiest building in downtown Schenectady," Richard DiCristofaro told me. He is the former owner and still the longest-working hair cutter at the Wedgeway Barber Shop. "I started here over a half-century ago, and just can't seem to get out of here," he laughed.

Today it is the oldest continuously operating barber shop in New York State. I asked DiCristofaro how he came to be a barber in the first place.

"I was in the Navy. Never cut a single hair in my life. I was on the USS *Sturdy*; it was the smallest minesweeper in the Pacific. A Filipino who cut the crew's hair quit, so they asked me to take over. And I have been snipping away ever since."

The Wedgeway opened its doors in 1912. A series of Italian barbers owned the shop over the next century. Great old names like Joe Vacca, Joey Cupo, and Patsy Gallo. And then DiCristofaro.

On my recent visit to the shop I remarked how busy it was, with each of the four barber chairs occupied and the waiting room full. "Yes, we stay busy. Some days are better than others. But you should have been here back in the old days, Chuck. In the 1950s and 1960s, oh boy! The big General Electric plant at the end of our street had nearly fifty thousand employees and on the other end the American Locomotive factory had almost five thousand. When we opened our doors at 8:00 a.m. there would already be a line going down the block waiting for a haircut. Oh, what a time that was," the barber said wistfully.

The barber shop was once in the same building as a major entertainment venue, and the famous Proctors Theater is right around the corner. So I asked him if any famous people came in for a haircut. "Well, we get a lot of famous people who come in all the time. Most are famous to those of us who live here. Political leaders, CEOS, and lots of lawyers. In fact this building once housed seventeen law offices. But I guess the most famous customer we ever had was Tom Mix, the Western movie star. I wasn't here at the time, but all the old-timers talked about it. Mix was appearing in the theater right behind us and he came into the shop, cowboy hat, boots, spurs, and all and got a haircut and a shave."

I commented that this must have brought a big crowd to the shop to see the star. "Well, yes it did. But the thing everybody really was amazed at was that Tom Mix even brought his horse, Tony, with him. Yessir, brought that big old horse right into the shop," DiCristofaro laughed.

I asked him why he has stayed at the shop for as long as he has.

"Well, I started here in 1957, and once I hit the fifty-year mark I sold the shop. I sold it to one of my own barbers, Dawn Taylor. But only after she agreed not to change things. I like the old traditions. I tried to stay away, but I just couldn't. So now I'm in here on a part-time basis still cutting hair a couple of days a week. I just really enjoy it. A famous golfer once was asked why he continued to golf every day at the same golf course. He said he never hit the same shot twice. I agree, only with me every head is different and every story I either hear or tell is different. I see four generations of customers from the same family now. This shop is a part of me. I love it."

The barber shop is exactly as you would imagine it. The old chairs, the big mirrors, gleaming porcelain sinks, the nostalgic newspaper articles on the wall. The cash register is the original one from 1912. In fact the keys only go up to a high of $9.99. "We finally hit the ceiling as far as the cash register goes," DiCristofaro said. "I like giving the penny back."

The twirling red, white, and blue barber pole out front is also the original one from 1912. "Back then it wasn't lit, and they had to start it up with a key. But it still works," he told me as we both looked out the window at the spinning relic.

In parting I asked him if, after well over a half-century in the same place, he would ever leave this old barber shop. His answer, like all of his answers to my inquiries, was direct and to the point. And funny.

"I can't leave. My working here supplements my losses on the golf course!"

At the time of the writing of this book, it is reported that the second-oldest barber shop in New York State is the Paul Mole Barber Shop on Lexington Avenue in Manhattan. It opened in 1913, a year later than the Wedgeway. And, here is one for you. Anthony Mancinelli was actually certified by the *Guinness Book of World Records* as the world's oldest active barber. Anthony, who works at the Anthony and Pasquale Mugnano barbershop in Vails Gate, was still cutting hair at the age of 104 as this book was being written!

Other Nearby Attractions or Sites

Downtown Schenectady is loaded with history. In fact, a historical marker across the street from the Wedgeway Barber Shop reads: "At this site Thomas Edison arrived in Schenectady, August 20 1886, to found his machine works, which in 1892 became the General Electric Company."

Proctors Theatre (two blocks from the barber shop) is one of Upstate's premier venues for live entertainment. It was built as a vaudeville palace by Frederick Freeman Proctor in 1926. In 2007 Proctors finished a $25 million dollar renovation and expansion. Today the theater can easily house the traveling shows of Broadway's biggest and most lavish musicals. Among its earliest acts were George Burns and Gracie Allen. The theater offers fascinating back stage tours of the premises and also has an in-house museum.

Essentials

What: The oldest barber shop in New York State

Where: 277 State Street, Schenectady; Schenectady County

Contact

Wedgeway Barber Shop: www.facebook.com/pages/Wedgeway-Barber-Shop

Proctors Theatre: www.proctors.org

81

The Stockade Indian Statue

Schenectady
Schenectady County

Lawrence the Indian.

The Stockade in Schenectady is one of the oldest neighborhoods in the country. It includes one of the largest single collections of Colonial homes found anywhere, with as many as forty houses in the neighborhood dating back over two centuries. As Schenectady's beginning footprint, the Stockade holds a wealth of history in just a few blocks. In 1962, the Stockade was made New York State's first local historic district.

And at the center of it all stands Lawrence.

"Yes, our statue is certainly an icon to all of us," Frank Gilmore told me. He is an architect who has worked in the Capital Region for over forty years. He is also a spokesman for the Schenectady County Historical Society.

"Many years ago, in the eighteenth century, lots of small towns wanted the elegance of statuary to commemorate something, anything that denoted the history of their community. But of course, many of these smaller towns and villages had little money for the expensive kind of statuary you would find in a city park. But several local foundries created a zinc covering which was poured over wood to preserve it and give a sculpture a three-dimensional appearance. The finished product would look like bronze and be quite impressive, even regal looking, and it was far less expensive than an actual bronze casting. Cigar-store Indians were a big industry for wood carvers, and that is really what our Lawrence started out to be. There are approximately twenty-four replicas of him around the nation, and many think the Indian referenced in the sculpture is the great Ottawa war chief, Pontiac."

It is believed the original designed was carved by Samuel Anderson Robb (1851–1928). The wooden sculpture was then purchased and recast by the J. L. Mott Iron Works Company of the Bronx, who sold copies of it from their catalog (identified only as Indian Chief No. 53) for five hundred dollars each.

"Our Lawrence is certainly one of the finest you will ever see. It serves as the historical centerpiece of our original Dutch outpost, the Stockade. It sits on a cast-iron base, and used to have water troughs around it to water horses from," Gilmore continued. "Even though the depiction is of a warrior, we believe the statue adds an element of quiet grace and dignity to our beautiful little corner of the city."

So was there really a Lawrence the Indian? The answer is yes. The village of Schenectady was already growing and becoming a busy trading center when in 1690 the stockade was attacked by French and Indian forces. The structures were destroyed and many of the residents were butchered. The marauders took twenty-seven men and boys with them as prisoners and force marched them back toward Canada through a brutal winter storm. Lawrence, a legendary figure and Christian Mohawk friend to all in the Stockade, tracked the attackers and rescued three of the men and boys and returned them to Schenectady. Later, he served as an advisor and supporter of the rebirth of the village. For this, many have referred to Lawrence as the "Savior of Schenectady."

The heroic statue of Lawrence, placed in the Stockade in 1887, is not only the physical heart of the Stockade but also its emotional heart. His image appears on every kind of bric-a-brac imaginable, from fine art prints to tchotchkes. Garden clubs keep the tiny park around his base well landscaped and colorful with seasonal plantings. One beloved, yet mysterious, tradition concerning Lawrence is the sudden appearance of flamingoes all around it on Valentine's Day. You know, those plastic flamingoes that are de rigueur in tacky suburbs across the land. For decades, a flamboyance of flamingos (yes, that is actually what a flock of these exotic pink birds is called) magically appears scattered around the grass at the base of the statue. When the sun goes down, the plastic birds disappear. Nobody professes to know exactly who is responsible for this tradition, but it is a cherished one, and many from throughout the city come to view this colorful, whimsical display.

If nothing else, Lawrence the Indian certainly is flamboyant!

Other Nearby Attractions or Sites

The Stockade is a great destination point when visiting the Capital District. Walking tours are available, and many historic buildings are open. The churches are awesome. The Stockade consists of winding, cobblestone streets not unlike those originally found in other historic cities such as Philadelphia, Boston, and parts of lower Manhattan. The neighborhood also sits right along the Mohawk River, which makes this neighborhood prone to frequent flooding.

There are several very interesting places to enjoy a meal or a drink in the Stockade. The Van Dyck is a venerable supper club, barroom, and jazz nightclub. It first opened its doors in 1947, and many entertainment luminaries have dined or entertained here, including Dizzy Gillespie, Dave Brubeck, Maynard Ferguson, and Thelonius Monk.

The elegant Stockade Inn is situated in one of the oldest buildings in the city. It was originally owned by Arendt Van Curler, the "Founder of Schenectady."

Clinton's Ditch is a newer tavern and restaurant that sits on the southerly edge of the Stockade. The owners have repurposed a couple of old buildings into a trendy multipurpose restaurant and popular bar that serves as a hub for Stockade social life. The business gets its name from the derisive epithet used to describe the Erie Canal when it was being built.

The Stockade is just a five-minute walk from the bustling downtown business district of Schenectady.

Essentials

What: Lawrence the Indian statue

Where: At the intersection of Front, Ferry, and Green Streets, Stockade, Schenectady; Schenectady County

Contact

The Historic Stockade: This website gives the history of the neighborhood, including the statue, and can give you tour information about events and other pertinent details for your visit here: http://historicstockade.com

The Van Dyck Lounge: www.vandycklounge.com

The Stockade Inn: www.stockadeinn.com

Clinton's Ditch: www.onefortheditch.com

82

The GE Sign

Schenectady
Schenectady County

The city (and sign) that lights the world.

It calls to you in an unmistakable manner. It draws you into a twenty-first-century city and pulls you back to the dawn of the electric age. It makes you smile. It's an old friend.

Since May of 1926, the towering GE sign has been the signature landmark of the "Electric City." It soars two stories above one of the largest headquarter buildings in Upstate New York at the General Electric complex in downtown Schenectady.

The sign is Ripley's Believe It or Not in size. It contains 1,399 light bulbs, and each of the two letters reaches up more than ten feet. The electric script signature is 40 feet across and the whole sign stretches for almost 170 feet. Amazingly, the sign, which can be read clearly from over a mile away, is lit with just twenty-five-watt bulbs. Hundreds of them. They are all put in at the same time, and when they all start to dim together, it takes a crew a full day to replace them all. Studies are under way about replacing the old-fashioned light bulbs with LED lighting to save cost and maintenance time.

The electric icon is one of the largest lit signs of its type in the country. The company, and the city of Schenectady, look at it as something of a playful cultural calling card. While on most nights the GE sign is a brilliant white, sometimes a touch of creativity is employed. During the Christmas season the bulbs are changed to red and green to kick off the holiday festivities. On the Fourth of July and September 11,the colors are those of the American flag. There have been times when the sign was completely dark, too. No lights blazed during the energy crisis of the 1970s, and the sign was blacked out for the duration of World War II. Obviously, the General Electric factory would have made a prime target for any enemy aircraft.

The sign was placed on the National Register of Historic Places in 1976.

General Electric was by far the largest employer in Schenectady for decades, and so the city with civic pride called itself "The City That Lights the World." As economic crunches came and went, so the fortunes of Schenectady's manufacturing plant ebbed and flowed. Thousands of jobs left the city over time as the company went on a national and international search for cheaper work forces and lower taxes. Lately, there has been a resurgence in interest in the Schenectady campus as the company has boosted hiring at what is now a thriving complex of manufacturing facilities and administrative offices.

Thomas Edison first moved to Schenectady in 1887, and General Electric was formed in the city in 1892. GE was one of the first twelve companies that helped create the Dow Jones Industrial Average and is the last founding company still on the list.

The GE campus, once known informally as "Schenectady Works!," is massive, at one time including over 250 separate buildings. There are no public tours of the complex because it still is very much an active workplace. The best place to view the GE sign is from a front green space near the parking lot of the giant administration building. Here you can also avail yourself of a small pedestrian walkway for a great photo opportunity. Traffic whizzes by at a breakneck speed, but you should be able to find a safe place to park and get out to admire the historic sign.

Of course nighttime viewing is strongly suggested. Seeing the sign for the first time, as it lasers its way through the ghostly Mohawk River fog, is pretty awesome.

Other Nearby Attractions or Sites

Schenectady has more than its fair share of historic sights and areas. One of the most interesting, and most easily accessible, is the GE Realty Plot. This is a ninety-acre neighborhood that features striking turn-of-the-century homes and manicured lawns. GE purchased the property from Union College in 1899 to help the college retire its debt. The plot was used to house scientists, administrators, inventors, and high-salaried employees of the GE manufacturing plant. The first fully electrified home in the United States was built here (by GE, of course) in 1905. Known as "The House with No Chimneys," it is located at 1105 Avon Road in the Plot.

It is said that more than four hundred important patents in the development of electricity and its usages were awarded to people in GE Plot residences. One house, that of Nobel Prize winner Irving Langmuir, is registered as a National Historic Landmark. In 1980, the entire ninety-acre development was listed on the National Registry of Historic Places.

Vale Cemetery is Schenectady's largest cemetery with more than thirty thousand burials. Many of the mythic figures who helped form GE in its earliest days are buried here, including Charles Steinmetz, a pillar of GE and the leading electrical engineer of his time; William Coolidge, who invented the X-ray tube; Ernest Berg, a radio pioneer who invented the first two-way radio transmitter; and Christian Steenstrup, a GE employee who personally held over a hundred patents and who invented the first electric refrigerator.

Essentials

What: The General Electric sign

Where: Schenectady; Schenectady County

Contact

General Electric Company (history): www.ge.com

Schenectady (city history): www.schenectadyhistorical.org

GE Realty Plot (walking tours): www.gerealtyplot.com

Vale Cemetery: www.valecemetery.org

83

Washington Irving's Grave

Sleepy Hollow
Westchester County

Tales of Sleepy Hollow.

There is a small selection of cemeteries listed in this book. Each one contains the grave of a singularly famous American, and it is well worth a few minutes to stop by each and pay respects to those featured within. Actress Lucille Ball, singer Kate Smith, abolitionist John Brown, painter Grandma Moses, and a few others are selected for you to visit.

But when does an entire cemetery become a major tourist destination?

The answer is simple. A cemetery becomes a destination when the list of those buried in it includes Andrew Carnegie (steel), Walter Chrysler (automobiles), Thomas Watson (IBM), Major Bowes (television), Leona Helmsley (hotels), William Rockefeller (oil), and all the members of the millionaire Astor family. Also here are Ann Trow Lohman, "The Wicked-

Many consider Washington Irving to be America's first internationally successful writer.

est Woman in New York"; Francis P. Church, the newspaper editor who penned the famous editorial "Yes, Virginia, there is a Santa Claus"; Elizabeth Arden, "The Cosmetics Queen"; Academy Award–winning actress Alice Brady; Samuel Gompers, founder of the American Federation of Labor; and Washington Irving, the author who gave us Sleepy Hollow and Rip Van Winkle.

The cemetery appears to have been laid out by one of the famous Hudson River School artists who painted the nearby surroundings. Covering almost a hundred acres, the cemetery winds and twists its way around the rolling hills and hollows of the forested area that abuts the Rockefeller family estate. Stone walls, creeks, little arched bridges, pavilions and gazebos, stone benches, and thousands of flowering bushes and trees make this one of the most pleasurable cemeteries you can ever visit. And, of course, the history of America is laid out in front of you (literally).

Some of the graves are great stories in themselves. Take William Rockefeller, for instance. He was the cofounder of Standard Oil with his better-known brother, John D. His mausoleum was the most expensive mausoleum ever built at the time, costing nearly three hundred thousand dollars. There are twenty family crypts inside, and some graves around the outside. The massive tomb is nearly forty feet tall; its walls are sixteen inches thick, and there are tall Ionic columns with pyramid roofs. Almost all of the other members of the sizeable John D. Rockefeller family are buried on the other side of the fence at the Rockefeller family estate, which is private and cannot be seen.

Hotel queen Leona Helmsley and her husband Harry, a wealthy real estate magnate, are buried in a $1.4 million tomb. It is thirty-six by thirty-seven feet of solid granite. Along the top border, snaking all the way around the twelve-thousand-square-foot mausoleum, is a custom-made stained glass window depicting the New York City skyline. It ends with the Empire State Building, which they owned, above their final resting places. The hotel matron bequeathed her dog, a tiny Maltese named "Trouble," $12 million in her will. The dog died in 2010 at the age of twelve and is now buried with her owners here in Sleepy Hollow Cemetery.

The cemetery is one of the most visited destinations in the lower Hudson Valley, although it can be tricky to find. At the eastern terminus of the Tappan Zee Bridge, traffic on New York State Rt. 9 whizzes past the cemetery entrance at a nerve-wracking speed, and if you don't keep your eye out for it, it can be easy to pass by. Once you are inside the stone walls, there is an office that can arrange tours and give you details about the locations of any of the dozens of famous gravesites. The cemetery gates are also open when the office is closed, and the staff has conveniently placed maps in a kiosk for the visitor to use.

Washington Irving (1783–1859) has been called the "Father of the American Short Story." Many of his stories were written using the area around the cemetery as a backdrop. His grave is one of the most visited in the cemetery. For a writer who gave America so many splendid and colorful tales, his gravesite can be a bit of a disappointment. It consists of a plain weathered headstone surrounded by a small black wrought-iron fence. The stone gives only his name, birth date, and death date.

The historic Old Dutch Church at the edge of the cemetery was mentioned several times in Washington Irving's Legend of Sleepy Hollow.

Perhaps the most famous cemetery in New York, Sleepy Hollow is a place of incredible beauty and interest.

Other Nearby Attractions or Sites

Washington Irving lives on in this place that he wrote about; it is where he grew up, earned his success, built his mansion, died, and was buried. It is possible to carve out an entire weekend of events and sights to see, all based around Irving and his Sleepy Hollow tales.

The Old Dutch Church is contiguous to the Sleepy Hollow cemetery. Irving wrote about this church and used it as a setting in many of his writings. The church is the second-oldest in New York. The church is a marvel of restoration, and the little cemetery in the rear has its own claim to fame. Here are the graves of the inspirations for many of Irving's literary creations. The real people who gave Irving his Brom Bones, Katrina Van Tassel, and Ichabod Crane are all buried here in this little five-acre graveyard.

"Sunnyside" was Washington Irving's mansion, located just up the road from the cemetery in Tarrytown. One of the finest Gilded Age mansions along the Hudson, Sunnyside has dozens of rooms, beautiful stained glass windows, lush gardens and public grounds, and sweeping views down the back lawn to the Hudson River. Costumed docents lead informative tours of this home, where Irving died of a heart attack at the age of seventy-six.

Keeping with the whole Washington Irving theme, Halloween is the most opportune time to visit the Sleepy Hollow area. Thousands attend "pumpkin glows" (in which masses of pumpkins are lit at one time), parades, readings, harvest festivals, costumed performances, and even a highly anticipated appearance by none other than the Headless Horseman himself!

It is no wonder Sleepy Hollow calls itself the "Halloween Capital of New York." The village was known as North Tarrytown for more than a century. In 1996 the citizens voted to change its name to Sleepy Hollow, in homage to its famous native son and with an eye to boosting tourism. When the name change was made officials, city fathers rang the three-hundred-year-old bell at the Old Dutch Church for fifteen minutes in jubilation.

Essentials

What: Washington Irving's grave; southern end of the cemetery overlooking the Old Dutch Church

Where: Sleepy Hollow, Rt. 9; Westchester County

Contact

Sleepy Hollow Cemetery: www.sleepyhollowcemetery.org

Old Dutch Church: www.odcfriends.org

Sunnyside: www.visitsleepyhollow.com/historic-sites/sunnyside

Tarrytown and Hudson Valley tourism and Halloween events: www.hudsonvalley.org

84

Mt. Utsayantha Fire Tower

Stamford
Delaware County

A watcher in the woods.

What a great job it must have been.

In the old days nearly a hundred fire towers stood guard over the vast mountain ranges of Upstate New York, with dozens in the Adirondacks and fewer in the Catskills. Sentinels would sit in their towers, scanning God's creation, always on the lookout for an errant wisp of smoke. The Adirondack bears and beavers and Catskill deer and foxes were their companions. It must have been just perfect—for the right person, that is.

"Fire observers led a very interesting life," Marty Podskoch told me. He is an expert on the history and lore of these fire towers and has written several books on them, including the popular *Fire Tower Stories*. "In fact, that is how I got started. I hiked up Hunter Mountain with a friend in 1987. At the base of the mountain it was quite nice, but by the time we reached the summit we were standing in four inches of snow. We saw the fire tower and went and chatted with the observer. He warmed us with his little fire, a drink, and some great stories. And I was hooked," he said.

There are five fire towers within the Catskill Park and thirty-one in the Adirondacks. The one atop Mt. Utsayantha is just outside the park's boundaries. The mountain is 3,215 feet high, and the tower rises another sixty-eight feet. A road allows you to drive a vehicle to the top. This is rare.

"Utsayantha is the only tower in the Catskills with a road. The other five in the area are staffed with volunteers on weekends, but you do have to hike to the top. There is no guide or staff in Stamford, but it is nice because you can drive right up the mile road to the top. The first tower opened there with great fanfare on July 4, 1882. It was four stories tall, made out of wood, and had a glass-enclosed observation cab. It quickly got blown down," he said.

The towers, in fact, succumbed to the wicked mountain winds and were destroyed in 1882, 1895, 1901, and 1916. "Then they built it with steel cables to hold it still," Podskoch said.

The view from the top of Mt. Utsayantha is wondrous. The patchwork quilt of the farms and fields below, the little white church spires of the village of Stamford piercing above the tree line, the deep blue sky with white cotton-ball clouds so close you could almost touch them. For the best view, a climb to the top of the tower will give you one of the only unobstructed 360-degree panoramas in the Catskills.

The long road to the top of the mountain is opened seasonally but is very treacherous even on a warm day if it has rained. Just before you reach the top, you will find a small clearing with a fantastic view on your right. There is an old wooden ledge from which to take photographs. This ledge was once a launching site for hang gliders. Continuing up the mountain to the top, you find a small park. Dr. S. E. Churchill, a wealthy leading citizen of Stamford, bought the twenty acres at the mountaintop in 1889 and deeded it to the village for a park in 1917. A large white observation building is the only structure there (it was once planned to be a museum). There are several wooden benches along the mountain ridge and several picnic tables and grills for public use.

"In the old days, people would come from miles around to visit the mountaintop. They would bring picnics and stay for the sunset. Some would even sleep up there overnight just to be around for the sunrise. In the 1950s and early 1960s, a group of Native Americans took up residence on the top of Mt. Utsayantha. They made a totem pole and sold trinkets to the tourists who came up for the view."

"The old fire observers were an important part of life in the woods. They really knew this area like the back of their hands. If they saw a plume of smoke, they would check to see if it was a dump or somebody who had the authority to start a fire. If not, they would coordinate by phone with fire departments and volunteer departments and use the art of triangulation to pinpoint where the fire was. The state eliminated all fire observer posts in 1990 for budget reasons. Now volunteers do what they can. Those guys did a valuable service for us all."

I noticed that Marty said "guys." I asked him if women did the job too.

"Oh, sure. There were lots of females up in those towers. In fact one of them, Ann Willis, used to stand guard in a fire tower up above Troy, N.Y. Last I heard she was over a hundred years old!

Other Nearby Attractions or Sites

One of the most persistent fables of the Catskill region is that of Princess Utsayantha. Lore has it that she committed suicide in a nearby lake following the abrupt end of an unrequited love affair, but other stories are also told. In any case, as you travel up the mountain road you pass a well-marked grave on your right. For years (with a wink to the tourist trade), the village of Stamford maintained a sign at this site telling one of the many tales about this doomed princess. There really is a grave at this spot, but it is so timeworn that no name or accurate dates can be made out. Fittingly, for a Catskill mystery!

At the foot of the tower hill, just off Rt. 23, you will come to the Stamford Cemetery. Here you can pull in at Section B and go five hundred feet. On your right, you will find a tall sand-colored obelisk bearing the name of E. Z. C. Judson. Edward Zane Carroll Judson was Stamford's most celebrated citizen. Under the pen name of Ned Buntline, he was a prolific writer, raconteur, international headliner, and journalist, and he was the man who discovered Buffalo Bill Cody. It is said that he also commissioned the design for the Colt .45 handgun (the "Buntline Special)." His prolific output as a writer earned him the sobriquet "The King of the Dime Novels."

Essentials

What: Mt. Utsayantha fire tower

Where: Stamford, N.Y. Rt. 23 East, take Mountain Road to signs to the park; Delaware County

Contact

Mt. Utsayantha: http://www.cnyhiking.com/MountUtsayantha.htm

Marty Podskoch: Books about fire towers: www.firetowerstories.com

Stamford history: www.stamfordhistory.org

85

The Old '76 House

Tappan
Rockland County

Oldest tavern in America.

Many of us enjoy going to historic bars, pubs, and taverns. I always seek out an ancient watering hole during my travels, not just for some cold refreshment but because I enjoy absorbing the ancient spirits that roam in some of these legendary "spirit" establishments. In New York State you can find lots of bars that are 150 years old without even breaking a sweat. But the Old '76 House in Tappan stands head and shoulders above all the others here, and across the nation, as the oldest tavern in America.

Before I go on, I can hear the faint hue and cry of those saying, "But what about McSorley's Old Ale House in New York City?" Yes, it is a classic old tavern with much history attached to it (it didn't allow women to come inside until the 1970s), but McSorley's opened in 1854, and although it holds the title of the oldest bar in New York City, by comparison to the Old '76 House, McSorley's is just a wee lad.

The famous tavern in Tappan opened its doors nearly two centuries before John McSorley ever poured his first draught.

In the days long before Colonial America was even a dream, the Dutch had a significant presence in the lower Hudson Valley. Part of the land they owned was in Tappan, and the story goes that the Dutch government would only recognize a community if they had a bona fide place for people, residents and travelers alike, to eat, drink, and congregate to discuss public issues. The present stone structure was erected in 1686. Later known as the Mabie House, it opened its doors in around 1750 as a public meeting house. One can only assume that owner Yoast Mabie poured a stiff one (or two) for those who convened in his front room, including General George Washington, who we know was a patron of the inn (now known as the Old '76 House) on several occasions.

In 1780, the British spy John André was discovered carrying plans in his boots for the surrender of West Point to the British. As a co-conspirator of Benedict Arnold, André was brought to the Old '76 House, where he was jailed until his trial. His trial, held at the historic Dutch Reformed Church a block from the tavern, was the biggest event in little Tappan's history. He was found guilty by a military tribunal of fourteen American generals, and he was executed by hanging nearby. Today a five-ton stone monument marks the spot where André had his date with the hangman.

All of these historic elements give the small eighty-five-acre historic district of Tappan almost a theme-park aura. The buildings are centuries old. At the Old '76 House, the actual room where André was jailed is now a dining room. The sidewalks are made of old stones. American flags and patriotic bunting give it all an air of a rural Revolutionary America re-enactment site. But it is the real deal, and all just a half-hour drive north of Manhattan.

To further contrast the comparison between the Old '76 House and McSorley's, one would actually have to visit both. I have.

McSorley's is a free-for-all scrum of conviviality. Beers are served two at a time, the men's restrooms have the original "walk-in urinals" (like I said, you have to visit it to know), a plate of raw onions and sliced American cheese is still one of the most popular items on the sparse bar menu, and the place is always packed to the walls—morning, noon, and night—with revelers, international visitors, students from nearby universities, tourists, and sailors who come here to savor their few last hours of shore leave. At any moment a rousing, red-faced, full throated sing-along of "God Bless America" can break out and rock the place. This bar is lively, fun and a little bit intimidating.

The Old '76 House is the complete opposite. Inside you will find an elegant, subdued dining area with white linen table cloths, candles, and fine silver on the tables. Historic prints and paintings can be found in virtually every room of the restaurant. Old muskets and Colonial memo-rabilia, including copper, pewter, and brass kitchenware, cover the walls. Framed paintings and documents, many of them pertaining to the inn's place in history regarding the Major André episode, are everywhere. One very interesting item on the wall is a rare self-portrait he drew in pencil while a prisoner.

The menu at the Old '76 House is one of the best in the Hudson Valley. Items prepared by their award-winning chefs include schnitzel with wild mushrooms, escargot Bourgogne, wild boar sausage, and American red deer. Ask for a plate of raw onions and a few slices of American cheese and you may be asked to leave.

And, while it's not quite as mirthful and exuberant as McSorley's, the Old '76 House does a have a tavern, which is comfortable, relaxing, and almost exactly the same as it was when the Father of Our Country bellied up to the bar for a cold one some two-and-a-half centuries ago.

Other Nearby Attractions or Sites

Five miles north of Tappan is the hamlet of Orangeburg. Here you will find one of the most poignant and important World War II museums in the state. Camp Shanks was the largest World War II embarkation camp built in the United States. Much of the hamlet was leveled to build this camp. More than 1,300,000 men trained here and left to go to war in Europe. Almost three quarters of them participated in D-Day. Of the twenty-five hundred buildings erected here for the camp, just one is left. This lone Quonset hut houses the small museum that tells the incredible story of what was once known as "Last Stop U.S.A."

Essentials

What: The oldest tavern in America

Where: Old '76 House, 110 Main Street, Tappan; Rockland County

Contact

The Old '76 House: www.76house.com

Camp Shanks Museum: www.orangetownmuseum.com/#!orangeburg/c1qav

86

Henry Burden's Water Wheel

Troy
Rensselaer County

The idea for the ferris wheel?

We can only imagine the sheer power the Burden water wheel must have been capable of producing. A massive towering structure, this behemoth in the hills was built just east of the Hudson River site of Henry Burden's iron factory. An enormous amount of power was needed to operate his company, which made and bent horseshoes and railroad spikes. That power came from water.

The Burden water wheel was the most powerful water wheel ever built. It was sixty feet tall and weighed in at more than 250 tons. When fully operational, the water from Troy's Wynantskill Creek would channel into the top oaken buckets and force the wheel to turn. It would grind and shake and churn its way completely around two-and-a-half times every minute. There was nothing ever like it, before or after. This harnessed power of water could produce more than five hundred horsepower of energy for the metal- and iron-bending machines of the Burden Iron Works. When the water was high and the wheel was spinning, Burden could make a half-million iron horseshoes a week.

Oh, what a sight it must have been! No wonder people came from far and near just to watch it operate. One of those observers was a young man attending the famed Rensselaer Polytechnic Institute in Troy. His name was George Washington Gale Ferris, Jr., and he later became an accomplished engineer. His most notable invention was the Ferris wheel, which he introduced to the American public at the 1893 Chicago World's Columbian Exposition. This wheel was used purely for entertainment, but it was clearly drawn from his memory of witnessing the giant Burden wheel in action during his school days.

Although the wheel is no longer around, having collapsed after years of neglect and disuse, we do have a couple of amazing touchstones to this glorious part of Troy's past. As you enter Troy from the south (on Rt. 4) you see a remarkable, heroic full-color mural depicting the wheel painted over a retaining wall. The exactitude of Kevin Clark's mural is astonishing. He even placed a human figure in the scene looking up at the wheel, just to give you perspective on the size of this technological marvel.

The Burden Iron Works Museum is housed on the actual site of Henry Burden's factory. Open by appointment only, it is a place where one could easily lose oneself for an entire afternoon. It mostly tells the tale of Henry Burden's great inventions and industriousness, but it also tells of Troy's other great contributions to the United States and the world. Troy gave the country the hull of the ironclad ship the *Monitor*, the metal valves on the locks of the Panama Canal, the modern-day fire hydrant, and pretty much all of the many cast-iron bells found in the country in the 1800s. Troy was the birthplace of the detachable shirt collar, and its citizens made millions of them. One of the earliest and most popular lawn and garden machines, the Troy-Bilt Rototiller, was invented here. Troy also gave the United States its very own "Uncle Sam," meatpacker Sam Wilson, who is recognized as the source of the patriotic name. Wilson was a meat inspector for the United States army during the War of 1812. After verifying that the contents of a meat barrel were fresh and safe to eat, he would stamp it with "U.S.," and when folks asked about the meaning of the initials, the answer was, "The 'U.S.' stands for Uncle Sam."

Other Nearby Attractions or Sites

History lovers will be hard-pressed to find a richer legacy than Troy's of historic chapters in an Upstate city. I would like to mention two aspects of that history that I would send a traveler off to explore.

It has been said that Troy, once one of the most successful, educated, and wealthy cities in the nation, has more original Tiffany windows than any city outside of New York. For those who study the history of Tiffany, a visit to St. Paul's Church in Troy is a must. Built in 1828, this large Episcopalian cathedral was basically designed from top to bottom by the Tiffany studios. Glass doors, decorative stenciling, wooden arches, dazzling chandeliers, an ornate altar, and a pageant of jaw-dropping original Tiffany Studio stained-glass windows add up to make this one of the most beautiful and historic churches in Upstate New York.

Another stop would have to be Uncle Sam's grave. Uncle Sam is Troy's beloved icon, and his image is everywhere, from posters to statues to flags. Samuel Wilson, the personification of the American symbol, lived to be eighty-seven. He is buried in Troy's historic Oakwood Cemetery, the final resting place of many great names from America's past, including Russell Sage, "The Money King," early pioneering educator Emma Willard, and many others. Wilson's grave is the most visited one in the cemetery. A local Boy Scout troop raises and lowers an American flag over his grave each day. A monument located at the flag tells the story of the connection between Mr. Wilson and Uncle Sam.

The view from the western ridge of the cemetery reveals Troy and the Hudson Valley beyond and is one of the best in the region.

Essentials

What: The Burden water wheel

Where: Route 4 at Mill Street; South Troy; Rensselaer County

Contact

The Burden Iron Works Museum: This is basically a museum about many of Troy's inventions and contributions, but it does focus heavily on Henry Burden's iron enterprise, and it is located at the former office of Burden Iron Works. It is run under the auspices of the Hudson Mohawk River Gateway. The museum has a very small staff and allows visitors by appointment only. It is well worth a visit. www.hudsonmohawkgateway.org

St. Paul's Episcopal Church: www.stpaulstroy.org

Oakwood Cemetery: www.oakwoodcemetery.org

Troy history, events, and tourism: www.visittroyny.com

87

Brotherhood Winery

Washingtonville
Orange County

America's oldest winery.

When one thinks of wineries in New York State, thoughts naturally turn to the Finger Lakes region. Dozens of wineries, large and small, proliferate across the undulating hills and gorges of that region. Naples celebrates the almighty grape with a Grape Festival; Canandaigua hosts the New York Wine and Cultural Center; Dr. Konstantin Frank opened his revolutionary wine cellar in Hammondsport in 1962, forever dispelling the notion that Upstate's cold weather would prohibit a robust wine industry; and in 1983, the wineries around Cayuga Lake established themselves as the first and, eventually, the largest wine trail in New York State.

But for the real history of the wine industry in New York, one needs to refocus attention on the lower Hudson Valley to find that indisputable wine fact that sets the Empire State's wine DNA apart from anyone else's. The Brotherhood Winery in Washingtonville is the oldest operating winery in America. It has been pressing grapes and serving glasses of wine continuously since 1839.

Today, what started out as a humble vineyard owned by John Jacques and his three sons is now a formidable commercial and public wine destination in tony Washingtonville, less than an hour from the George Washington Bridge. The winery achieved its legendary status and historical asterisk, that of being the "oldest continually operating winery" in America, by staying open during the dry years of Prohibition and changing course to produce sacramental wines for religious purposes.

The winery produces many varieties of wine and is the recipient of numerous national and international awards for its rieslings, cabernets, pinot noirs, merlots, and more.

Brotherhood Winery today sprawls over hundreds of acres and includes a large modern wine-making facility, vineyards, and a wine store and gift shop. Thousands visit each year to take tours of the facility and enjoy tastings in any of their three attractive wine-tasting rooms. The winery cherishes its heritage and its place in the pantheon of New York State wine history. Several original buildings are still intact and are part of the very interesting winery tour. The white brick mansion that John Jacques built in 1837 for his family still stands, now a fully stocked gift shop.

Perhaps the most interesting part of the tour is a narrated walk through the underground wine cellars. These are the original hand-dug earthen vaults built by the Jacques family. Here you will find over two hundred massive solid oak barrels used to hold wine since the founding of the winery. A private room, seen by the public but sealed from entering, contains a priceless collection of some of the oldest and finest wines ever made in America. The room, protected by a wrought-iron gate, is adorned with the large, ornate family crest of the winemakers at Brotherhood.

There is an air of a small European village at the winery. Visitors may stroll along the little "main street," viewing buildings of all sizes and descriptions. Colorful flags flutter in the summer breeze, and the air is often filled with music provided by street performers. The "village" is usually bustling with tourists (the winery is a favorite of motor coaches and tour buses), and the number of international visitors has grown over the years. The winery keeps things lively with an active series of events all year long.

Among the favorites are a Mother's Day celebration and tasting, wine and sangria pig roasts, a Valentine's Day candlelight wine and chocolate

The oldest winery in America is now a major destination for tour buses.

380

tour, and an interactive grape stomp in the fall (all they request is that you bring "clean feet"). One of the most highly anticipated events is the Haunted Halloween at the Winery. This event, laden with spooks, ghosts, and merriment, takes visitors, young and old alike, on a Halloween trip through the appropriately scary and dimly lit underground cellars for a unique Halloween trick-and-treat experience. Costumes are suggested!

The original 1839 winery building now operates as the full service Vinum Café. The restaurant sheathed in the original bricks and dramatically located under two towering ancient brick smokestacks, seats over 150 for dining.

The most elegant and stunning building on this historic property is the Grand Salon. This is an eighteenth-century stone building with hand-hewn wooden plank floor and towering open-beamed ceilings. The grand space (more than five thousand square feet in size) is an exquisite setting for weddings, parties and private functions.

Other Nearby Attractions and Sites

Washingtonville got its name after General George Washington stopped in the then-unnamed hamlet to water his horse at a trough underneath a giant elm tree at a crossroads.

Sarah Wells was one of the first white settlers in the area of Orange County. She was just a teenager when she married John Bull and they came to live among the Indians, in the wilderness among wolves and mountain lions. It was a hard life for them, but Sarah Wells was indomitable and persevered through incredible hardships. She bore twelve children and helped her husband build a large stone home on their two-thousand-acre property atop a hilltop outside of Washingtonville. Sarah carried most of the heavy stones up the hill to her husband, where he, an excellent stone mason, cut and fit them into the foundation. Sarah Wells died at the age of 102 and is revered as a legendary pioneer in this region.

The Bull House, built by John Bull and Sarah Wells, still stands today in Campbell Hall. The house is located about halfway between the communities of Goshen and Washingtonville and is open for public tours by appointment.

The road between the two communities is known as the Sarah Wells Trail.

Essentials

What: The oldest winery in America

Where: Brotherhood Winery, Washingtonville; Orange County

Contact

Brotherhood Winery: www.brotherhood-winery.com

1722 Bull Stone House: www.bullstonehouse.org

Washingtonville history, tourism, and events: www.washingtonville-ny.gov

88

The Eastern Overlook

Wilton

Saratoga County

Grant's last view.

In the last weeks of his life, former president Ulysses S. Grant, suffering from terminal throat cancer, came to a mountaintop just north of Saratoga to write his memoirs. Grant was heavily in debt at the end of his life, and the promise from publisher Mark Twain of substantial royalties compelled Grant to finish his life's story before the clock ran out.

Grant came to Wilton and stayed at the cottage of Joseph Drexel, a Philadelphia millionaire who owned the entire mountain and built a hotel and a series of cottages near the summit. Mount McGregor would be the last place Grant would reside. His six weeks at the cottage were spent with his family and well-wishers as well as periodically with Twain to collaborate on the memoir. The president finished his manuscripts just days before he died on July 23, 1885.

The cottage today is a wonderful museum and repository of artifacts having to do with Grant's final time here. His handwritten notes to family and staff are here (he could not speak near the end of his life), as

Although he was wracked with pain from terminal cancer, President Grant found peace and solace on this remote mountaintop just outside of Saratoga Springs.

are personal items, photographs, clothes, and the bed he died in. In fact, the entire cottage (seen in the background of this chapter's photograph) remains remarkably as it was the day he passed away.

Nearby is a magnificent overlook to the east. It is one of the most spectacular vistas you will find in Upstate New York. From this overlook you can see for more than a hundred miles in each direction. On a clear day you will see a breathtaking unobstructed view of the Champlain Valley, the Saratoga Battlefield, the Hudson River, the Empire Plaza in Albany, the Catskill Mountains, the Green Mountains, and the Taconic Range.

"After we take people on a tour of the cottage, we take them through the woods to the overlook," Jonathan Duda told me. He is the former executive director of the U.S. Grant Cottage Historical Site. "About three-quarters of the way in, we start to hear people oooh and ahhh as the vista starts to come into view. When we come out to the clearing, they are literally speechless. We know Grant came here to collect his thoughts and take a break from writing his memoirs. We call it Grant's Last View because near the end, on July 20, 1885, he asked to be brought down here in his bath wagon. His son, Col. Fred Grant, and a servant wheeled him down. We can only imagine the thoughts the old general had as he took in the historical sweep and natural grandeur of the view here. Seventy-two hours later he was dead."

There is a marker that acts as a memorial to Grant located on the ledge.

"Yes, people always ask about that," Duda told me. "As I try and explain the geological nature of the overlook, the fact that it was created ten thousand years ago and that some of the rock on the ground actually displays the markings of the glacial Ice Age, people still want to know about the memorial stone. The story is that shortly after President Grant died, a marker was placed here as a tribute to him. It is supposedly at the location where he took in his last view. Today there is a large black wrought-iron fence surrounding it. After the stone was erected people came and chipped away pieces of the memorial to take as souvenirs or mementos of their visit to Grant's final home. The fence has allowed us to preserve the marker for future generations."

I have driven thousands of miles over the years I've spent writing and researching my many books about Upstate New York. This is one of the most stunning views I have ever come across.

From the Eastern Overlook you can see the Capital District, the Adirondack Mountains, the Northway, the Hills of Vermont, the Saratoga Battlefield, and much more.

Other Nearby Attractions or Sites

The Saratoga battlefield is twenty miles from Grant's cottage. Now a National Park, the battlefield is famed as the "Turning Point of the American Revolution." Here, in the fall of 1777, the American Army defeated the larger British force led by General John Burgoyne. The battlefield is four square miles in size, and many tour options are available. A visitor's center features video presentations, a gift shop, display cases of military artifacts from the battle, and a computerized database portal where you can look up information about ancestors who may have fought here.

One of the most popular sights on the battlefield tour is the famous Arnold Boot Monument. American General Benedict Arnold was a key player in the Battle of Saratoga. He was severely wounded in the leg during the Battle of Freeman's Farm, and suffered other injuries in following battles. The monument is a rare oddity on any battlefield—it is located where Arnold fell and his leg was pinned under his horse. It depicts a replica of Arnold's leg, boots, pants, stirrup, and all, without ever mentioning Arnold by name. Of course he went on to ignominy when he turned on the Americans and was implicated in a plot to hand over West Point to the British. The nameless boot is the only recognition on this hallowed battlefield of the shamed officer.

The Saratoga Monument, a part of the Saratoga National Historical Park, is located in nearby Victory, N.Y. It is also part of battlefield tours. The giant obelisk soars 156 feet into the air and features a staircase that allows visitors to climb to the observatory windows at the top. Along the four sides of the monument are recesses for life-sized sculptural tributes to the heroes of Saratoga. The monument is located at the site of the British surrender and features the likenesses of Gen. Horatio Gates, Brig. Gen. Daniel Morgan, and Gen. Philip Schuyler.

One recess is conspicuously empty. This was to be the place of tribute for General Benedict Arnold. His treason prohibited him from being honored here, so the recess remains empty.

Essentials

What: Grant's last view

Where: Grant Cottage, Eastern Overlook, Mount MacGregor; Saratoga County. (Note: Although Grant Cottage is in the foothills of the Adirondack Mountains, it is not technically within the "blue line" borders of the Adirondack Park.)

Contact

U. S. Grant Cottage: this website is for the cottage and overlook. Please note when visiting President Grant's cottage that it is on the grounds of a recently closed New York State prison. Some security is always in effect when visiting, and you may be asked to show identification when entering; www.grantcottage.org

Saratoga Battlefield: This website includes history, directions, and tour information; www.saratoga.com

REGION FIVE

North Country and Adirondacks

Including parts of Essex, Franklin, Jefferson, Oswego, St. Lawrence, Warren, and Washington Counties

89

Horne's Ferry

Cape Vincent
Jefferson County

America's oldest family-run ferry.

The Horne family has been ferrying travelers from the United States to Canada for well over two centuries. And lest you think this is a major, bustling international transportation hub, think again. In what must be the quickest and easiest way to go from one country to another in North America, the Hornes will sandwich in as many cars, bicyclists, motorcycles, and people as they can and jaunt over to Wolfe Island, Canada, from Cape Vincent, New York, in about ten minutes. It is quite an operation to experience, and sometimes they can squeeze as many as ten vehicles on the ferry at once.

Yes, that's right. Ten.

The Hornes started plying the international waters of the St. Lawrence River in 1798. A Horne family descendant still operates it. The ferry dock is an official point of entry into the United States, and all legal papers must be shown to come on land in Cape Vincent. Wolfe Island, Ontario, Canada, is the largest of the Thousand Islands at fifty square miles. It sits at the mouth of the river where it joins Lake Ontario. In fact, Cape Vincent has adopted as its slogan "Where River and Lake Meet." That would be Wolfe Island.

There are about fourteen hundred permanent Canadian residents on the island. The largest community is Marysville, a typical small, rural community not unlike a New England village. Churches, a small school, a bakery, small mom-and-pop grocery stores, specialty shops, and family farms are the order of the day in this "pass-through" community between the United States and Canada. Another ferry on the north side of Wolfe Island takes you to mainland Kingston, Ontario, Canada.

There could not be a more jarring juxtaposition than the one between the ports of entry into the two countries. Kingston, Canada, has a growing population of around 125,000. Cape Vincent, New York, has a population of around 2,500.

Tens of thousands of travelers jam the international bridges between the two countries every day at major cross-over points such as the Rainbow Bridge in Niagara Falls, the Peace Bridge in Buffalo, and the Ogdensburg-Prescott Bridge, among others. But for a real slice of Americana, nothing beats this little ferry service owned by the same family since it was founded, chugging its way out of little Cape Vincent on a daily sail to Canada.

If a ferry can be charming, the Horne's Ferry is.

In doing my research on Horne's Ferry I was quite surprised to find a whole fan base of ferry lovers in the United States. To be sure, there are several documented older ferries than the one in Cape Vincent. In fact the two oldest are just thirty miles apart, in Connecticut. But try as I might I just could not come up with a ferry service in the United States still being run by the same family continuously for over two centuries. Congratulations, Horne family!

Other Nearby Attractions or Sites

Like so many of its sister communities along the St. Lawrence Seaway Trail, Cape Vincent exudes a certain seaside lightness to it. Because it is located where river and lake meet, virtually every vista shows wide expanses of blue, turquoise, and green. People can be seen walking on the shoreline of Wolfe Island across the river. Giant Canadian windmills slowly dance in the stiff breeze that always seems to be blowing in off Lake Ontario. The

The Tibbetts Point lighthouse is one of upstate's most beautiful.

business district is quaint and offers a smattering of nice little restaurants, pubs, and gift shops.

All of the Seaway communities have something to offer the Upstate traveler. Alexandria Bay is the center of summer up here, with its honky-tonks, midway games, hot dog stands, and the magnificent Boldt Castle. Morristown has McConnell's windmill, a stone masterpiece and the only windmill on the American side of the river. Ogdensburg has one of the best museums in Upstate, the wonderful Frederick Remington Museum of Western Art. And little Clayton has the Antique Boat Museum and is the birthplace of Thousand Island salad dressing! Plus, the entire region is dotted with historical markers telling of events that happened here during the War of 1812.

Cape Vincent is steeped in history. French history, that is. Many of its earliest settlers were French or French-Canadians, and the French language rivaled English as the native tongue of residents here for a long time. An influx of French refugees came following the French Revolution, and it is said that Emperor Napoleon wanted to "retire" to Cape Vincent in his twilight years and even sent emissaries here to check it out.

Today, one of the largest American-French festivals is held at Cape Vincent to celebrate the long, rich history between the two countries. A large parade is one of the event's highlights, a parade led by none other than Emperor Napoleon himself.

At the far western end of Cape Vincent, literally at the water's edge, is the Tibbetts Point lighthouse, built in 1854. Of the many lighthouses along the river and the Great Lakes, this may be the most beautiful, not so much for its design, but for its locale.

The stark white, sixty-nine-foot round tower is situated on a spit of land at the very point where the river and lake meet. The vast expanse of Lake Ontario offers a shimmering, ever-changing pageant of pastoral sunsets and massive white cloud formations exploding across a wide, deep-blue sky. An unending parade of ships, large and small, passes in review. On the other side of the lighthouse is the St. Lawrence River and the nearby Canadian countryside. Here the water is darker and more animated and short, choppy whitecaps can be seen dancing along the crowded, rocky shores on both sides. A small 1920s-era light-keeper's house sits next to the tower. A sweeping, well-manicured lawn invites the visitor to stroll down to both the lake and the river's edge. It is a serene, quiet, and yet majestic location.

The Tibbetts Point lighthouse light-keeper's house is one of the only places in New York where you can actually spend the night at a working lighthouse. Comfortable modern amenities such as bathroom facilities, a kitchen, and overnight accommodations make a stay here a rare treat for the adventurous traveler.

Essentials

What: The oldest family-run ferry in America

Where: Horne's Ferry, Cape Vincent; Jefferson County

Contact

Horne's Ferry: Note that the ferry does not run in the winter; www.hornes-ferry.com

Tibbetts Point lighthouse: www.capevincent.org/lighthouse

Cape Vincent French Festival: www.capevincent.org/frenchfestival

90

Edward J. Noble Tribute

Gouverneur
St. Lawrence County

The world's largest roll of life savers.

It is the oddest welcome sign in New York State.

As you enter the city of Gouverneur, you are quickly drawn to the unusual towering oddity perched high in the air on two poles at the end of the village green. Is it? Could it be? Yes, it is.

A giant replica of a roll of Pep-O-Mint Life Savers candy.

Edward J. Noble (1882–1958) was born in Gouverneur and remains its most famous native son. Noble was a broadcasting entrepreneur who founded the ABC (American Broadcasting Company) network in 1944. He had interests in a variety of businesses, also owning at one time the Rexall Drug Store chain. But it is his association with the little round hard candy that, well, looked like a life preserver, that endeared him to his hometown.

Noble did not invent the hard candy, but he is credited with making it a household name and a candy phenomenon. While working as an advertising executive in New York City, Noble approached the candy's inventor, Clarence Crane, about an advertising campaign. Crane seemed uninterested in the ads, and in fact wanted nothing to do with his creation anymore. He offered the company, lock, stock, and Life Saver, to Noble for the sum of twenty-nine hundred dollars. Noble added another thousand dollars to his investment and opened up a candy factory in a one-room loft in New York City. He started with six employees.

The secret to his incredible success (his company was a million-dollar business within a decade) was his decision to wrap the candy in tinfoil. For years candy makers had wrestled with the problem of candy (mostly chocolates) going stale and soft. Noble's tinfoil solution ended those problems and sent sales skyrocketing.

Noble made millions over his career and was considered a true titan of business. Yet he never forgot his small Upstate hometown and gave freely to the betterment of the community.

His largesse to the region of his birth includes several hospitals, including the Edward J. Noble Hospital in Gouverneur as well as a hospital network that provides medical care in small towns in northern New York, including Alexandria Bay, Canton, and Potsdam.

The multimillionaire owned several lavish estates spread across the St. Lawrence Seaway region, including, at one time, the most famous residence in the area, the famed Boldt Castle on its own island in the middle of the St. Lawrence River.

So how to honor the memory of one of Upstate New York's greatest philanthropists? How does a little town pay tribute to such a giant, such a legend? Well, with a roll of his own candy, that's how.

For many years Life Savers was based in a massive, newly built (1920) five-story building in Port Chester (Westchester County). It was a state-of-the-art facility built out of concrete, brick, and terra cotta. Over six hundred employees worked there making the candy that was responsible for the "sweet scent" that wafted over the city. Even today, long after Life Savers ceased to base its operations there, the building evokes the era when Life Savers was a prominent part of the Port Chester success story. Over the front entrance you can still see the Life Savers logo, and several little images of the white candy are carved into the arch over the front doors.

At the peak of its time in Port Chester, the building itself became a bit of a tourist stop. Visitors would walk around and into the magnificent structure and marvel at the attention to detail on the exterior and the interior. Of course the most charming accents to the building were the five ten-foot rolls of Life Savers candy that rose from the ground-floor facade and were attached to the sides of the building. Each roll represented one of the original Life Savers flavors: lemon, orange, cherry, lime, pineapple, and of course the original Pep-O-Mint.

The company left Port Chester and closed the building in 1985. It has since been converted into condominiums.

The whereabouts of four of the giant steel-and-porcelain candy rolls is unknown. But we do know that the one in Gouverneur, appropriately representing E. J. Noble's first successful flavor, was donated to the town by the local Rotary Club and erected in the village park on November 10, 1987.

Rumors say that the city fathers grumbled under their breath at the size of the quirky donation and its location smack dab in the middle of town. But affection for the sweet as well as for the beloved Mr. Noble overrode any embarrassment regarding the new city icon and it is there for all the world to see.

Like I said, it is the most unusual welcome sign you will find in Upstate New York community.

Other Nearby Attractions or Sites

This is military country. The largest entity and employer in the region is Fort Drum. This Army base has been in use since 1908 and sprawls over a hundred thousand acres near Gouverneur. Home to the famed 10th Mountain Division, Fort Drum trains more than sixty thousand soldiers annually. The base is vast, and although its northern border reaches close to Gouverneur, you have to drive thirty miles to the main entrance to enter the base.

Tours are offered at Fort Drum by appointment only. These can be fascinating and they are very popular. Motor coaches take you around the base on a guided tour and inform you of the history and the operation of the base. These are called "installation tours." They also offer youth and school group tours. Those tours are similar to the installation tours, but for the young people on tour an emphasis is put on allowing the kids to interact with the soldiers on active duty.

Essentials

What: The world's largest roll of Life Savers

Where: Main Street, Gouverneur; St. Lawrence County

Contact

Governeuer history, events, tourism: www.gouverneurny.us

Fort Drum Army Base: This is the website for base tours: www.drum.army. mil/iso/Pages/pa_InstallationTours

91

Kate's Smith's Grave

Lake Placid
Essex County

God bless America.

She was the most unlikely star. She was a large girl whose 250-pound frame could still dance a mean Charleston. Despite her girth she was an excellent golfer, tennis player, and outdoorswoman. She starred in early vaudeville presentations in blackface. At the height of her career in the 1930s, Paramount signed her to star in her first major motion picture. It was a failure, and she never starred in another movie. She never married, battled weight problems for a half-century, and was the butt of many insensitive jokes about her persona as well as her rah-rah patriotism.

So how did this woman become one of the most popular, legendary figures in American entertainment history? Through her conviction of who she was, through an inimitable "come, sit a while" personality, and through a once-in-a-lifetime voice that resonated with millions of her countrymen for over six decades.

Kate Smith was the first major female star on both radio and television. Her radio show was top-rated for more than a decade, and her television appearances were frequent well into her sixties. She connected with her massive media audiences with her folksy manner; her opening line was a simple "Hello, everybody," and her closing signature was equally simple: "Thanks for listenin', folks." And of course she gave us our stirring unofficial national anthem, Irving Berlin's "God Bless America."

If Kate Smith were enshrined in the National Baseball Hall of Fame in Cooperstown, she would need her own separate wing to accommodate all of her accolades, honors, and milestones. Her radio ratings could never be matched. She recorded a Ruthian three-thousand-plus songs, six hundred of which she introduced. More than twenty sold over a million copies. She received more fan mail during her career than any other performer (the *New York Times* put this figure well into the millions of letters), she raised a mind-boggling six hundred million dollars' worth of World War II bonds, and she was the recipient of the highest civilian award in the nation, the Medal of Freedom. Smith was an honorary Texas Ranger, an honorary U. S. Army colonel, one of just a handful of female Grand Marshals of the Tournament of Roses Parade, and a member of the Radio Hall of Fame. In the twilight years of her career, she was the ebullient good luck charm to a Stanley Cup winning hockey team (Philadelphia Flyers). In 2010, she was honored with her own U.S. postage stamp.

During Word War II, Kate was a tireless supporter of home-front efforts. She is personally credited with selling an astonishing six hundred million dollars' worth of War Bonds.

Despite all of this, Kate was really a small-town girl at heart. She was born in little Greenville, Virginia, and summered for four decades in the Adirondack community of Lake Placid. Kate had a rustic residence and boathouse on Buck Island in the middle of the lake. She named her home Camp Sunshine.

The locals looked on Kathryn (as friends and family called her) as more of a neighbor than a world-renowned celebrity. She would leave the network studios of *The Dean Martin Show* or *The Ed Sullivan Show* or *The Tonight Show with Johnny Carson*, shed her star trappings and entourage, and motor to Lake Placid. There she would don a floral print housedress, put on her glasses and a pair of sensible shoes, and go down to the dock and wave to the tour boats as they passed by. She was a frequent visitor to area flea markets or tag sales, always trying to save a few dollars (despite her estimated thirty-five-million-dollar fortune). She also worked part-time in a Main Street gift shop owned by her elderly godmother, was frequently ensconced in a booth at Howard Johnsons enjoying a stack of blueberry pancakes, and was a reliable Sunday fixture in the front pew of St. Agnes Roman Catholic Church, praying with the faithful and lending her unmistakable bell tones to the choral offerings.

When Kate Smith, seventy-nine, died on June 17, 1986, many in America felt as if they had lost a member of their extended family. Her death was announced on the front page of virtually every newspaper in the country. Her burial service in Lake Placid was attended by a large crowd of fans, local dignitaries, and just plain folks. People who had known her for years in the Adirondacks came to say thanks. Her gardener, her neighbors, her card-playing partners, the shopkeepers along Main Street, and her priest all came to mingle with a throng of fans who came from around the country to say goodbye to this good and beloved woman.

Kate Smith's large rose-pink mausoleum in St. Agnes Cemetery is a popular site in the village. Fans, music lovers, and tour buses seek out this beautiful cemetery a mile from the lake to pay their respects to a woman they may never have met, but always felt they knew. Kate is buried in the only above-ground mausoleum ever allowed in the cemetery. The capstone reads "Kathryn E. Smith," and her tomb is adorned with seasonal plantings, subtle landscaping, and of course, an American flag.

In June of 1939, President Franklin D. Roosevelt invited the king and queen of England to visit the United States. The royal couple were the guests at a party hosted by FDR. The entertainer was Kate Smith, a personal favorite of the king. The president introduced the singer to the gathering with these words: "Your majesties. This is Kate Smith, this is America."

Today, in a quiet rear corner of this Adirondack cemetery, you can still thrill to that moment. If you peer through the wrought-iron gates of the singer's mausoleum, you will see a beautiful stained-glass window above a large photograph of the entertainer. On the back interior walls of the chamber you can easily read the glittering gold lettering chiseled there for all time: "This is Kate Smith, this is America."

Other Nearby Attractions or Sites

John Brown's farm and final resting place are also in Lake Placid. A larger-than-life monument pays tribute to the legendary abolitionist near his grave. The Olympic ski jump, which soars overhead near Brown's site, is a jarring juxtaposition of the old and the new at the John Brown farm.

Essentials

What: Singer Kate Smith's grave

Where: St. Agnes Cemetery, Sentinel Road at Cascade Road, Lake Placid; Essex County

Contact

Kate Smith book: Kate Smith: A Biography, by Richard Hayes (McFarland & Co.)

St. Agnes Church (a large photographic tribute to Smith): www.stagnes lakeplacid.com

Lake Placid Boat Tours (the singer's former Camp Sunshine is highlighted on the tour): www.lakeplacidmarina.com

Lake Placid Crowne Plaza Resort (contains the Kate Smith Library meeting room): www.lakeplacidcp.com

A historical plaque, located on Main Street near the Olympic Center, describes Miss Smith's career and connection to Lake Placid.

John Brown Farm State Historic Site; http://parks.ny.gov/historic-sites/29/details.aspx

Lake Placid sights, events, and attractions: www.lakeplacid.com

92

Almanzo Wilder Homestead

Malone
Franklin County

Little house in the North Country.

The famous writer Laura Ingalls Wilder is forever associated with her immortal books about life in a little house on a prairie. Her books have sold millions of copies, and the award-winning television show, Little House on the Prairie, is certainly one of the great classics. But Laura Wilder wrote about another little house, and that book too was a big success. The house is still located just a few miles south of the St. Lawrence River in Malone.

Laura Ingalls married Almanzo Wilder on August 25, 1885, in De Smet, South Dakota. He was twenty-five, she was fifteen. It was in this wild, untamed territory of the blossoming United States that Laura began writing her recollections of growing up on the prairie. The books garnered her widespread fame. After her marriage to Almanzo, he began to tell her of his own upbringing in the harsh conditions of remote northern New York State. It is on these tales that she based her second book, *Farmer Boy*, which also became a popular hit. *Farmer Boy* is a quaint retelling of the simple pleasures and hard realities of rural life without modern accessories to aid in the back-breaking daily chores.

Her book is now considered a classic. Although life could be difficult in Malone (where Almanzo's farm was located), it was full of promise and mystery to a boy not yet ten years old. The chapter names reflect the nostalgia of the book, including "Sheep Shearing," "Early Snap," "The Little Bobsled," "County Fair," "Independence Day," and "The Strange Dog." Many grade-school teachers across the country today have used *Farmer Boy* as a text for young students learning about the hardships and joys of early farm life in the United States.

The Almanzo Wilder Homestead is today an important cultural destination in the sparsely populated area in Upstate New York around Malone. Many buildings at the farm evoke farming life in the mid-nineteenth century. While many of the buildings are historically accurate for the time and place, the main house is the only original building that existed when Laura's husband was young.

The homestead is a popular place for tourists and school groups, and it hosts many Little House–themed events throughout the year. In the farm museum you can see antique equipment of the type used by Wilder and his brothers to do their chores. Farming in the 1860s was not for sissies. A well-stocked gift shop offers a wide variety of homemade craft items, pottery, jewelry, jams and jellies, and books. Copies of all of Laura Ingalls Wilder's Little House books are available here.

Tours of the grounds are offered. You may wander at your leisure or be accompanied by a docent. School groups are welcome with advance notice. The large property consists of outbuildings, reconstructed barns (the originals fell victim to lightning strikes in the 1960s), the original family homestead, pastures, the adjoining Trout River, a pump house, orchards and fields, a covered picnic area, and the gift shop ("general store") and farm museum.

The Wilder Homestead is a busy gathering place for those who enjoy a slice of Upstate history just twenty-five miles south of Canada. Art shows, walking tours, Civil War re-enactments, horse shows, baking contests, concerts, and more keep the museum and homestead busy on weekends throughout the tourist season.

One popular event is "Christmas with Almanzo." An actor reads the chapter from *Farmer Boy* titled "Christmas" while sitting in the actual parlor to which the book refers. A large crowd gathers, and holiday treats are served. In the book, Laura Ingalls Wilder describes her husband as a child, enjoying the delicious smells of Christmas cooking and all the chores he had to tend to while the women prepared the meal. He had to fill the woodstove, prime the water pump, polish the silver, and make the candles. As you listen to this chapter, while smelling the cookies being baked and hearing the gay jingle of the sleigh bells on the horses outside, it is not hard to transport yourself back to the 1860s and get a sense of life as they knew it here in the little house in the North Country.

It is not an overstatement to say that a visit to this place by avid Laura Ingalls Wilder fans can be quite an emotional and humbling experience. It remains the only structure in the country still in its original place from any of her Little House books.

There are plans to expand this site and add more outbuildings on the eighty-eight-acre site. Among the buildings currently being planned are a one-room schoolhouse and an ice shed.

Other Nearby Attractions or Sites

The Wilder Homestead is actually located in the tiny community of Burke. Malone is just down the road. The city has about fourteen thousand residents and hosts one of the oldest historic county fairs in the country. The Franklin County Fair has been operating for well over 150 years. In fact, it was to this very fair that a young Almanzo Wilder and his family came each summer. In Farmer Boy, Almanzo tells of bringing his milk-fed pumpkin here one year to be judged, and how Eliza Jane and Alice also brought their homemade pickles and jams to be judged. It was at this fair that the young boy was mesmerized by the man in the tall hat playing the "shell game" for his audience. It was also here that the boy and his father sat for a hearty meal of turkey and dressing, succotash, boiled beans, and rye'n'Injun bread. Yes, it was a great day at this fair for the Wilders. And Almanzo went home with the blue ribbon for his milk-fed pumpkin!

The fairgrounds have changed over the last 160-plus years. But not by much.

Essentials

What: The boyhood home of Laura Ingalls Wilder's husband

Where: The Wilder Homestead, 177 Stacy Road, Malone; Franklin County

Contact

The Wilder Homestead: www.almanzowilderfarm.com

Franklin County Fair: www.frcofair.com

93

The North Creek Train Station

North Creek
Warren County

"Welcome aboard, Mr. President.

Things went downhill fast after President William McKinley was shot at the Pan-American Exposition on September 6, 1901.

Vice President Theodore Roosevelt had been attending a luncheon along Lake Champlain in far northern New York when word reached him of the tragedy. He immediately embarked for Buffalo as McKinley's life hung by a thread. Shortly after Roosevelt arrived, the president's condition got better. The vice president conferred with his family, and they decided to go ahead with a long-planned vacation in the Adirondacks to calm the fears of the anxious nation.

McKinley lived for over a week following the shooting. While the Roosevelt family and their entourage were ensconced at a summer retreat called the Tahwas Club near Mt. Marcy, New York's highest peak, a runner appeared. A local man, Harrison Hull, had made the arduous trek up the mountain looking for the Roosevelt party. He carried news that President McKinley was at death's door.

Theodore Roosevelt then began what is known in the Adirondacks as "Teddy's Midnight Ride." This harrowing nighttime thirty-five-mile journey, along winding forest paths and some uncharted roads, took Roosevelt all night. It was a rain-soaked ride, and the roads were rivers of mud. Several wagons were used, fresh horses were procured, and new drivers met the wagons carrying Roosevelt along the way.

Mike Cronin, a local lodge owner, drove the final wagon carrying his important passenger the last sixteen-mile leg to the North Creek train depot. Here waited the fastest locomotive the Delaware and Hudson Railroad could find, all fired up and ready to whisk Roosevelt to Buffalo. The vice president's own private secretary, William Loeb, Jr., was also waiting at the depot with a telegram addressed to Roosevelt stating that President William McKinley had succumbed to his wounds at 2:15 in the morning.

Roosevelt entered that big D&H train at the tiny North Creek station no longer as vice president, but as the new president of the United States.

"I still love to share that story with our visitors," Sarah Liebelt said. She is a ticket agent at the historical site. "People love our museum and are so surprised by the Teddy Roosevelt connection to us." The museum has many exhibits and displays relating to "Teddy's Midnight Ride," and it is a popular spot in this little Adirondack community of under two thousand.

And the North Creek train station is not just a dusty old relic of the past. It is a bustling, active train station carrying passengers up and down the Adirondack hills of Warren County.

"We are the Saratoga and North Creek Railroad, the route of the Hudson Explorer," the ticket agent told me. "We have short rides and round-trip excursions to Saratoga. We have leaf-viewing trips, snow trips, and party trains. It is a very popular place."

I asked Sarah about the magnificent train that was purring next to the railroad depot getting ready to take passengers down the line to the small community of Thurman.

"We actually have two trains. Both are big 1950s-era diesel locomotive passenger trains. Some of the cars are double-decker, and both trains have dome cars for better viewing of our wonderful Adirondacks. They have their roots in Alaska."

Alaska?

"These trains started out there and over the years made their way right here to North Creek," Sarah said. "We fixed them up and operate them much as they did in the old days. Families, skiers, tourists. Everybody enjoys a train ride," she laughed. "The one thing we didn't change are the names of the cars. They were named in Alaska and we have kept it that way." I took a little tour of the "Matanuska."

The seats, floors, and ceilings are well appointed, ensuring that the rail ride will be comfortable. The dome cars sparkled in the afternoon sun. The dining service looked impressive. Kind of like a rustic American Orient Express.

"One of our most popular events is 'Dark Tuesdays.' On these nights you can reserve dome-car seat and enjoy an evening train ride while reveling in a five-course gourmet meal with complete bar service. You can even see a spectacular sunset over the Hudson River," Sarah told me.

Wait a minute. "We are a long way from the Hudson River," I said.

"No sir. The Hudson River actually runs right behind our train depot. It begins just up the road in Lake Tear of the Clouds. In fact, that is one of the things I hear the most up here at North Creek. 'I can't believe that little stream is the Hudson River,'" she laughed.

Other Nearby Attractions or Sites

This is ski country. Gore Mountain is one of the largest ski areas in the Adirondacks and is located in North Creek. As well as the beehive that is the mountain when the snow falls, the ski-lift ride to the top of New York State–owned Gore Mountain in the summer is also very popular. The mountain has more than a hundred trails and a variety of ways to get to the summit.

In 1967, Gore Mountain became the first New York ski center to use ski-lift gondolas. Today, more than a half-century later, these curious little red "cherry gondolas" can be found dotting the landscape of the village of North Creek. They are popular photo ops for tourists and are even used for wedding backdrops. One sits at the entry to the North Creek Depot Museum.

Essentials

What: The North Creek Depot Museum and the Saratoga and North Creek Railroad

Where: North Creek; Warren County

Contact

The North Creek Depot Museum: www.northcreekdepotmuseum.com

Saratoga and North Creek Railroad: www.sncrr.com

Gore Mountain Ski Resort: www.gore mountain.com

94

The LT-5 Major Elisha Henson

Oswego
Oswego County

The last active U.S. Army D-Day invasion ship.

The D-Day invasion included one of the largest masses of men, ships, planes, and equipment ever assembled for a military action. The invasion, code name Operation Overlord, included an assemblage of nearly seven thousand seagoing vessels from eight different navies. Twelve hundred of the ships were heavy warships, but the smaller craft played an important role in accessing the beach with troops and supplies. More than four thousand landing craft brought tens of thousands of soldiers onto the beach on June 6, 1944. Other ships brought tons of materials. Many ships were lost, mostly to mines and rough seas, and the loss of life was significant. Of course, we now know that the invasion was ultimately successful and led directly to the end of the war in Europe.

A small but hardy flotilla of tugboats plied the waters of the English Channel that day. Ferrying barge after barge of munitions, pre-assembled piers, and supplies to the ever-growing contingent of men on shore, these tugs were tireless in their efforts. One hundred fifty-eight tugboats took part in the invasion, from several countries. The United States provided around three dozen, both small and large, to the action. These boats were built at the Jakobson Shipyard at Oyster Bay, Long Island, expressly for use in D-Day. They then sailed to Florida, where small American crews and stranded Scandinavian sailors who could not get back to their countries piloted them with to England for staging. The Henson sailed the Atlantic dragging behind them their first cargo load: eight railroad boxcars.

The L-T 5 (large tugboat) *Major Elisha K. Henson* served valiantly during Overlord and today is the last surviving operational U.S. Army vessel from the thousands that took part in the invasion of Europe. It is located in Oswego and is now a part of the H. Lee White Maritime Museum located on the Oswego River. At the end of the war, the tugboats that survived were sent to Detroit where they were dismantled and sold for scrap. The *Henson*, however, was sent to Buffalo, where it provided harbor maintenance until 1986. Headed for the scrap heap in 1989, the boat was secured by the Port of Oswego, which in turn handed it over to the H. Lee White Maritime Museum. It is open for tours, and on rare occasions can actually be seen sailing on Lake Ontario.

The proud boat, christened the *Major Elisha K. Henson* and then renamed the *John C. Nash* in 1946 (and then later back to the *Henson*), has been the focal point for many civic and patriotic ceremonies over the

414

years, hosting large gatherings of veterans and military enthusiasts, who converge on its dockside berth for various momentous occasions. One of the largest military gatherings was on the seventieth anniversary of D-Day in 2014. The large tug, 115 feet long and able to reach eleven knots (thirteen mph), is fully functional and has been reconditioned to much of the way it was on June 6, 1944.

This last tug has quite a dramatic story to tell. Being a workhorse and not a killing machine, the tugboats of D-Day operated only in supporting roles to those ships actually shelling the shore. The tugs were armed with just two small .50-caliber machine guns, which under normal conditions would never be fired. However, on June 9, 1944, just three days after the invasion and with the beaches of Normandy crowded with men and supplies, the *Henson* faced a date with destiny. While lugging tons of equipment through the choppy waters of the English Channel, a group of German planes came into view in the skies above. With little to do other than act as sitting ducks, the crew of the *Henson* scrambled to the gun mounts and started blasting away at the enemy planes. They were successful and sent an enemy plane crashing into the waters nearby.

As if it were a routine action, the boat's logbook recorded this historic event in typical maritime stiff-upper-lip fashion: "June 9, 1944. Planes overhead. Everyone shooting at them. Starboard gunner got a FW [a German Luftwaffe Focke-Wulf fighter plane]."

So when you go to the White Maritime Museum in Oswego to visit this heroic relic of D-Day, be sure and glance up to the top of the gray metal smokestack. There, above the colorful battle ribbons flying in the lake breeze, you will see two little white-painted emblems. One is a plane and the other is the Nazi swastika. These "kill marks" represent the only enemy aircraft downed by a tugboat in wartime.

In 1992, the *Henson* was named as a National Historic Landmark.

Other Nearby Attractions or Sites

The H. Lee White Maritime Museum tells the story of Oswego, its port, lighthouse, and maritime activity. Of note are several massive paintings by artist George Gray depicting the history of the city and the region. These paintings, from the early 1930s, were originally hung on the walls of the iconic Pontiac Hotel, an Oswego landmark. When the hotel went out of business, the paintings were saved by local art lovers, who donated them to the museum in 1985.

Across the Oswego River, behind the museum, you can view the hulking profile of Fort Ontario. This was the site of a several War of 1812 and other engagements. Also on the grounds of Fort Oswego is the Safe Haven Museum. This small yet powerful museum tells the story of the 982 Jewish refugees saved from death in Europe and housed in the (then) empty fort during World War II. This was the only place in the United States that welcomed Jewish refugees during the war.

Essentials

What: The L-T5 Major Elisha Henson, he last U.S. Army vessel from D-Day

Where: H. Lee White Maritime Museum, Oswego Harbor, Oswego; Oswego County

Contact

H. Lee White Maritime Museum: http://www.hleewhitemarinemuseum.com

Fort Ontario: http://fortoswego.com/

Safe Haven Museum: http://www.safehavenmuseum.com

95

Potsdam Sandstone

Potsdam
St. Lawrence County

Upstate history written in stone.

If you drive into Potsdam on a sunlit summer morning you will notice something different from almost every other community in Upstate. You will not be able to put your finger on it at first, but there is something magical about the aura that surrounds this place and its old buildings.

Potsdam sandstone was quarried out of the banks of the Raquette River here for more than a century. Some say the luminous pink-and-red natural stone was discovered early on when Sir John Johnson, a British soldier and land agent in central New York, spied the rose-colored rock along the river as he fled to Canada through Potsdam at the outset of the American Revolution. The sandstone is unusual in that it is pure silica, it has a definitive and unique red to pink color, and it is one of the hardest substances minable and will for all intents and purposes last forever.

One of the earliest and most successful quarry owners was Thomas Clarkson. His efficient quarry mined untold tons of the rare sandstone, which made him a millionaire many times over. He was not an ivory-tower hands-off business owner, however. In fact, he died when he was crushed by a giant pump at one of his quarries where he was assisting his employees. His family raised an educational monument to his memory in Potsdam—Clarkson University.

Today, there are dozens of buildings around the city made out of this sturdy, lovely building material. And these buildings, when hit directly by sun, can be quite gorgeous as their ancient walls reflect a gentle pinkish hue on all that surrounds them. Homes, churches, businesses, college buildings, and more all shimmer in the glow of the city's indigenous jewel, Potsdam sandstone.

Let's take one of the many buildings built with Potsdam sandstone and explore its history. The Potsdam Presbyterian Church is located near the downtown business district. After outgrowing a series of previous church structures, the congregation decided to erect a massive new one made entirely of sandstone. Construction began in 1868 and took four years to complete. Hundreds of tons of multihued sandstone were carted to the site from the Clarkson quarry for the project. It was finished in 1872. The price tag for this minicathedral was a shocking thirty-eight thousand dollars. Amazing!

Each of the original sandstone edifices still standing is marvelous in its own way, large or small. The quarries and mines closed down in around 1920, so the stockpile of sandstone ended a century ago. That does not mean that Potsdam's famous stone is gone forever. At one time, the city sidewalks were paved with sandstone. As years went by and the ground underneath the sidewalks shifted and moved the stone, residents were allowed to replace it with cement and keep the original stone. Stories have been told of the huge amounts of money turned down by bidders asking for some of the rare sandstone now stockpiled in many residents' backyards. Also, a relatively new company to the area, Graymont Potsdam Quarry and Concrete, has just discovered a previously unknown vein of rich, red Potsdam sandstone. So there might be a whole new generation of buildings in the city sporting a red veneer.

The aura that the sandstone lends to Potsdam is really quite remarkable. I am sure that many of the locals today, while well versed in the history and the importance of the stone, might wonder what all the fuss is about when a newcomer asks about the unique color of the buildings. I guess sometimes living inside of history prevents you from realizing its impact on others.

Recently, I was in Potsdam researching the sandstone. I went to the museum, the library, the Clarkson campus (which has original sandstone buildings), and out to where the quarries were. After a day of researching, and never having been in the city before, I decided to have a slice of pizza and relax and write down my day's observations.

I chose an eatery on Main Street called Little Italy. It was a busy evening at the restaurant with a mix of locals, families, and college students (there are two colleges in Potsdam: Clarkson University and the State University of New York at Potsdam). As the crowd died down, I chatted with my server, who was curious about seeing me jotting things down in my travel journal. I told her I was researching Potsdam sandstone. She looked surprised and said with a wink, "Well, you better check out the sign on the side of our building when you leave."

I finished my slice, paid, and hurried outside. And there it was: "Little Italy restaurant is the oldest standing sandstone structure in Potsdam." All right here at a pizza joint. The building was erected as a private residence in 1821.

While this family-owned pizzeria might be the smallest example of Potsdam sandstone still standing, plenty of buildings could vie for the title of largest. In fact, the towering All Saints Cathedral in Albany and the Canadian House of Parliament in Ottawa both relied heavily on Potsdam's beautiful stone in their construction.

The city holds a Potsdam Sandstone Festival in the fall. During this time, many of the public buildings made of the famous red stone are open to the public. .

Other Nearby Attractions or Sites

St. Lawrence County offers much for the outdoorsman. The county covers forests, lakes, rivers, and mountains. And although there is much to explore, be prepared to bring some extra gas money. St. Lawrence County is the largest county in New York State, covering a whopping 2,680 square miles! The county touches both the Adirondack Park and the St. Lawrence River.

Essentials

What: Potsdam sandstone buildings

Where: Throughout the city of Potsdam; St. Lawrence County

Contact

Potsdam Public Museum: This is a great local museum and an important stop for visitors exploring the history of the region's sandstone. They can provide you with a walking map of the existing sandstone buildings in the city; www.potsdampublicmuseum.org

96

Madison Barracks

Sackets Harbor
Jefferson County

Defender of the north.

Even though the United States won the American Revolutionary War, our erstwhile enemy, the British, was in no mood to roll over. Not yet.

A mere thirty years after Britain surrendered at Yorktown they were itching for another fight, and this time their focus was on northern New York. After the War of Independence, many British ended up in Canada, where they were neighbors with thousands of Loyalists, Americans who had thrown their lot in with the wrong side during the war. Britain and France were at war in 1807, and wishing to stay neutral, the United States authorized the Embargo Act, which prevented any American business from exporting goods to England. This created a web of black-market smuggling across the jagged, porous border with Canada along the St. Lawrence River and Lake Ontario.

The U.S. Navy chose Sackets Harbor for its naval center at this time, changing this sleepy bayside outpost into one of the largest military encampments in the Northeast. Thousands of soldiers and sailors descended on the village, and more than a hundred buildings were erected for housing, warehousing, shipbuilding, and training. The population swelled at one point to over five thousand—in a village that had never seen five hundred residents before. During the War of 1812, only two cities in the state had greater populations than Sackets Harbor: New York City and Albany.

Two major battles were fought here, both on land and sea. The Americans were ultimately successful, and the village returned to its prewar routine. Deeming a military presence vital to our nation's northern defense, the government constructed a large, elaborate military barracks after the war. Many of those original buildings and much infrastructure have been left in place exactly as they were, so the village of Sackets Harbor is a treasure trove of discovery for those interested in Upstate history.

The village itself has many fine old buildings and a delightful main street. The waterfront is developed and is the scene of much summer activity. But it is the Madison Barracks where the real history of Sackets Harbor glory lies.

Named for President James Madison, the Barracks housed the military men and today stands as a tribute to the might poured into this village more than two centuries ago. They include nearly a hundred stone buildings, which were used to house and train as many as six hundred troops. The majestic gray limestone edifices line up like soldiers at attention all around a large, manicured parade grounds. Each building today carries the name of a famous soldier who either led the troops here or trained here.

On my most recent visit to the Barracks, I read the descriptive plaques on each separate building. "Ripley, General Ebenezer. War of 1812, Sackets Harbor." "Forsythe, Col. Benjamin. Commander of Rifle Regiment at Battle of Ogdensburg." "Brown, General Jacob. War of 1812 Commander of U.S. Army until 1828." One unit declares itself "Grant's Quarters." I didn't realize that President Grant did time up here, but the history of Sackets Harbor tells us that as a young soldier, he and his wife, Julia, were stationed in this very barracks. Another large boulder reads "Birthplace of General Mark Clark." Clark, a World War I, World War II, and Korean War hero, was the youngest soldier ever to be promoted to general. He was born at Madison Barracks on May 1, 1896. Former New York City mayor Fiorello LaGuardia as well as President Martin Van Buren also served at Sackets Harbor.

Brig. Gen. Zebulon Pike, who had the famous western mountain named after him, is buried in the military cemetery here.

The solemnity of this place is akin to that of West Point, albeit on a much smaller scale. The buildings are all in original condition, although efforts have been made to modernize them to today's standards. The row houses that make up "Stone Row" were constructed out of Lake Ontario limestone, which was carried by the troops up from the lake at a cost of $150,000. There was once a bakery, chapel, hospital (where the first use of chloroform during surgery took place), dining halls, and a theatre on the grounds. All of the buildings here overlook the harbor and Lake Ontario.

One of the most unique features of the Barracks is its water tower. It was built totally out of limestone in 1892, and is the most outstanding structure found on this sprawling campus of buildings. A plaque at the base lists the names of soldiers and sailors who left here to serve their country and were killed in battle.

Other Nearby Attractions or Sites

The Sackets Harbor battlefield is about a mile from the Madison Barracks. Tours are given.

The Madison Barracks has been converted into private use with apartments, condominiums, a health center, retail shops, and a marina. The conversion has been done tastefully and the air of history here is still remarkable. One block east of Madison Barracks is the Military Cemetery. Many of those who served at Sackets Harbor over the years are buried here. The great soldier and explorer Zebulon Pike was based in Sackets Harbor. He was the first person to document the mountain that carries his name today, Pike's Peak in Colorado. Pike was killed in battle during the War of 1812, and he and his men are buried in their own section of this cemetery

Perhaps as a tip of the hat to their worthy adversary, the British gifted Sackets Harbor with the wrought-iron fence that surrounds the Military Cemetery. It once guarded London's Buckingham Palace.

By the way, Sackets Harbor was named after a local businessman and founder of the village, Augustus Sackett. Nobody knows what happened to the second "t."

Essentials

What: Madison Barracks

Where: Sackets Harbor; Jefferson County

Contact

Madison Barracks: This is a private residential complex, but there is plenty to see and absorb on a walk around the complex; www.madisonbarracks.com

Sackets Harbor Battlefield: Many re-enactments and public events take place on the battlefield over the course of the year; www.sacketsharbor battlefield.org

97

Cure Cottage

Saranac Lake
Franklin and Essex Counties

Little Red.

In 1873, Edward Livingston Trudeau was diagnosed with tuberculosis. In that era this was pretty much a death sentence. Despite many attempts to find a cure for the dreaded disease, thousands died of it every year. Trudeau, twenty-five years old at the time, moved to the Adirondack Mountains of Upstate New York to seek out a new concept in fighting tuberculosis. The concept of battling the illness with a combination of a healthy lifestyle, relocation to a cold, clear environment, and total rest and relaxation had been pioneered in Germany. Trudeau found the perfect place to practice this regimen in Saranac Lake.

After he got better, he moved his family to the region from New York City and began studying the "miraculous cure in the mountains." He began a medical practice in the village and started researching tuberculosis and how to battle it. In 1892, he founded the first institute committed solely to the eradication of tuberculosis. His Adirondack Cottage Sanatorium, later called the Saranac Laboratory for the Study of Tuberculosis, was a ground-breaking effort that became a model for other medical research facilities in the state.

The core of Trudeau's TB rehabilitation regimen can be found in his "cure cottages." The remnants of this phenomenon can still be seen throughout the village of Saranac Lake. As patients came from around the world seeking the health cure at Trudeau's institute, many in the village began building "cure cottages," and even "cure porches," designed to maximize exposure to sunlight and cold, fresh mountain air. The cure porches were simply glassed-in additions to existing homes, which were then rented out to patients. Dozens of these can still be seen, conspicuous additions to the Victorian homes of that era clearly meant for a special use.

One of the most famous personalities to come to the village seeking a cure was the writer Robert Louis Stevenson. His arrival was dutifully recorded by the local press, resulting in even more patients and curiosity-seekers flooded this rural lakeside community. During this period the little village grew by thousands in population and became the focal point in the battle against TB. The home occupied by Stevenson during his medical stay in Saranac Lake is now a museum to him.

Physicians even created "cure chairs" for patients of the disease. Basically a chaise lounge, these padded wooden reclining-chair beds made breathing easier and made patients' stay in the cottages and on the porches as comfortable as possible. Several companies produced thousands of these

The Robert Louis Stevenson Memorial Cottage and Museum in Saranac Lake.

cure chairs in the Saranac Lake area, selling them for about fifteen dollars. Many residents still have these little pieces of local history.

Dr. Trudeau's very first cure cottage can be seen today on the grounds of the Trudeau Institute. Called "Little Red," the small building looks much like a typical red, rural one-room schoolhouse. It was built at a cost of $350 in 1885. The tiny structure measures only fourteen by eighteen feet and consists of a single room with two beds, two chairs, a desk, a wood stove, and a pair of kerosene lamps. The first patients here were Mary and Alice Hunt, factory workers from New York City. Both sisters recovered from the disease while living at Little Red.

Many famous people, themselves or family members afflicted with the disease, came to Saranac Lake and built their own cure cottages. TB was so prevalent at the time that several companies actually came to Saranac

Lake and built cure cottages for use exclusively by their ill employees. Among these companies were DuPont and Endicott Johnson Shoes. The National Vaudeville Artists organization built their own residence to house sick circus performers.

Although Trudeau's experimental "rest cure" had a high rate of success, some famous people came to the mountains and succumbed to the deadly disease. The most famous of these is Baseball Hall of Famer Christy Mathewson. He made several visits to this curative community over the years and eventually had a home built here. Erected in 1924, his mansion is one of the most spectacular residences in the village. It is more than two stories high and had five bedrooms and two long "cure porches" for the afflicted baseball star to rest in. Mathewson's tuberculosis had been triggered by exposure to poison gases during World War I training. He died in Saranac Lake on October 7, 1925, at the home that still bears his name at 21 Old Military Road.

An interesting side note to the whole story of the "miracle in the Adirondacks" is that Garry Trudeau, creator of the award-winning cartoon *Doonesbury*, is the great-grandson of the institute's founder.

Other Nearby Attractions or Sites

Saranac Lake is a beautiful community of about five thousand residents. Much of the town's social activity is centered on its lakeside location. The lake (known as Flower Lake) freezes over each winter, and the ice is harvested to use in one of the oldest and most popular winter carnivals in the state. The historic Saranac Lake Winter Carnival was first held in 1897. The centerpiece of a weekend filled with sports, food, and entertainment activities is the building of the Ice Palace, a tradition that began in 1898. Built with as many as four thousand large hand-cut ice blocks, the palace is complete with turrets, drawbridges, and "ice furniture."

Essentials

What: Little Red cure cottage

Where: Trudeau Institute, 154 Algonquin Avenue, Saranac Lake; Franklin and Essex Counties (they meet in the center of the village)

Contact

Trudeau Institute: mwww.trudeauinstitue.org; it is not open to the public. However, the Little Red cure cottage is located right next to the parking area and is easily viewed. Visitors are welcome to go up on the cottage's porch and look inside at the furnishings, which reflect the era during which the cottage was constructed. Also, if you go around behind the Institute's main building, you will see a dramatic statue of Dr. Trudeau peering out over the lake. The stark sculpture depicts the good doctor in the throes of the dreaded tuberculosis while resting in one of his cure chairs. The bronze statue was by Gutzon Borglum, who also carved Mount Rushmore.

Saranac Lake Winter Carnival: www.saranaclakewintercarnival.com

Robert Louis Stevenson Memorial Cottage and Museum: 44 Stevens Lane; www.robert-louis-stevenson.org/107-baker-cottage-saranac-lake/

98

Paddock Arcade

Watertown

Jefferson County

Oldest indoor shopping mall in the United States.

For over a century, Watertown's Public Square was the main focal point of the bustling city in the North Country. Political gatherings, business meetings, public markets, holiday celebrations, and the city's transportation all revolved around the large commercial square with an oval park in the middle.

After World War II, Watertown saw greater expansion to the west of the city, and the central business district began a slow decline in its fortunes. A great turn-around came in the 2000's, when people began to refocus interest on center-city development and the incredible architecture that reflected the city's halcyon days.

The Paddock Arcade (named after local businessman Loveland Paddock) opened as a sheltered market space in 1850. It was designed by famed architect Otis Wheelock, who had helped design many of the buildings in Chicago that went up after that city's great fire. The arcade was enclosed and topped with an arched ceiling of glass to allow sunlight into the business space. The tiled floor led from the main entrance in the front on Washington Street and went all the way to another a block, Arcade Street, in the rear. The main floor consisted of retail, restaurants, and open-stall markets, and the second floor was rented out as office space.

The Paddock Arcade is designated as the oldest continuously used shopping mall in the United State.

On my most recent visit to the arcade, I was struck by how lovely it still is and how active life is in the arcade. Businesses do a brisk trade, especially during foul weather, and the glass ceiling is still intact, affording the place a cheery atmosphere. Many of the restaurants, cafés, and pubs in the Paddock Arcade provide seating under the arched ceiling outside their front doors. There seems to be a distinct air of Merry Olde England to the place, maybe because I have seen too many old movies set in Victorian London. I found it quite charming especially on a dark, cloudy afternoon when the lights come twinkling on in the arcade.

The arcade is listed on the National Registry of Historic Places.

The front entrance to this historic shopping mall is directly on Watertown's Public Square. The square is ringed with a variety of small businesses around the park. The architecture is nineteenth and early twentieth century, and parking is plentiful. More than fifty historic buildings surround the four sides of the square. A heroic statue of New York Governor

The interior of the Paddock Arcade as seen today.

Roswell P. Flower by famous French sculptor Augustus Saint-Gaudens was erected in the park in 1902. Flower was born near Watertown in the little hamlet of Theresa.

One of the many notable businesses on the square is the Crystal Bar and Restaurant at 87 Public Square. This is the oldest restaurant in Watertown, and they still serve three meals a day in an ambience of amber-coated nostalgia. From the floor tiles to the tin ceiling tiles, little has changed in over a century in this popular eating place. For more than eighty years, the Crystal has been serving up their own holiday drink concoction called a Tom and Jerry. People come from all over the North Country to imbibe and take part in this beloved tradition between Thanksgiving and Christmas. I have had a Tom and Jerry at the Crystal, and it is great. You can drink it at the stand-up bar in the front of the restaurant. This is the last bar without stools or seats in Upstate New York. I was told by the current owners that the original proprietors of the Crystal said that if people couldn't stand up any longer, it was time for them to go home.

It should be noted that the Paddock Arcade was not the first enclosed mall in the United States, but rather is the oldest continuously open one. The first enclosed mall was the Westminster Arcade in Providence, Rhode Island. It was built in 1828 and closed many years ago. Today it has been refigured as a mixed-use residential and commercial building.

Other Nearby Attractions or Sites

Watertown is one of the great surprises you will find traveling north of the New York State Thruway. It appears that the economy is on a good footing, no doubt because it is basically the home of tens of thousands of military personnel and their families at nearby Fort Drum. And the history here reveals what once was a major business hub in the North Country and as well as a cultural center.

Watertown is home to Thompson Park. What a gorgeous public space this is. It is located high on a hill, offering some beautiful views of the city and the surrounding Adirondacks. It is no surprise that this hill is the perfect setting for the city's large fireworks celebration on the Fourth of July. The 365-acre park was designed by landscaper Frederick Law Olmstead, of New York's Central Park fame.

The New York State Zoo at Thompson Park is a one-of-a-kind zoo. It is the only one in the state that houses New York State birds and animals exclusively. The thirty-two-acre park includes dozens of exhibits featuring more than a hundred animals, including cougars, wolves, bears, eagles, mountain lions, and more. More than fifty thousand visitors come to this unique zoo every year. It was opened in 1920.

As a topper to all of the historic attributes of Watertown, the Jefferson County fair is held here every summer. It was started in 1817 and is the oldest continuously operating fair in the United States.

Essentials

What: The oldest indoor shopping mall in the United States

Where: The Paddock Arcade, 1 Public Square, Watertown; Jefferson County

Contact

Paddock Arcade: No website, (315) 786-6633

New York State Zoo at Thompson Park: http://www.nyszoo.org

Jefferson County Fair: www.jeffcofair.org

99

The Birthplace of the American Navy and a Castle on the Hill

Whitehall

Washington County

Birthplace of the American Navy.

It is one of the most startling welcome signs you can come upon while traveling around Upstate New York. As you wind your way north on Rt. 22 where it is about to connect with Rt. 4 and enter Vermont through its "back door," you see it. Somewhere way in the back of your memories of grade school it hits you as a jarring mistake. "Welcome to Whitehall, New York: The Birthplace of the American Navy."

Huh?

What about Annapolis? Boston? New York City? No, the sign is correct. By act of the New York State legislature in 1960, Whitehall, population four thousand, was officially declared the birthplace of our country's navy.

Let me explain.

In the mid-1700s, this area situated on the southern end of Lake Champlain was a wilderness outpost. In fact British Army Captain Philip Skene carved out a village here, the first located along the 125-mile-long lake. Skene transformed this forested spot into a bustling maritime and manufacturing center called Skenesborough. During the American Revolutionary War, Benedict Arnold swept through the area, captured Skenesborough, and built a small naval flotilla. He sailed his ships north along the lake until he found and engaged the British Navy in the straits surrounding Valcour Island. Although Arnold's ships were mostly caught or destroyed, the battle itself is recognized as the first naval engagement of an inchoate American navy, thereby giving Skenesborough (the name changed after the war to Whitehall) the prestigious "birthplace" claim.

The village has a proud naval history. One of her most storied ships was the schooner USS *Ticonderoga*. During the War of 1812, she took part in the Battle of Plattsburgh and caused the surrender of several British ships. One great story they like to tell in this area is that of midshipman Hiram Paulding. The young sailor was in charge of firing a ship's cannon during the naval battle, but all the firing matches were dead. Frustrated but undaunted, Paulding pulled out his pistol and fired it at the cannon fuse, sending a cannonball crashing into a British ship. Paulding eventually ended his long naval career as a rear admiral.

After the war, the *Ticonderoga* was scuttled in Lake Champlain. In 1958, the ship was "found" and preservationists and historical groups united to raise it from the lake bed and reassemble it for the village's bicentennial. Today it sits next to the Skenesborough Museum along the canal that runs through the heart of Whitehall. To say that the restoration is incomplete is an understatement. This hundred-foot historic ship appears to be a pile of wooden boards faintly resembling a sailing vessel. The remains are encased in a crude open-air enclosure of chicken wire.

Other Nearby Attractions or Sites

The Skenesborough Museum and Heritage Visitors Center is situated in a 1917 concrete canal terminal building. It has been open as a museum since 1959. The remnants of the USS *Ticonderoga* are on the adjacent grounds. The museum tells the rich history of the village, naval and otherwise. The canal that lolls along in front of the building is the Champlain Canal, which connects Lake Champlain with the Hudson River. Whitehall is located at Lock 12, the northernmost canal lock on the waterway.

The view of the village and waterfront of Whitehall from the front of Skene Manor is gorgeous.

From virtually any point in the village, the most recognizable focal point is Skene Manor (seen in the background of this chapter's photograph). This enormous white castle-like residence appears to hang off the side of a mountain overlooking the canal and downtown area. The home, one of the largest sandstone homes in this part of the state, was built by Judge Joseph Potter in 1874. The sandstone was quarried locally by Italian stone artisans. The three-thousand-square-foot residence has eight fireplaces, ten bedrooms, and a clock tower. The astronomical cost of building this exquisite home was twenty-five thousand dollars.

After many years as a residence (and traveler's curiosity), the home fell into disrepair. The village bought it just ahead of the wrecking ball, and it has been renovated and is now used for community purposes. Tours are given, and the mansion is filled with great stories. Several periodicals have called it one of the most haunted places in Upstate New York. It was placed on the National Registry of Historic Places in 1974.

Essentials

What: The birthplace of the American Navy

Where: Whitehall; Washington County

Contact

Skenesborough Museums and Heritage Visitor's Center: http://www.skenes-borough.com/skenesborough-museum; this eclectic museum contains everything from priceless early naval documents to antique firefighting equipment to a baseball signed by Babe Ruth. Next to the museum is a twenty-two-ton railroad caboose on a thirty-five-foot section of track. This is homage to the village's railroading history. Also next to the museum is the shelter holding the remains of the historic USS *Ticonderoga*.

Skene Manor: www.skenemanor.org

100

Santa's Workshop, North Pole

Wilmington

Essex County

America's first theme park.

It had been more than fifty years since I last visited Santa's Workshop in the shadow of Whiteface Mountain. The last time I came here I was just ten years old. I remembered it through the amber prism of nostalgia as a wondrous place of fun, laughter, games, rides, Santa, and live reindeer. A half-century later it did not disappoint.

Santa's Workshop is located on the long highway that takes you to the peak of the fifth-highest mountain in New York. You know the minute you pull into the parking lot that this is going to be a place where the young and the young at heart can really have a fun time. Christmas songs emanating from hidden loudspeakers echo off the mountains and throughout the forests. The buildings are constructed to look like a little Alpine village. Once inside, the names on the various rides and venues give you a clue that Christmas is king here. There is the Jack Jingle Theatre, Santa's Bake Shop, Elmer's Wishing Well, Mother Hubbard's Restaurant, the Peppermint Swing, the Christmas Tree ride, and much more. Some of the time-tested and most beloved stops here are Santa's House, the brightly colored carousel, the post office where you can mail letters to Santa postmarked "North Pole," and, well, the actual physical North Pole itself. More on the pole later.

The idea for this magical dream park came from Julian Reiss, a successful Lake Placid entrepreneur. Well, actually it came from his little daughter, who wanted to know where Santa lived and worked. Reiss and several others seized on this childhood wish and carved out a little piece of the North Pole at the base of Whiteface Mountain. Artist Arto Monaco was the genius behind the whimsical concept of the park, and local contractor Harold Fortune oversaw the construction of it. On a hot July 1, 1949, the little park, dubbed "The North Pole, Home of Santa's Workshop," opened its doors to 212 paying visitors.

Although the crowd on opening day was small, the power of the press soon came into play. More than five hundred newspaper articles soon described this new, wondrous place in the Adirondacks. Reiss and his friends had come upon a unique and daring new entertainment design called the "theme park." Many believe that this was the start of an exciting new wave of venues across the land. With costumed characters strolling the gaily colored streets interacting freely with the customers, and with buildings, concessions, and rides all staying true to the singular theme,

America's obsession with theme parks was born here in tiny Wilmington, New York.

And all of this occurred more than five years before Walt Disney's Magic Kingdom opened its doors in Anaheim, California, in 1955. It is widely believed up here that Uncle Walt actually sent some "spies" to the North Pole to see what all the excitement was about before he opened up his own, much larger theme park.

The folks that operate Santa's Workshop will insist that this is not an amusement park. It is a theme park. You won't find dazzling water rides here, or dizzying roller coasters either. All of the rides are geared to the little ones, say those under ten. And, just because there are no thrill rides doesn't mean there are no thrills. When Santa and Mrs. Claus make their daily entrance into the park, the feeling is electric among the crowd of youngsters. Santa is clearly the rock star at this theme park.

Now back to that famous pole. Near the entrance to the park is perhaps its iconic feature. I remember it vividly from my first visit here in the 1950s, and I couldn't wait to see if it was still there during my most recent trip. I noticed a knot of kids gathered in a huddle, laughing and acting all stirred up. I knew this was it. I approached, and there it was, the North Pole! This pole, which seemed to lord over the landscape when I was a tyke but now meets me at eye level, is literally a tower of ice. Dubbed the "North Pole," it is frozen solid 365 days of the year. Kids poke it, scrape it, rub it, and yes, some even lick it. I doubt that there is a place in the whole of the Adirondack State Park that has been captured in more photographs than this pole of ice at Santa's Workshop.

When no one was watching, I stepped up to the North Pole and slid my hand over the shiny, slick ice covering. For an instant I was back here as a kid with my family, laughing and running around with abandon at "our" theme park. It was just the right size for kids then, and it really is just the right size now for those of us who wish to return, if just for a moment, to the time we spent in "vacationland" in Upstate New York, chasing down the varmints at Frontier Town, driving our own cars at Gaslight Village, watching Rapunzel let down her hair at Fantasyland, entering the giant whale from Pinocchio at Storytown U.S.A., and, yes, touching the North Pole here at Santa's Workshop.

On December 16, 1953, the United States Postal Service officially gave Santa's Workshop its very own post office, designated North Pole,

New York. Today, thousands of "letters from Santa" come out of this rural postal station, to the delight of kiddies around the world.

Other Nearby Attractions or Sites

While visiting Santa's Workshop, it is hard to ignore the shadow of Whiteface Mountain. Continue up the highway from the North Pole and you can drive to the top of the forty-eight-hundred-foot mountain. The view is among the best in the Northeast, including (on a clear day) a glimpse of the skyline of the city of Montreal, Canada, some eighty miles to the north. Note that despite the thrilling experience you can have at the top of Whiteface, extreme weather causes the summit (and the highway) to be closed on and off during the winter.

Whiteface Ski Resort is one of the most popular skiing destinations in the East. The mountain was used as the major skiing event venue for the 1980 Lake Placid Winter Olympics.

Essentials

What: America's first theme park; Santa's Workshop at the North Pole

Where: Wilmington; Essex County

Contact

Santa's Workshop at North Pole: http://www.northpoleny.com

Whiteface Mountain Ski Resort: www.whiteface.com

Index

445